DELUSION

Internal Dimensions
of Political Life

DELUSION

Internal Dimensions of Political Life

James M. Glass

THE UNIVERSITY OF CHICAGO PRESS

Chicago and London

JAMES M. GLASS is professor of government and
politics at the University of Maryland. Since 1977
he has been a research affiliate of the Sheppard and
Enoch Pratt Hospital.

The University of Chicago Press, Chicago 60637
The University of Chicago Press, Ltd., London

94 93 92 91 90 89 88 87 86 85   54321

LIBRARY OF CONGRESS CATALOGING IN PUBLICATION DATA
Glass, James M.
   Delusion: internal dimensions of political life.
   Bibliography: p.
   Includes index.
   1. Schizophrenics—Language. 2. Political
science. I. Title.
RC514.G5318   1985   616.89′82   84-16193
ISBN 0-226-29797-7

To my parents

Contents

Foreword

It is hard to imagine that the world of madness could enrich the field of political theory. Yet the present work by Dr. James Glass, a professor of political theory, demonstrates that the everyday goings-on of a mental hospital can indeed serve as a frame of reference to broaden our understanding of politics. The bringing together of two seemingly unrelated disciplines in this volume is a prime example of the potential for cross-fertilization between areas of study.

When Dr. Glass came to the Sheppard and Enoch Pratt Hospital, the observation and conceptualization of individual human development, as applied to psychosis, had already resulted in a high degree of understanding of the clinical manifestations of severe mental illness. The psychological development of the infant, child, and adult came to be seen as an interaction of biological and experiential components.

In a larger context, culture and civilization have been approached by an exploration of the influences of the derivatives of human development. In speculating on the origin of religion, Sigmund Freud, in *The Future of an Illusion* (1927) and *Civilization and Its Discontents* (1930) conjectured that illusions derived from human wishes, and he regarded religion as just such an illusion. In making use of the developmental framework, Freud's emphasis was on infantile helplessness. According to Freud, this helplessness led to the creation of the concept of God (= father). Other psychoanalysts have utilized psychological concepts in the understanding of various phenomena, particularly in the field of anthropology. Erik Erikson has made seminal contrubutions to the understanding of culture and personality in his studies of the influence of contrasting ecologies of the Sioux and Yurok Indians.

Dr. Glass elected to do his "fieldwork" not in an unfamiliar culture, or alongside an analytic couch, or in a library. Instead, he spent several years listening to and talking with patients who, although severely mentally ill and disordered in their thinking, were able to convey something of their experience to him. Since I have spent thirty-five years of my professional life with comparable patients, I can testify to the frustration, fascination, and resonating range of feelings—ranging from omnipotence to impotence, isolation, bleakness, and despair—one can experience if one allows oneself to become immersed in the inner life of these human beings. One cannot help but be changed as a result of this kind of participation. Intensive experience with psychotic patients becomes a rich source for the understanding of a wide range of human behavior, for the magnification provided by psychopathology gives one a clearer perception of the normal everyday phenomena involved in motivation and behavior.

I approached the task of introducing readers to this book with some apprehension, since I am not at all grounded in political theory. As I read through each chapter, I became progressively more absorbed and caught up in the author's presentation. I began to realize his was a very special experience conveyed in a very special book. This study represents a natural historical link with Dr. Harry Stack Sullivan, who sixty years earlier learned from schizophrenic patients at the Sheppard and Enoch Pratt Hospital. Later, Sullivan, too, attempted to forge a link with the social sciences through his collaboration with political scientists such as Harold Lasswell.

Dr. Glass, in an utterly readable account, shows schizophrenia as a vivid human experience. His use of visual and tabular material (a reflection of his academic background), for example, to outline the process of the therapeutic transformation from delusion to reality, is particularly apt. The results demonstrate how his status as participant-observer allowed him to learn simply by being with patients over a long period of time and having the opportunity to discuss his experience with colleagues. Today, the opportunity to be with delusional patients over an extended period is seldom available to trainees, even in modern psychiatric residency programs. I shall return to possible reasons for this when I speculate about society's—and psychiatry's—reluctance to engage with these patients.

The purpose of the book, as I understand it, is to demonstrate how political theory can be enriched by including data about peoples' inner worlds rather than limiting its scope to conventional, conscious, external, "rational" institutions. Just as psychotic phenomena have helped psychiatrists to understand normal infant and child development, Glass uses these same phenomena to shed light on political processes. One can say he explores political anthropology from a developmental, psychological frame of reference as opposed to, for example, the narrower use of psychological testing. To cite but one example, it has been recognized that early in development children view the world in all-or-nothing terms; nuances and in-between attitudes have not yet developed. There are either "good" people or "bad" people. Later on a more integrated approval develops, with the ability to negotiate, to break down tasks into intermediate steps, to postpone gratification, and to forgive others. It might be possible, in a similar way, to assess societies on a spectrum from primitive (immature) to advanced (mature) according to the degree to which these societies resort to all-or-nothing thinking. In this regard, one could probably make a case for applying Glass's use of the development model to other social sciences, such as social anthropology.

The reluctance of political theorists to delve into the realm of the unconscious is representative of the culture as a whole. In the past, psychotic experience as well as dream experience have been dismissed by Western civilization as meaningless. Even some present-day psychiatrists avoid dealing with these processes out of the fear of the threat of reactivation, in their patients, of dissociated systems of primitive experience. Since Dr. Glass uses the term "countertransference," it may be helpful to explain that this term refers to the feelings that the therapist and other staff members have toward the patient. If unrecognized and unresolved, these feelings of countertransference can act as blindspots and interfere with treatment. In contrast to other more traditional somatic medical attitudes, where one is supposed to be "objective" and free of personal response, psychiatrists recognize and often make use of their reflective responses to obtain clues about processes going on within their patients. Throughout the book Dr. Glass gives us glimpses of his reactions as a result of his involvement with these deeply ill patients.

That Dr. Glass has been able to produce such a vivid phenomenological description of the patients' inner lives is due in large part to the fact that he did not have to facilitate therapeutic change or make clinical management decisions. The unique opportunity simply to observe or, at most, to encourage elaborations of the patients' communications permitted the author to view the patients' inner worlds without having to act on what he heard. Clinicians, on the other hand, must direct their attention to making order out of chaos, responding to suicidal ideation, or pointing out reality in a field distorted by delusions.

In sum, this is a ground-breaking work. In additon to its relevance to the field of politics, the book is invaluable both to students of psychiatry as a description of the phenomenology of schizophrenia and to practicing psychiatrists for the insights it can provide in their efforts to fathom the schizophrenic patient's experience. Psychiatric nurses involved in the daily care of such patients could also benefit from reading Dr. Glass's case descriptions. Dr. Glass's lucid, organized presentation of his detailed clinical examples makes the complex concepts with which he deals accessible to all.

Clarence G. Schulz, M.D.

The opinions of the world, both in antient and later ages, concerning the cause of madnesse, have been two. Some, deriving them from the Passions; some, from Daemons, or Spirits, either good or bad, which they thought might enter into a man, possesse him, and move his organs in such strange, and uncouth manner, as mad men use to do. The former sort therefore called such men, Mad-men: but the Later, called them sometimes *Daemoniacks*, (that is, possessed with spirits;) sometimes *Energumeni* (that is agitated or moved with spirits;) and now in *Italy* they are called not onely *Pazzi*, Mad-men; but also *Spiritati*, men possest.

Thomas Hobbes, *Leviathan*

I have now to say that there is no *general* stuff of which experience at large is made. There are as many stuffs as there are 'natures' in the things experienced. If you ask what any one bit of pure experience is made of, the answer is always the same: "It is made of *that*, of just what appears, of space, of intensity, of flatness, brownness, heaviness or what not. . . ." Experience is only a collective name for all these sensible natures, and save for time and space (and, if you like, for 'being') there appears no universal element of which all things are made.

William James, *Essays in Radical Empiricism* and *A Pluralistic Universe*

I am the curator of delusion . . . I live in the rain of pain.

A patient at Sheppard/Pratt Hospital

The psychoanalytic experience has rediscovered in man the imperative of the *verbe* as the law which has formed him in its image. It manipulates the poetic function of Language to give to his desire its symbolic mediation. May that experience bring you to understand at last that it is in the gift of the Word that all the reality of its effects resides; for it is by way of this gift that all reality has come to man and it is by his continued act that he maintains it.

Jacques Lacan, *The Language of the Self*

Preface

What appears in the delusional world contains a story, an emotional fable; the language draws out ideas and tendencies. Its imagery possesses a resonance, a structure and significance that reveal the agony experienced in an internal psychological universe. Delusion derives from what psychoanalysis calls the "unconscious"; and while the structure of the unconscious is inaccessible directly, its existence is inferred from the evidence provided by delusion, hallucination, fantasy, dream, slips of the tongue, and symptomatic behaviors of various kinds. In schizophrenic patients, the most obvious demonstrations of an unconscious lie in utterance that appears at times to be insensible, that lacks any ostensible thematic center or organization.

Delusional speech is generally regarded as regressive, an indication of severe mental illness. It is, however, utterance motivated by meaning. It is a form of intentional thought that requires decoding and a sensitivity to complex emotional logics. What is remarkable about delusional knowledge is its refusal to consider any aspect of experience that might involve feelings of ambivalence. Delusion provides a certain, often unbreakable identity, and its absolute character can maneuver the self into an unyielding position. In this respect, it is the internal mirror of political authoritarianism, the tyrant inside the self. The authoritarian regime dominates through the application of terror to the polity's political and social life; delusion terrorizes through the often horrifying scenarios (or spectacles) of an internal regime that take shape in bizarre symbolizations. For the schizophrenic delusion encloses the self in oppression; it destroys freedom and possibility; it reduces the self to the status of hopeless victim. As one patient put it, "hope is the last pearl in Pandora's box."

Delusional imagery frequently evolves around critical political relationships: victimizer/victim; master/slave; controller/controlled. In terms of their effect, these internal structures exercise as much power over the self as any external tyranny. Is the schizophrenic any less imprisoned in the internal cell of delusion than the prisoner facing solitary confinement? Is someone who feels in imminent danger of annihilation—from whatever cause—in any sense of the word "free"? The schizophrenic is a classic victim, and while the reasons for that victimization may often include external settings (conditions in mental hospitals; attitudes of families, friends, and employers), what is even more compelling is that the victimization (and its source) lie inside the delusional introject. The self creates its own victimization (delusion as defense), an internal feat that immobilizes action and brings any pursuit of social life to a standstill. It is this situation that constitutes the tragedy of being schizophrenic. What I want to focus on in this book are these internal sources of victimization (and their psychodynamic reasons), an inner psychological world that not only imparts identity to the schizophrenic self, but gives it an affinity to individuals and groups that find themselves excluded from freedom by intolerable forms of domination.

Delusion represents the victory of the internal over the external, the projected over the existent, the imaginary over the consensually real or validated (the social world). It is a system of thought (defined by *unconscious* intentionality) that torments and frightens. The great difference between the schizophrenic delusion, held inwardly and the delusional projections of a political or religious fanatic appears in the historical relations of the system. The political fanatic uses delusion to create a specific history, to link the project to an ongoing historical event; the schizophrenic retreats to the delusional fortress and severs the self's contact with historical reality. The fanatic fuses delusion with a talent for organizing the "intentionality" of others; the schizophrenic desperately tries to avoid all forms of social (even instrumental) contact. The fanatic imposes delusional structures onto political priorities (and enthusiastically engages the surrounding environment); the schizophrenic lacks interest in almost all organizational projects.

For the fanatic, delusional readings of reality, hallucinations, divinations, revelations—all coalesce as claims to power and draw on a community or group's own uncertainty and fear. The fantasy of power depends on domination; it may even become the vehicle for a collective identity, with the delusional world being shared publicly as national policy or revenge. As the source for political definition and concepts, delusion may replace more consensually derived or historically conceived values and ideals. Delusional calls to action, in the fanatic's world, are turned outward as belief and may succeed in inducing (or producing) an extraordinary amount of suffering. Fanaticism, fueled by delusional certainty, is capable of concrete acts of destruction and annihilation.

For the hospitalized, withdrawn, and internally oriented schizophrenic, however, delusion (a substitute life-world) is a reparative movement, an attempt to recapture or recover emotional connections lost at an early developmental stage. Even though it is authoritarian in structure, the schizophrenic retains that delusional world inside; it is not set upon the world; it appears in the form of language; its intentionality is to be discovered by examining the defensive functions of the introject itself. Delusional identity (and I will have a great deal to say about this) rests on premises that have nothing to do with the consensual or social universe; it is knowledge held within, a retreat to private concerns and an implicit repudiation of public modes of being. In cutting the self away from the social world, delusion projects an alternative form of life populated by bizarre figures that haunt consciousness. Consensual relationships fall away; and the ego, preoccupied with an incessant parade of distorted images, turns inward.

In the clinical literature, the therapist or clinician who is examining delusion looks for keys that might generate an understanding of emotional reasons lying behind the use of complex imagery, information about the self's withdrawal from social relationships. Psychotherapists are not likely to linger on the content or meaning of delusional systems; their priorities lie in process, in the way self masks contact with others, in emotions defining the therapeutic alliance (assuming one is established). It is rare for any clinician to be directly concerned with the structures of delusional utterance, with this inner world understood as an expression of political conception and structure. It is unlikely that clinical interest will focus on the "political" content of language. To my knowledge, no work in either psychiatry, psychology, or political science looks specifically at the political forms embedded within delusional utterance itself. Nor have clinicians been particularly concerned about connections between political theory and delusional statements. Nor should they; it is simply not their concern.[1] Political theorists, too, have shown little interest in looking at delusional language (utterance involving unconscious intent) as a source for understanding the construction of political phenomena. Psychiatry addresses itself to clinical and management issues; political theory turns toward history, formal models, mathematical logic, scientific method, and so on. Even psychiatrists who have examined political relationships (R. D. Laing and Thomas Szasz, for example) turn their

---

1. Part of my task is to translate the concepts and theories of a psychoanalytic psychology into a language accessible to a political audience, particularly as this involves an understanding of the delusional content and structure of schizophrenia. While it is at times essential to use psychoanalytic terminology, where possible I try to interpret and explain. But even more importantly, psychoanalysis retains a humanistic and highly personal view of the person called schizophrenic. Delusion is central to what it means to be schizophrenic, and psychoanalytic theory as an interpretive method is persuasive both in explaining what schizophrenia is and in providing a framework to undertake an analysis of the "politics" of language as it appears in delusional utterance and in the contextual psychological environments of the schizophrenic self. Psychoanalysis, in contrast to major directions in a more formal physiological or psychopharmacological psychiatry, retains a respect for inner or unconscious mental processes and a commitment to language in treating the schizophrenic person. In the words of Theodore Lidz, one of the most respected physicians in the treatment of schizophrenia, "Those who have followed the transformation of patients who have been withdrawn, disorganized and delusional into well-functioning persons know that psychotherapy can accomplish and has accomplished what no other treatment has even approached."

analytic critiques toward contradictions, biases, and definition within the field of psychiatry. To take then as an object of inquiry the delusional utterances of schizophrenics and what these utterances say about concepts in the history of political thought (and the study of political life generally) is a major shift from paradigmatic models in political science *and* theory.

I hope this project initiates a dialogue about different ways of conceiving the "political" and provokes an exchange that looks at the proposition that "politics" owes as much to internal sources within the self as it does to external institutions and processes traditionally called political. It would be a mistake, therefore, to read this book as an attempt to disprove any given theory of politics. It is a series of reflections on the political content of delusional phenomena in theoretical and empirical contexts. By examining the utterances of schizophrenics, I intend to argue that, if the existence of an unconscious cannot be proved, it can with reasonable plausibility be inferred. And if schizophrenia demonstrates a single hypothesis, it is the existence of an unconscious (brought into imagery through the ego's regression) specific not only to the delusional self, but present and active in all human life. Further, within the schizophrenic's internal world lies a form of political domination as severe (and demanding) as any external oppressor.

From the perspective of political theory and debates within the tradition, the argument to be advanced here lends credence to the notion (common to social contract theorists) of a human nature that precedes the development and implementation of social forms of life. The schizophrenic's delusional world is precivil, a rejection of social life and a movement back toward what Rousseau called the "language of the heart" (as opposed to the knowledge, language, and assumptions of civil society and rationality). Delusional utterance is a highly symbolic language commenting on wounds suffered by the self prior to the acquisition of formal linguistic structures. And to listen to the schizophrenic is to hear stories of hearts broken at very early stages in the psychodevelopmental process. If the origins of schizophrenia (in part) are to be found in the nonverbal or what Freud called the "oceanic" feelings of infancy, then the utterances of delusion provide a graphic illustration of psychological hurt that lies deeply embedded in the self. Delusion recreates the pain, the defenses against this early hurt. It portrays in language and image trauma suffered during the first year of life.

I would at the outset like to forestall several objections. I do not treat the schizophrenic as a hero. Nor do I argue that schizophrenic language should be the basis for political or social order. Schizophrenia is not a state that should be regarded as desirable or taken as a sign of revelation. Nor am I particularly troubled about debates over etiology. Whether schizophrenia is caused by a gene, chemical, brain dysfunction, or psychological factors (although I find psychodynamic explanations to be the most persuasive) is not here the relevant consideration. What matters is that there exist millions of individuals with histories, aspirations, hopes, and feelings who, for whatever reason, are diagnosed or classified as schizophrenic.[2] What, from my point of view, "describes" this group are its language, its internal psychological structures, the relation of utterance to the surrounding social community, and the impact of a psychological universe separated from the terms and conditions of the social (and historical) contract.

Undoubtedly, physiological and genetic factors play a major role in certain individuals diagnosed as schizophrenic. There is strong evidence for such conclusions.[3] Yet the issue is not so much cause or etiology but how to treat, interpret, and respond to individuals who manifest schizophrenic symptoms. I am perfectly willing to concede an organic or physiological causality. I do not, however, believe that debate over etiology affects the real problems of the schizophrenic's adaptation to internal and external reality. Medication certainly diminishes the intensity of delusion, but it is not at all clear that pharmacologic intervention frees the self from its preoccupation with delusional frames of reference. It is ultimately how the delusional self finds its way to consensual sources of knowledge that controls or eliminates symptoms (the so-called thought disorders). And it is not likely there will be a pill or machine or any technological instrument that will magically eliminate delusional thought and replace it with the "cured" foundations of consensual knowledge. Until that magic is developed, it is essential to look at the schizophrenic

2. A variety of behaviors are classified as schizophrenic, and I am not suggesting that delusion is the only symptom covered by this diagnostic category. For example, *DSM III* (1980) (the APA's official *Diagnostic and Statistical Manual of Mental Disorders*) lists several types: catatonic, paranoid, undifferentiated, disorganized, residual. I focus here primarily on paranoid delusional systems, although in the other types delusional thinking is often present but not in such complete form. I return to issues of classification in chapter 3.

3. There are hundreds of studies concerned with various aspects of schizophrenia as a medical issue. A representative selection might include the following: F. J. Kallman, *Heredity in Health and Mental Disorder* (New York, 1955); S. S. Kety, "Current Biochemical Research in Schizophrenia," in P. N. Hock and J. Zubin, *Psychopathology of Schizophrenia* (New York: Grune and Stratton, 1966); S. S. Kety, "Biochemical Hypotheses and Studies," in L. Bellak and L. Loeb, *The Schizophrenic Syndrome* (New York: Grune and Stratton, 1969); H. E. Himwich, S. S. Kety, and J. R. Smythies, *Amines and Schizophrenia* (New York: Pergamon Press, 1967); A. R. Kaplan, editor, *Genetic Factors in 'Schizophrenia'* (New York: Charles Thomas, 1972); I. L. Gottesman and J. Shields, *Schizophrenia and Genetics: A Twin Study Vantage Point* (New York: Academic Press, 1972), C. E. Frohman and J. S. Gottlieb, "The Biochemistry of Schizophrenia," in S. Arieti, *American Handbook of Psychiatry*, vol. 3 (2nd ed., New York: Basic Books, 1966); Don D. Jackson, editor, *The Etiology of Schizophrenia* (New York: Basic Books, 1960). For a review of the physical therapies that accompany schizophrenia, including drugs, shock treatments, and insulin injections, see Arieti, *Interpretation of Schizophrenia*, pp. 677–75.

self as a person, with problems in relatedness, and to respond to those problems with a linguistically based psychotherapy.[4] Delusional reality represents a hopeless and often tragic withdrawal from a set of social relations the self regards as intolerable, a retreat into a form of life that precludes any contact with external reality.

To view schizophrenia not from the perspective of a psychiatric professional but as a political theorist working with concrete, clinical experience is to see in the condition considerable evidence about theories of human nature. I take seriously the argument that human nature and political life have something to do with each other, and that what is called "political" depends in some measure on inner psychological structures whose effects appear in the organization of political institutions, in values and perceptions, in boundaries separating public from private.[5] Take for example the concept of power: if the evidence of schizophrenia is any indication, the preoccupation of the delusional self with power demonstrates the importance of feelings of power (grandiosity, omnipotence) from the very beginning of life. Delusional concepts of power are not those of sharing and cooperation; what appears are images of domination, absolute sovereignty and command, force and control. Invariably, such inner regimes are split between victim and victimizer; but the relationship is defined by power. What matters in the delusional world are the flows of power and the impact of delusional projections on how the self reads or interprets events in the external world (a cup of coffee seen as a deadly poison sent by hostile invaders; or the chirping of birds understood as a message sent about an impending atom bomb explosion). These images comment (although indirectly) on the distribution and structure of power relations.

It is important, however, to distinguish between the emotional hurt lying at the center of the delusional self and the kinds of images, particularly those involving power, utilized to defend against pain. When a patient describes the fluids in her veins as "liquid magnesium and iron ore, mixed with rocks and stones," she experiences her inner reality as

4. When I speak of psychotherapy in this book I refer to the therapist as an actor in a delusional drama, a central figure who grapples with delusional introjects. In this sense, I would argue that the therapeutic process with schizophrenics emerges as a form of "politics," a commitment to self-governance and an inner democracy of the self. For the clinician, delusions are defenses that for the sake of the patient should be dismantled, and the urgent therapeutic is to help the self establish a connection or relatedness with another human being.

5. For example, research into schizophrenia may shed some light on the distinction Hannah Arendt (1958) draws between public and private. I disagree, however, with her contention that the public and private spheres are separate and should be understood as mutually exclusive. From a psychodynamic perspective, it mystifies psychological reality to suggest that each area can be kept separate and to maintain that the public is not infused and driven by intense private needs and desires.

cold, dead, and empty. It is easier for her to tolerate these images than to look directly at feelings of self-contempt and self-hatred that persistently define her utterance. Worthlessness—the sense of being nothing or being dead—disguises an enormous inner hurt, a fear of trust and empathy, and the defenses against acknowledging this unbearable hurt appear in frightening and frequently grandiose imagery. To be filled with the coldness of unrefined metallic ores offers an implicit commentary on how the self perceives its being (and power) amid a world of other human beings (an instance of delusion commenting on victimization). Delusion becomes rigid defense, often unbreakable, against emotional connections such as trust, compassion, and love of self—essential aims in any therapeutic effort at reintegration.

To look closely at the utterance of the schizophrenic is to witness the self not as a culture hero, but as a tragic representation of a flawed relation between culture and human nature, and its patterns of fragmentation, withdrawal, and social alienation. It is to see the despair of a human nature forced backwards in its own psychological time, and an often desperate attempt to confront the dreadful and live in an inner universe that mirrors victimization in all its forms. The world of the schizophrenic is one without empathy, compassion, or kindness; the "I" finds itself devoured by monsters, devils, gods, objects, and messages that absorb boundaries, perform acts of immense cruelty, and speak to the self in the language of sadism and torture. Yet, for the schizophrenic, delusion defends against human desires: this "waking nightmare" provides a place untouched by the ambivalence of real human beings. As strange as it may seem, it is easier for the delusional self to manipulate and ward off intensely paranoid intrusions, to sustain the torment of delusional introjects, than it is to seek out social relationships based on compassion or empathy.

Delusion demonstrates what Lévi-Strauss (1969) and Freud (1930) see as the perpetual struggle between the interests of nature and those of culture. Delusion moves the self away from culture and toward nature. Psychotherapy takes the self in the other direction: away from the boundless images of delusional nature toward the integrated and differentiated world of consensual reality. If delusion demonstrates anything for the student of political life, it is the phenomenon of a human self taken quite seriously in the literature of the social contract: an existence and consciousness "in nature" that precedes the entrance into the laws of civil and communal life. I do not suggest that such inwardness (the withdrawal from social rules and logic) is preferable to life in community. Quite the contrary: all the ex-schizophrenics I have spoken to affirm the life-sustaining properties of intersubjective (social) experience. Each possesses a vision of communitarian existence that might provide relief from despair and loneliness, a refuge from unhappiness and isolation. Each is acutely aware of the pain accompanying the withdrawal and absorption into a delusional world; each expresses a desire never to return to any kind of psychotic state. And each acknowledges the bases of the social compact. It is also true that the experience of being in delusional "nature" affects how these expatients view, in their current lives, the structure of social rules, judgments regarding appropriateness, and methods used to regulate social exchange and the kinds of behaviors society finds unacceptable (and therefore deserving of exclusion). Ex-schizophrenics, in particular, have a difficult time with social expectations and often express hostility toward values society tends to reward and encourage.

To conclude: the analysis of delusion is touched upon from several perspectives: as an issue in a cultural "politics" (chapter 1); as an instance of the rupture between nature and culture (chapter 2); as a langauge that articulates the intense emotional oscillations of infancy (chapter 3); as an alternative theory of knowledge, a linguistic way of life, obsessed with power and domination (chapter 4); as a psychological prison ruled by a tyrannical psychical world (chapter 5); as a precivil or "natural" state that reflects properties Hobbes describes in *Leviathan* (chapter 6); as a descent into psychological terror (the mind's "state of nature") described from the perspective of the day-to-day phenomenology of one patient's treatment (chapter 7); as a defense against compassion and empathy from the perspective of ex-schizophrenics who have experienced the movement away from nature (delusion) to culture or community (consensual reality) (chapters 8 and 9). The final chapter addresses some general questions that pertain to the study of political theory and the importance of the "data" of the unconscious.

I make no claim in these pages to be scientifically objective; my position is one of participant-observer involved in looking at language forms that come from a radically alienated view of human experience. What the delusional self conveys both through the use of imagery and gesture defies analysis in any "purged" or hyperrational language. The hermetic world of the schizophrenic requires a language sensitive to ambience and nuance, to confusing patterns of communication. Interpretive language attuned to the schizophrenic state of mind should itself be a language willing to forego some hypothetical objectivity for the greater purpose of conveying mood, sense, and feeling in a psychological universe distinguished by its feints, deceptions, obscurities, and symbolic meanings. In addition, objectivity might distort essential meaning structures embedded in utterance; and to attempt the stance of a scientific neutrality interested only in measurement might alter the content and structure of such elusive and metaphoric utterance.

Further, from what I witnessed in over six years of clinical research, it would be absurd to pretend scientific distance. Such a position would violate the inner reality and feelings of patients who revealed (with often considerable pain) thoughts they knew I would find bizarre, if not horrendous. The humanistic basis of this study (and its grounding in a psychoanalytic methodology) requires a language sensitive to the symbolic contours of the schizophrenic's inner world. "Science," in the form of measurement, quantification, questionnaires, tests, and so on distances the object of inquiry; what I wish to do in this book is to bring the language of delusion as close as possible to the audience, to unravel the utterance as a commentary on meaning and value.

As a political theorist observing first-order experiences, what I offer here is a reflection on the structure and politics of inner psychological states. The arguments touch on concerns in the historical tradition and on specific political theorists and concepts, particularly the psychological meaning of the nature/culture opposition, the "state of nature," the making of the social contract, and the implications of precivil or prerational states of mind. The human condition that is called schizophrenic acts as a psychological refraction of experiences that may have about them a universality suggesting a picture of human nature in its most primitive and natural state.

I am not, however, unmindful of another argument: the schizophrenic represents a self broken or fractured in a process of enculturation that, for whatever reason, has assaulted the ego. What this shattering suggests is not regression to a hypothetical "natural" or precivil state, but a self in a relative condition of "brokenness" (in the context of what society considers to be selves in whole or healthy states). Further, since individuals live within social conventions that depend on agreement and a certain cooperative effort, those who resist those conventions or who reject their governing assumptions may be said to be repudiating not society but constructions of its rules, laws, and methods of thinking. The issue becomes not that of a natural versus a social self, but of selves in *relative* states of wholeness or fragmentation (with the schizophrenic as an extreme instance of a self fractured by the social nexus and withdrawing to a position of radical alienation). While much in this argument is useful and compelling,[6] I find that the clinical evidence portrays a more starkly defined split between outer (social) and inner (natural). Further, as I shall argue, if schizophrenia embodies in language the screams of an infant in severe psychological distress, then these feelings come from a period of human development that precedes even the existence of social conventions or regulations associated with civil community.

---

6. See, for example, the intellectual tradition represented in the work of Simmel, Mead, Pierce, and James. I should add that a more phenomenological analysis may be useful in disentangling the complex threads of schizophrenic symbolization (see chapters 6 and 7).

Acknowledgments

At the Sheppard and Enoch Pratt Hospital (Towson, Maryland), I would like to thank Dr. Gerald Whitmarsh (Director of Research), whose encouragement, conversation and support were essential in delineating the resources for this project. I am also grateful to Dr. Wolfe Adler (director of in-patient services) and Sheppard/Pratt's Institutional Review Board for granting me access to the hospital's patient population and clinical environment.

Several psychiatrists at Sheppard/Pratt generously contributed their time and interest. I would like to thank Drs. Maria Klement, Roger Lewin, Richard Mehne, Charles Peters, Miles Quaytman, Cass Ragin, Julie Soler, and Jerome Styrt. Because of their insight and advice, I was able to clarify and sort out difficult problems in clinical interpretation and process. I am especially grateful to Dr. Sally Winston, who, from the very beginning, offered her resourcefulness of interpretation, perceptiveness, and friendship. I am also indebted to the nursing staff, particularly Rosalie Alsop, Jane Cole, Jane Goldsborough, Carol Miello, and Jonathan Sachs, for their help in facilitating contact with patients. Finally, with much respect and gratitude, I would like to thank Dr. Clarence Schulz, Sheppard/Pratt's senior psychiatrist and director of residency training, a teacher and clinician whose guidance, support, and example were invaluable and whose containing presence focused and clarified many jagged edges throughout this project. If, in the book, there is a sense of the nature of psychotherapy with schizophrenics and its psychoanalytic foundations, it is derived from the work and compassion of Clarence Schulz.

My intellectual debts in political theory are many, and a number of individuals over the years gave support and direction. I am grateful to Benjamin Barber, Brian Barry, Richard Claude, Fred Dallmayr, Jean Elshtain, Robert Goodin, Ralph Hummel and John Gunnell. I find my excursion into political theory to be an activity that moves through different phases, a journey into both conceptual formulation and the concreteness of emotional life. It is this synthesis that informs my approach to political concepts and ultimately I alone stand responsible for whatever conclusions come from this inquiry.

Acknowledgments

I would like to thank the University of Maryland and its General Research Board for financial support at various stages of this project.

I would also like to thank Michael Diamond, Charles Levine, Sam Postbrief, and Seymour Rubenfeld, who spent considerable time just listening, and to my wife Janis, who patiently tolerated the moments of my own astonishment and confusion in trying to come to grips with the language of madness. The efforts of Judy Staples in typing and retyping the manuscript and her skill in deciphering my handwriting are gratefully acknowledged.

Finally, I owe a profound debt to the patients of the Sheppard and Enoch Pratt Hospital, to their willingness to explore difficult and painful events and to reveal, with often great anguish, states of mind that were as intricate as they were compelling.

NOTE: Chapters 4 and 10 originally appeared, in slightly different form, in the following publications:

Chapter 4: "'I Am the Curator of Delusion': Knowledge and Power in Schizophrenic Symbol Systems," *Psychoanalysis and Contemporary Thought* 4 (1981):567–606.

Chapter 10: "Political Theory and the Internal Structures of the Self: Reflections on Where Should Political Theory Be Now," pp. 338–57 in John Nelson, ed., *What Should Political Theory Be Now* (Albany: State University of New York Press, 1983).

Although extensively revised for this volume, some of the material in chapters 2 and 3 originally appeared in the following publications:

Chapter 2: "The Schizophrenic and Primitive Thought," *Politics and Society* 6 (1976):327–45.

Chapter 3: "Schizophrenia and Language: The Internal Structure of Political Reality," *Ethics* 92 (1982):274–98.

one

The Meaning of Delusion as Knowledge

The Inner World: Delusion and Language

The language of politics is a language that with few exceptions accepts the primacy of externality over internality, that defines the origins of ethics in the context of externally given phenomena. It is a language that looks at institutions and historical structure. It is concerned with the system's functioning, with theory drawn from visible forms of political life and action. To view politics as an event possessing roots in an external world is to see it as a process through which individuals organize their lives—who gets what, when, and where.

It is equally legitimate to look at the politics of the inner self, internal structures and perceptions that reflect political properties. What Harold Lasswell argued over fifty years ago still retains significance for political science: "There exist in modern society sizeable collections of such material which have hitherto been accorded slight attention by students of social science. I refer to the case histories of those individuals who have been ill, and especially those who have been cared for in hospitals and sanitariums" (1930, 3). The structure of internal mental processes appears in these histories, and in Lasswell's view the study of psychological motivation and intention, the "prolonged interview technique as a method of personality study (especially psychoanalysis)," enhances political analysis. Lasswell concerns himself with specific political types, styles of leadership, and the effect of psychopathology on the leader's ideology, sense of self, and behavior. While my focus is quite different, it is important to acknowledge Lasswell's assumptions, which include the importance of the case history and interview, the status of the internal world, and the impact of internality on public forms of action. It is a mistake, he argues, to think of political or public relationships as independent of inner psychodynamics that mold personality and belief.

The schizophrenic self transmits complex messages about human need and the structure of gratification, and uses a language that cannot be known in terms of its attachment to a significant social or historical other. "The [schizophrenic] scream is a protest . . . the scream means, 'stop, stop, surrounding malevolent forces. Don't overcome me, don't drown me. I want to live, I am alive, I scream'" (Arieti 1974, 307). To determine what this scream or message means requires a sensitivity to the symbolic

1

content of language and to experience that reflects the unconscious laws of mental organization. As one clinician puts it: "In such [a] human organism, there is a unique form of words which, properly heard, reveal the reality peculiar to that person" (Siirala 1964). Or compare the following observation by an "ex-schizophrenic":

> Let us say that when you awake tomorrow you find standing at your bedside a man with porpoisescale skin who tells you that he has just arrived from Mars, that he is studying the human species, and that he has selected your mind for the kind of on-the-spot examination he wants to make. While you're catching your breath, he walks casually into your best chair, drapes his tail over it, and informs you that he will be visible and audible only to you. Fixing his three eyes sternly upon you, he warns you not to reveal his presence; if you attempt to do so, he threatens he will kill you instantly. [O'Brien 1975, 1]

Delusion, a world held within, exercises considerable power over the self. "Regardless of their individuality," delusional systems "seem to have certain characteristics in common . . . figures of authority . . . command with considerable expectation that the [self] will obey" (ibid., 129). Delusional figures requiring obedience and action "live or exist beyond human control"; they are "superhuman and beyond the power of human authorities who might interfere. . . . Once they appear [the self] speedily gets the general drift; either you do what these characters say, or else; for no other human being can help you" (ibid., 112). Clinically delusion entraps the self: "In the acute phase, the patient is overwhelmed by organismic panic and cannot distinguish what is inside him from what is outside of him. He exists in a dreamlike state. . . . He does not know that he is hallucinating or has a delusion. He is the delusion or hallucination" (Pao 1979, 245). And "he knows that his 'new' delusional self is his self. Similarly he no longer needs to lament, 'where was he' for his 'old' self is long buried and forgotten" (ibid., 247). Delusion creates its own, specific imprisoning effect: "The schizophrenic existence has been likened to the person who lives in a glass prison pounding on the walls, unable to be heard, yet very visible" (Mendel 1977, 129).

In delusion, levels of emotional function, subject to incessant oscillations, are "abrupt and catastrophic in extent," experienced by the schizophrenic as "outside his voluntary control—thus the uncanniness and terror of schizophrenic states" (Edelson 1971, 126). Most importantly, delusions organize emotional and physical experience: "a delusion may not be simply the creation of a false reality substituted for a painful true reality in the interests of gratification, but rather might involve the patient's use of a particular and for most of us peculiar, kind of language to represent, think over and communicate certain conceptions he has of his object world, self and his past experience" (ibid., 123). From this point of view, psychotherapy with schizophrenics involves a process of liberating the self from the delusional knowledge system, a "process of becoming more fully awake" (ibid., 116).

Delusions bracket reality, define the coordinates of an inner world that organizes experience with great intensity, and reject any reality considered to be part of the social language game. Nothing links delusional utterance to a consensual or ordinary reality, although schizophrenics may speak in ordinary language. "Delusions and hallucinations represent in part efforts to create a new reality, in the form of thought or image, to replace the rejected reality. The new reality has elements at least more favorable to gratification than the rejected reality" (ibid., 72). Such systems act as defenses against other human beings—it is safer to be in your own constructed universe than to deal with others who may be unpredictable and demanding.

Linguistic experience of these images, which is essential to the schizophrenic self, indicates an ongoing survival activity. Language links the self to a world that requires participation, no matter how fantastic it may seem. And attachment to the utterance, to the ability to speak, affirms what remains of a self-image. In being able to speak, the schizophrenic demonstrates the capacity for human communication. Notice how Edelson describes the process:

> Hallucinating, frightened, fascinated [the schizophrenic] may feel trapped in a world of vivid images, from which he cannot escape. Think of that same patient lurching and staggering from one word to another, and suddenly blank, motionless, from words to silence. Think of the strained attention and effort such a patient may then bring to the creation of some order, any kind of order—how he focuses on words, how he weaves and strings them, how he scrutinizes each word, how he doubts and backs up and repeats, refusing to let anything pass without clearing and placing and clarifying and connecting it. Is not that how you or I might try to awaken ourselves from a nightmare? [ibid., 79–80]

Freud speaks of this kind of linguistic event as an attempt to protect the self from external stimuli. It is also the method the psychological victim uses to defend against what are perceived as externally hostile agents (the internal language of power as defensive structure). Delusion shields consciousness from the "unacceptable" threats posed by others.

> *Protection against* stimuli is an almost more important function for the living organism than reception of stimuli. The protective shield is supplied with its own store of energy and must above all endeavor to preserve the special modes of transformation of energy operating in it against the effects threatened by the enormous energies at work in the external world. [Freud 1920, 27]

3

Delusion then surrounds the self, provides refuge, creates explanation. It constitutes itself as a form of knowledge with origins inside the self and language games peculiar to the self's internal, psychological reality. It is a prison that absorbs, transforms, and devours the ego.

The Recovery of Delusional Utterance:
An Empirical Environment

Initially, my effort to seek out a clinical reality involved a simple proposition: to speak meaningfully about human nature required more than introspection and reflection on commentaries. It seemed imperative to witness "human nature" or the expressions of the human self in a form that could touch on primitive or basic developmental structures, what might be called the self's "original position." If delusion derives from the precivil unconscious, the environment where society contains that language would be the most logical place to seek it out. A mental hospital that encouraged linguistically based psychotherapies seemed the most likely source for evidence of the self in its natural condition. There, it seemed, the abstractness of the classical concept of a "state of nature" and its presentation in liberal political theory could be made accessible through what the schizophrenic projects as linguistic description. There "natural states" appearing as psychological forms or models could be explored as living realities.

What cannot be missed in the literature on schizophrenia, no matter how formal, is the stark contrast between the "rational" social ego and the primitive, nonsocial, nonconsensual worlds of an inner life. That distinction is clear enough: a schizophrenic who says "bears are coming out of my eyes" or "muskrats are running around in my head" begins from logical or inferential premises having little in common with historically defined consensual systems. Nor is the schizophrenic self particularly interested in social habits and routines. The person who suffers from schizophrenia denies implicitly the terms of both the psychological *and* social contracts, especially as the latter emerges in the use of language. The ego withdraws from social representations, constructs a universe separate from meanings and relations generated in a social milieu, rejects assumptions about normality, and speaks to internal audiences completely dissociated from any autonomous social or historical other or tradition. Nothing in the schizophrenic's universe exists independently of the terms and definitions of the inner world.

My intention in seeking out a clinical environment was to enter delusional worlds, observe their structure and transformations, and look at precivil forms of psychological reality (the infant's object-relations) embodied or recreated in language. It would be (or so I thought) a fairly straightforward task: to find a suitable environment for observing madness (i.e., a mental hospital), actively delusional patients who enjoyed talking, and a long enough period of time to explore in a participatory relationship the nature and structure of what patients believed "reality" to be. I decided not to administer questionnaires (since they would objectify the process and interfere with the phenomenological flows of delusional imagery). Nor would I put an arbitrary limit on the interviews—it was to be the patient's decision when to end the dialogue.

Given these guidelines, I arranged a research project with the Sheppard and Enoch Pratt Hospital in Towson, Maryland, a suburb just north of Baltimore. Sheppard/Pratt, as it is known locally, is a private, nonprofit mental hospital. It has been regarded since its founding by Quakers in the late nineteenth century (it was first chartered in 1853 and opened its doors to patients in 1891) as a center for progressive and humane care. Taking his model from the eighteenth-century founders of what has come to be known as "moral" psychiatry, Moses Sheppard in his bequest to the trustees insisted on the "courteous treatment and comfort of all patients." The hospital was to "combine every feature that science and experience might indicate as requisite or desirable to minister to the greatest possible advantage of the patients" (Forbush 1972, 20).

Sheppard left the trustees over three hundred acres of rolling, wooded hills in Towson (much of which has subsequently been sold to local colleges and hospitals), in addition to a capital fund (with the stipulation that only the interest be drawn on) to finance the hospital's construction and maintenance. "I desired to invest the estate in such a way as to meet some need that would not otherwise be met and to see that the money would continue to be a blessing to men and women on down through the generations" (ibid., 239). Moses Sheppard's original intent has been upheld by the present hospital administration. In the words of a former patient, Sheppard/Pratt gave her a "home, a family, a world that meant something to me, where people cared and listened. Leaving there was the most difficult thing I ever did."

Sheppard/Pratt's physical structure is not that of a conventional mental hospital. It has no dingy rooms or wards; it is kept immaculately clean and airy; its grounds are spacious and expansive. It does not engage in the exploitation or brutalization of patients. Nor is it an institution designed for the management of recalcitrant physical and psychological behavior. Patients are encouraged to take advantage of its extensive activities programs, including recreational facilities and a well-stocked patient library. The hospital's adult services involve about 260 patients, but it also runs a high school for its younger patients. Everything is done to make patients as physically comfortable as possible.

The psychiatric and psychological staff represent a number of different perspectives. The orientation is primarily psychoanalytic, and Harry Stack Sullivan's interpersonal psychiatry exercises considerable in-

5

fluence. In addition, a great deal of importance is attached to milieu treatment and to participation from all sectors of the treatment environment. The hospital runs an extensive psychiatric residency program and supports postdoctoral fellowships for psychologists; the nursing department sponsors its own education and development programs. Outpatient services (including a day treatment center and a highly successful agoraphobia clinic) are offered to the surrounding community. Sheppard also sponsors symposia for the general public on different approaches to psychiatric interventions and the treatment of a variety of mental disorders. In all respects, Sheppard/Pratt is an enlightened, multipurpose mental hospital. Given current conceptions of institutional care, its philosophy of treatment is as far as possible from the "warehouse" or "snake pit" mentality.

Sheppard/Pratt gave me access to its patient population and made available its research services and staff library. I could, with the appropriate consent, sit in on patient interviews, case evaluations, resident supervision, hospital seminars, hall meetings, service conferences, and residency training classes. I had the opportunity to participate in all aspects of the life of a sophisticated mental hospital. Conversations with patients were governed by two conditions: (1) the patient's voluntary consent, both oral and written, and (2) the therapist's consent (with the understanding that occasional meetings would be held regarding the nature, substance, and content of the dialogues). Through interviews, I found patients who felt reasonably comfortable speaking with me. I explained why I was at Sheppard, who I was, and asked them if they would, on a regular basis, join with me in a free-floating conversation on any topic they wished to talk about. In each instance I informed the patient of the purposes of my research, and that I was not formally on the hospital staff or employed by Sheppard/Pratt in any way. I explained to them, as clearly and simply as I could, the nature of their contribution to my research project. I assured them I would not reveal their identities in any published work, that my presence at the hospital would not interfere with or be dependent on services they received from Sheppard/Pratt, and that they would be free to withdraw from the conversations any time they chose.

In some instances my position as outsider, an individual not formally entrusted with patient care, made it easier for the patients to reveal what they often called their "secrets" (which I took to be knowledge claims made on the psychological environment). I never promised not to reveal these secrets to their therapists, nor did the patients insist on this. Occasionally I received the impression that what the patients were frightened of or even ashamed to tell their therapists they shared with me, knowing full well that secrets would be conveyed to their therapists.

6

Sheppard/Pratt's treatment program involves active collaboration among staff at all levels: psychotherapists, nurses, activities therapists (dance, art, work, skills, occupation, recreational, and so on), mental health workers (usually local college students in some field pertaining to mental health), volunteers, and consultants. Considerable give and take characterizes meetings devoted to the clinical progress of patients, and the treatment milieu encourages an open exchange of views. Occasionally differences arise or political alliances develop within the hospital regarding the allocation of resources or treatment philosophy. Yet during the period of my research, these alliances never undermined the effectiveness of the hospital's primary therapeutic aims.

I spent all my time on the long-term adult halls (in the facilities devoted to adult services, the majority of the beds are occupied by patients whose stay is longer than thirty days). Each hall houses about thirty patients in usually (with a few exceptions) two or three to well-lit, comfortable rooms. The impression is certainly not that of a typical ward; rather, the visitor to any hall sees a nicely furnished commons area with brightly decorated rooms. The hospital's central buildings reflect their origins in a late-nineteenth-century architecture (although the interiors have been completely renovated). Red brick, intricate spires, a liberal use of copper flashing, slanted, slate roofs, and native stone give an impression of solidity and enormous expense in the initial construction. Surrounded by well-tended lawns, gently sloping hills, huge maples, poplars, and pines, Sheppard/Pratt appears to be a quiet oasis, a refuge, an asylum from the cares of the world. However, Sheppard is definitely not a hospital for the indigent. Its population comes primarily from middle- and upper-middle-class families with, for the most part, liberal health care and hospitalization plans. Table 1.1 gives some indication of the composition of the Sheppard patient population, the nature of the diagnoses, and the type of patient. The mean length of stay is six months, although the hospital has had a few patients whose residence has lasted over ten years.

The hospital's concern for the patient's welfare is manifested in a number of ways. Patients and staff dress in their own clothes; indeed, in six years of research I only saw one white-jacketed staff member, a consultant neurologist. Far from being mistreated, in some respects the patients are overcared for; the hospital's approach to mental illness treats patients as individuals suffering from considerable pain who need attention and empathy. Psychotherapists, nurses, activities therapists, mental health workers, volunteers—all contribute to an atmosphere in which the patient is rarely treated as a nuisance, and there is considerable effort, with even the most difficult and nonresponsive patients, to engage in some kind of dialogue or interaction. Patients at Sheppard are not drugged for convenience or for purposes of management; tranquilizers

Table 1.1:[a] Composition of the Hospital, Nature of the Diagnoses, and Types of Patient

Inpatient admissions data: General adult units	Males	Females
Voluntary	89.9	88.8
Married	18.9	36.0
Separated/widowed divorced	10.7	14.9
Age		
10–19	20.1	15.5
20–29	52.2	35.4
30–39	11.9	24.8
40–49	8.2	8.7
Educational Level		
(less than) H.S. graduate	20.1	14.9
H.S. graduate	37.7	35.4
Some college	28.3	32.9
College graduate	6.3	11.8
Provisional diagnosis		
Schizophrenia	42.8	34.8
Major affective disorders	11.9	17.4
Depressive neurosis	15.1	16.8
Symptoms on admission		
Depression	54.1	68.9
Delusions	35.8	37.9
Social withdrawal	53.5	49.1
Sleep disorders	32.7	52.8
Confusion	30.2	42.9

Length of stay around 6 months on average (mean).

NOTE: Evaluation date for FY 80 SEPH inpatient admissions indicate that 38% had prior family psychiatric history (treatment of evaluation), 29% attempted suicide at least once, 78% had received previous outpatient treatment, and 62% previous inpatient treatment. Symptoms reported most frequently were depression (68%), social withdrawal (46%), and sleep disorders (44%), with schizophrenia (26%), major affective disorders (15%), depressive neurosis (15%), personality disorders (15%), and alcoholism (10%) the primary diagnoses at evaluation. Treatments of choice indicated most frequently were individual therapy (92%), group or intensive group therapy (56%), psychiatric medications (70%), social services (78%), and activity therapy (70%).

a. SOURCE: *Selected Clinical, Management and Patient Data: Fiscal Year 1979–80*; Research Report 23, the Sheppard and Enoch Pratt Hospital, Baltimore (Towson), Md., pp. 150–60, 186.

and antipsychotic medications are administered judiciously and with concern. The issue of medication is constantly discussed and analyzed among the staff.

For my purposes, the physical environment of the hospital, combined with the attitude of its staff, made it easier for patients to tolerate not only my presence as a researcher but to respond to questions over an extended period of time. Patients were never treated as inmates, and I did not receive the impression I was interviewing prisoners (although at times patients felt unnecessarily restrained and hemmed in by hospital regulations, particularly regarding signouts and the willingness of staff to allow unsupervised excursions on hospital grounds). Sheppard's tranquil surroundings, its use of the patient as a person with needs and problems, its refusal to succumb to the management model, and the very real commitment to a linguistically based psychotherapy enabled patients to regard my presence as an extension of their hospital life.[1]

All patients regularly undergo intensive psychotherapy, usually three or four times a week for periods of up to an hour. The verbal aspects of treatment are crucial, although patients also have available an extensive range of activities programs. Psychotherapy implies work within the context of a linguistic exchange, and this awareness of the importance of language extends throughout the hospital's treatment plans. Since words mean a great deal to patients, communication signifies considerably more than the transmission of information (although it is frequently difficult to establish any regular pattern of communication with schizophrenics). The shifts in mood, the inner feelings of terror and panic may last for long periods of time and patients may refuse human contact by sitting and staring or lying in bed for hours or sitting rigid in a chair and uttering random phrases. Each hall has a carefully monitored quiet room for patients undergoing severe reactions or exhibiting impulsive behavior that threatens or bothers other patients and staff (such as kicking, hitting, and screaming).

My conversations with patients took place in a private recreational room on the hall or in an office provided by the hospital. The dialogues lasted anywhere from thirty seconds to an hour, depending on the patient's inner turmoil and capacity to speak without crippling anxiety. I found several patients receptive to my project, if somewhat puzzled by my interest in them; indeed, the dialogues may have provided some relief from the expectations and predictability of hospital routine. Although

---

1. It should be emphasized that many schizophrenic persons are quite lucid; the caricature of the schizophrenic as a "raving lunatic" does not describe the patient at Sheppard/Pratt. Because of medication, most patients keep to themselves and appear quite withdrawn and quiet.

the patients were initially puzzled over my status and amused that a political theorist could find their thoughts useful, I was able to establish with each a long-term relationship. Over my six years of clinical contact, dialogues with individual patients lasted anywhere from three to twenty-four months.

I received advice and suggestions from therapists and senior staff in my effort to decipher complex delusional systems and to understand the psychodynamics of schizophrenic defenses. Therapists, nurses, mental health workers, activities therapists, and social workers all generously shared their time and experience; and at particularly difficult moments, this sort of collaborative feedback contributed to the ends of the project.

My goal then with patients was to avoid objectifying the research relationship. I set up a routine that included being at the hall on certain days at specific times. I immersed myself in theoretical orientations that focused on psychotic and schizophrenic process, and I sought out staff whenever possible for informal guidance. I spoke with therapists, and received suggestions on how to proceed, impressions on the course of clinical treatment, interpretations of relevant psychodynamic material, any background information that might be relevant, and the patient's reactions to my presence. I attended hospital seminars, hall meetings, case presentations, case reevaluations, and observed staff supervision. If I was going to have any success in explaining delusional systems, I felt it was essential to be intellectually and emotionally involved with patients and hospital. Research, learning, and understanding: each became part of an inquiry into the projections of the inner self. To penetrate this tricky and unsettling universe required both a sensitivity to the world itself (in language) and a willingness to see that world through specific clinical and theoretical orientations.

Schizophrenia and Culture: Some Introductory Remarks

In listening to this language and its symbolic content, I became increasingly aware of a realm of expression that functioned as knowledge. It seemed that a logic or message system internal to the delusional utterance was determining the structure of the patient's existential world. Utterance, no matter how bizarre, spoke about the world and represented value in fantastic images. Truth (for the patient) appeared to lie in the inner meanings of the delusional system, not in any social or consensual constructions linking time, history, tradition, and culture. For the delusional self, knowledge of the inner has little to do with what comes before or what happens tomorrow. It is an imaginary world (taken as real) strictly understood as a happening in the present, a reel of images unraveling in vivid immediacy. Every reference, feeling, thought, or action develops according to a logic that derives solely from the internal structures of the delusion itself; the self retreats from formal assumptions about language and thought.

The language and images of delusion should not be understood as sympathetic to the languages of the polis or to theories of citizenship and obligation. Indeed, from the point of view of the rationally analytic political philosopher (Aristotle, for instance), delusional utterances constitute an immediate danger. Social and political language protect the polity from the expressiveness of precivil impulses, Further, political philosophy supports the efforts of the rational ego in directing energy that, uncontrolled, would inevitably lead to entropy. It would be naïve and romantic to think of the political philosopher as supportive of the "id"; and from Socrates onward political philosophy makes a fetish out of the rational (the efforts at control and domination) and sacrifices inner desire (as an expression of unconscious energy) for structure in the external world. Even a political philosopher like Rousseau, sensitive to the inner self, assimilates the conditions of the emotional life to the juristic and political embrace of the general will. The institutional and formal mechanisms in his social contract are designed to move away from the lack of definition and motivation of the state of nature. Whether the general will ever assured the sovereignty of the "languages of the heart" at the core of the participatory process is another question. Yet the "rationality" of arrangements in the social contract possess a depth, structure, and meaning missing in the amorphous emotional reality of Rousseau's natural condition.

Political philosophy consistently shies away from the hidden, the unknowable, the unseen in the self. Plato banishes the poets; no well-organized polity can allow such disturbances. Aristotle refuses the "beast" admittance to "polis life" (I assume here that a modern variant of an Aristotelian beast might appear in the guise of the modern delusional schizophrenic). Hobbes in the *Leviathan* guards against the presence of madness and delusional speech. Adam Smith forces nature into a beneficient pose and assures the survival of such "beneficience" by implanting in the breast of all citizenry an "Impartial Spectator" (what today might be called a sadistic superego) that guarantees compliance with social and political law. Even Marx ignored the possibility that the mad might justly claim a psychological affinity with the proletariat. And it was Kafka in the *Metamorphosis* who demonstrated that economic and social structure intensifies the internal experience of delusion and distorts the self's ability to contain its energy and relate to things external to its perceptual field. While the political philosophers banish the mad, it remains for writers like Kafka and Freud to remind us that madness is both a social and intrapsychic event, that it may be integral to the culture's experience of itself. In fact, to deny the expressions of the unconscious through

11

"reason" and domination might be to increase its pathogenic properties. There is then an aspect of madness or delusion that is quite unsettling, even threatening, to the political philosopher. Why banish or otherwise make invisible the psychological reality of delusional utterance? Yet it is not at all clear what the nature of that threat is, what it implies, or even how legitimate it actually is.

Nevertheless, it would be absurd to argue that madness and mad speech should be included in the philosophical justifications of political, social, and economic order. Such justification would be so bizarre that it makes sense only as fantasy (in the movie *King of Hearts*, for example). Yet the mad occupy a place within the social order and their exclusion by political philosophy and the demands of social organization may signify more than a disruptive presence and unacceptable behavior. Mad speech contains certain symbolic truths that focus attention not only on the conscious orientations of power, but also on the unconscious or primary processes that precede our fundamental affective attitude toward power and authority—two concepts central to the organization of political interests and the recommendations of political philosophers. Delusion is an implicit commentary on the inner origins of power and authority.

It may be the expressiveness, the unsettling imagery of an imaginative inner universe that disturbs political philosophers and scientists. Delusional utterance seems little concerned with the externally constituted political world of institutions, laws, and codes. It is not involved in what we normally call history. The language of madness, then, situates the "gaze" (of the observer) within the self and implies that to be a citizen involves certain internal considerations that if not resolved or dealt with can only bode ill for the political world. Sick selves make ineffective and withdrawn citizens, and a schizophrenic cares little for the political process as an arena of activity. As one patient put it to me, "I hate the superego." He then elaborated a complex theory about a benign civilization lacking all superego controls. The schizophrenic reminds us with considerable clarity that politics begins within the self; that the values, meaning, and orientations toward power and authority have psychodynamic foundations. Political scientists skirt this issue by arguing that the inner self is not open to investigation, or that it is not quantifiable, or that it is more appropriately part of the "private" realm of experience and therefore peripheral to considerations of the political and public world.

Dialogue with schizophrenics is no ordinary conversation. Frequently I found myself refracted in the translucent and penetrating gaze of another human being who could see in a way inaccessible to my world of "normal" consciousness. The "gaze" inwards, so characteristic of the delusional utterance, encircles the external world; and what we judge to be solely a function of externality depends in large measure on the action of internal, psychological structures. Schizophrenic language is vivid evi-

12

dence for this link between the internal and external. It symbolizes a cultural pathology hidden and disguised through the maneuvers and control of rational ego operations. It is also a language that reflects the extremes of the human community. The schizophrenic's expressiveness, then, is not a perversion of the community but an integral part of it.

Language and Description: The Meaning of Schizophrenic Messages

The patients I knew at Sheppard/Pratt were intelligent, sensitive, and aware human beings, yet they had little hope of ever becoming part of any social process and structure. They often voiced a despair about the future, about how they would be stigmatized, how family, friends, and employers would look down on them as former residents of a mental hospital, ex-mental patients, "schizos," "loonies" and so on. Participation is a real and troubling issue for people classified as separate and undesirable in the culture. Even in an institution as enlightened and humane as Sheppard/Pratt participation was rarely discussed, and when it was, the issue appeared to be tangential to the hospital's primary therapeutic objectives. But it is a fact that the person who utters strange and confounding words ceases to participate in the society's common purposes. That exclusion is political. What we do not want to see stirred up in ourselves—extremes of scorn, hate, fear, dread, and need—we make invisible by hiding the persons who exhibit these extremes and by objectifying their speech, studying it as some aberrational, sick dynamic. We refuse to listen to the ontogenesis of our own values. The institutions refuse to listen. But delusional utterance contains profound meaning: delusions are about human experience; they touch on universal issues.

It is of course impossible to speak about delusional reality as "philosophical" or "logical" in the normal way these terms are used. While the schizophrenic speaks in ordinary language not much different from everyday speech, it is not language that would be recognizable as displaying normal or formal logic. The schizophrenic possesses a deep and thoughtful mind that makes sense within a framework that has to be understood and decoded.

If common structures unify the garbled messages of schizophrenia, the impact of those structures implies a consequence that is *political*—political in the sense that withdrawal from the conventional codes of communication, from the historical messages, from the language paradigms, implicitly represents a rejection of culture. Overwhelmed by the pain of social values and forms and by domineering messages the self finds impossible to accept or internalize, consciousness turns away from society and from its history, and embraces the logic of nature as opposed to

13

those mental operations learned through socialization and acculturation. Delusion, then, may be seen as a denial of history, the language of history, and the archives of a historical culture.

Delusion produces a type of knowledge, but not a knowledge, as I have been arguing, understood as a logical series or as a historically defined or determined philosophical system. This knowledge appears as "organization" of the inner world, what Margaret Sechehaye (1956) calls the *Ordnungsprinzip* or a basic attitude or position toward experience and need. I am suggesting that once the *Ordnungsprinzip* of delusion has been deciphered, it should be considered a form of knowledge. Such knowledge is not socially useful, nor does it create a therapeutic orientation toward the social world. It is unconscious, and its origins are obscure. But it is nonetheless knowledge that should be taken seriously and not dismissed as the "ramblings" of the mad, or as crazy speech against which to measure "normal" speech. For a person to feel compelled to use delusional utterance means that something in that person's particular culture, milieu, or family produced the need for an active, symbolic language. And in the absence of a clearly discernible genetic, physiological, or chemical imbalance or defect, it should not be argued that the schizophrenic is innately disposed to madness, nor should madness be seen as the product of a temporary aberration in body chemistry.

It was a source of continuous fascination to me to feel the subtle (and often not so subtle) effect delusional utterance had on what could be called "normal" or "rational" intellectual structures. If even with support from experienced staff and therapists I could be rattled by what I was hearing (and if psychiatric residents and, less frequently, seasoned clinical staff could undergo similar reactions), the effect of delusion on individuals not professionally involved with the "mad" and "disturbed" must be immense and in some respects intolerable. A family is thrown into considerable disarray when one of its members is diagnosed as schizophrenic. To compound the problem, there is almost no instruction in popular culture regarding communication with mad people. Thus delusion is usually met with shock, dismay, and utter confusion. Since delusion disrupts the relations between cause and effect and the sense of a past, present, and future, it is inevitable that the delusional self will affect the way of life and the ordinary day-to-day patterns of closely associated individuals. By confusing the order of things and by delving beneath the surface of experience, the schizophrenic initiates a way of seeing life that is strongly felt by those who exist within the schizophrenic's life world. Delusion therefore possesses the power to involve others in its terms and definitions and to disrupt the habitual patterning of experience and the routinization that accompany any form of organized social life. Delusional language alone is unsettling since it confounds a historically given semiology and the accepted meanings of words with ideas and behavior often perceived as bizarre. It is utterance that should be understood as part of a culture, continuous in time, whose historical fragmentation, in experience and value, finds itself reflected in the language and behavior of those we call delusional.

The schizophrenic's threat to the community's sense of its own integrity depends on political frames of reference that have become part of our linguistic life. For example, Wittgenstein argues in *On Certainty* (1969) that "knowledge is in the end based on acknowledgement" (par. 378). Yet the schizophrenic refuses to accept the terms of acknowledgment and moves from the culturally defined "language game" to an inner world that denies any sense of acknowledgment. What Wittgenstein argues about the importance of language games and the nature of acknowledgment applies with considerable force to the linguistic plight of the schizophrenic:

> It is quite sure that motor cars don't grow out of the earth. We feel that if someone could believe the contrary he could believe *everything* that we say is untrue, and could question everything that we hold to be sure. . . . We should like to say that someone who could believe that does not accept our whole system of verification. [ibid., par. 279]

For the schizophrenic however, motor cars *do* grow out of the earth, and it is this recognition that distinguishes delusional conceptions of verification from the normal, routinized and historically defined language games and sources of acknowledgment. The schizophrenic occupies a very peculiar language environment, but it is one that possesses its own system and patterns of verification.

Society rightly refuses to accept the legitimacy of the schizophrenic's lingusitic and ontological constructions. After all, if we were to believe that motor cars grow out of the earth or the clouds contain atom bombs, the entire productive and consensual world would cease to exist (which is what happens for the schizophrenic). Obviously madness cannot be the norm, nor should it be. It should, however, be acknowledged as a language filled with meaning and representation, and not be shut away and denied. Delusion not only reveals part of who we are, our unconscious human identity, but also draws attention to failures in a whole range of social activity. What is important here is not the fact that society refuses acknowledgment of delusional utterance, but that the linguistic forms of madness (and their messages) are excluded and regarded as being ontologically inferior, a sickness holding no meaning at all. What the schizophrenic speaks as message is denied. And the politics of normal language, particularly the scientific languages of interpretation, translate that message into an aberrational statistic. In rejecting the entire system of social verification, the schizophrenic stands outside the normal linguistic modes of life. That does not imply, however, that the schizophrenic is "wrong" or, more importantly, that the messages he constructs lack significance. What the schizophrenic utters constitutes his "truth."

> Suppose we met people who did not regard that [a proposition of physics] as a telling reason [for a given action such as taking precautions in boiling water or insulating pipes against freezing]. Now, how do we imagine this? Instead of the physicist they consult an oracle. (And for that we consider them primitive.) Is it wrong for them to consult an oracle and be guided by it? If we call this "wrong" aren't we using our language game as a base from which to combat theirs? [ibid., par. 609]

The schizophrenic lives out an inner life that opens itself to view through language. While it appears strange to the outsider, it accurately reflects the ordering principles of an inner reality and indicates a willingness to survive psychically through the agency of language. Delusional language (in Wittgenstein's sense of a "form of life") defends the self against dread and an impending sense of annihilation. This use of language may be understood by society as "wrong" or as gibberish, but for the self uttering delusional words language serves to orient experience, to explain and interpret. Meaning may be kept hidden or may appear in fragments, in phrases lacking an obvious coherence. Yet each word uttered possesses a significance, a reference deriving from the *Ordnungsprinzip* of delusion rather than from the language of socially rooted assumptions and values. While the language violates social forms of understanding, it is certainly "right" and essential as a psychological defense and a commitment to survival, and should therefore be taken seriously and not dismissed as nonsense.

Wittgenstein writes that "at the end of reasons comes persuasion." But the schizophrenic is not interested in persuading any audience. The true interest here lies in an internal audience, and any attempt to suggest that delusional reality is "untrue" will be quickly rebuffed and denied. "It would be more disturbing to [the patient] to realize that [the delusions] were symptoms of an illness rather than real" (from a patient chart at SEPH). For the schizophrenic, delusion does not lend itself to argument, and persuasion is not the issue. Delusion means survival; to give up delusion would mean to relinquish not only the self's only knowable reality but also the very terms and conditions of life. It is unthinkable to the schizophrenic that the delusion is wrong. Only by replacing delusional attachments with consensual ones can the schizophrenic begin willingly to shed the delusional identity.

In this regard correspondence with social reality is equally irrelevant. For example, a patient may say that he is a double agent for the C.I.A., and the C.I.A. will reward him with 650 million dollars if he does certain things, or he may insist that his therapist is controlled by a satellite run by the C.I.A.—all these "delusions" manifest a "truth" that preoccupies the self and defines psychological boundaries. Such utterance also allows the self to survive the enormous pain that floods its consciousness. To live in a grandiose fantasy, a complex delusional system, is to deal effectively with the pain without confronting it directly. To acknowledge (as this patient's therapist did) that the idea of being a double agent for the C.I.A. may have something to do with the patient's perception of radically opposed qualities in his parents involves an encounter and recognition of a personal past and history that may involve intolerable pain. It is much easier and safer to relate to delusional images than it is to confront the meaning of that imagery in the context of an intrapsychic conflict or the recollection of serious developmental trauma.

Conclusion

Delusional utterance has been excluded from society's common fund of meaning, even though that utterance forces the "common fund" to look more closely at its processes of definition and its assumptions about identity. The afflicted or delusional self is regarded as something other than an extension of the community's organic integrity, since the politics of utterance defines what will and will not be said. Language and its use become political issues manifest in any number of forms: the limits of allowable speech; the conception of nonsense; the definitions of reliability, comprehensibility, and predictability; and the kinds of language appropriate to the duties of the "good citizen" and the "good person." The exclusion of the schizophrenic ultimately protects the society's sense of its psychological reality and security, the inherent justice of its values, and the structures that stand behind and motivate the historically accepted language games.

Society's political integration depends on the controlling dynamic of modern, scientific, technological languages that regard linguistic deviation as pathological "eruptions" on the body politic. It is here that Wittgenstein's views regarding language are particularly important, especially in relation to the power of a given language game to define the nature of utterance and the structure of the relationship between words and meaning. It is frequently the case, for example, that the information processing model used to study linguistic deviation in schizophrenia makes certain assumptions about language that depend more on the socially approved conception of language use and logic than the internal psychological processes that generate delusional utterance.

It is a mistake to view the schizophrenic as participating in a historically defined language game that requires some form of consensual validation. Yet to treat schizophrenic utterance as a commentary that verifies structures hidden in a peculiar internal logic requires a psychodynamic framework capable of describing the relation between knowledge and desire. The reality of the schizophrenic's linguistic productions possesses internally consistent verifiers. Decoded and interpreted, the relative meaning of the inner dialogue becomes accessible. What I should like to emphasize here is that a patient whose knowledge references lie in inner, hidden forms and who speaks to an inner voice or spirit constantly engages in the expression of meaning through language. The utterance may appear ridiculous to the outsider, but it holds enormous importance for the self whose life revolves around delusion. The capacity to engage in this inner dialogue, to express it to an other, to carry on a conversation with inner spirits and presences, means the difference between psychological life and death.

To conclude: in an emotional sense, schizophrenic delusion represents a triumph of survival over death. In its desperation, delusion signifies at least a momentary ascendance of the life instinct. However, delusion rapidly degenerates into a manifestation of the death instinct when the internal voices begin speaking about suicide and physical mutilation. To maintain to the schizophrenic that his or her inner world rests on erroneous assumptions is to deny the self's reality. An ex-patient remarked: "If I ever become psychotic again and tell you delusional ideas, don't tell me I'm wrong or even interesting. Just say that you and I hold different views about things and my views are all right to hold." Thus delusion should not be confused with aimless rambling; it makes a claim as knowledge. It is not the knowledge of persuasion, nor is it philosophical or social knowledge. It is the knowledge of survival: it gives reasons for being, for speaking to someone, for maintaining a connection with an other. Delusional knowledge systems represent a commitment to life.

two

Delusion and Nature:
A Theoretical Perspective

**Schizophrenia and Regression: The Movement
of Consciousness "Backwards"**

The notion of schizophrenia as raving lunacy is
an overdrawn caricature. Most schizophrenics suffer from an inability to
communicate, what Silvano Arieti (1974) calls the "retreat from society"
or "desocialization." Within the self a struggle is going on with perception, language, and value. Most therapists (including psychiatrists,
psychologists, and social workers) who attribute a psychodynamic etiology to schizophrenia see the condition as a regressive process: "disintegration is not a state that nature accepts." It is unnatural, and therefore
seems to violate inherent "codes" or movements to sociality implanted in
"nature." "Then how does the patient defend himself from [disintegra-
tion]? With further regression. The same mechanism is repeated all over
again. Regression engenders further regression" (ibid., 935), pushing the
person "backwards" in psychological and developmental time.

The psychodynamic argument emphasizes the deviant aspects of
schizophrenic thought. The patient regresses to primitive modes of thinking and lives in a universe of what Arieti calls "paleosymbols" or "clusters" of thoughts peculiar to primitive modes of expression. A paleosymbol (a set of images that for Arieti lacks the sophistication of more
complex, social symbols) consists of a "particular mental cognitive construct which stands for something that exists in external reality"; but
generally the experience of the paleosymbol is not a shared one. "It has
symbolic value, but this value remains private to the individual who
experiences it." Paleological thinking (i.e., delusional thought) is a somewhat more complex form of paleosymbolic representation, but it is still
not as sophisticated or "logical" as social (or what Arieti sees as "Aristotelian") thought: "As thinking progresses from the level of primary
aggregation and becomes more and more organized, it eventually reaches
that order of organization which is called logic or 'Aristotelian' logic"
(Arieti 1967, 68, 108).

From the perspective of the regression model, normal social language
disappears and paleological thought reflects no analogue in conventional
social experience. There are no language structures or paradigms that
govern the exchanges of paleological or delusional thinking. The condi-

19

tion is an "abnormal" way of dealing with an "extreme state of anxiety, which originated in childhood and was reactivated later on in life by psychological factors." It is aberrant because it reflects cognitive modes more appropriately belonging to earlier or less complex stages of existence. Paleological thought "uses a category of specific mechanisms which belong to lower levels of integration and ordinarily play a much less prominent role in life" (ibid., 698).

The concept of "lower levels of integration" or "primitive thinking" determines much of the formal attitude toward delusion—primitive thought is seen as less complex, more concrete, less differentiated than thought in advanced or scientifically oriented cultures. The paradigmatic statement of this position appears in Heinz Werner's *Comparative Psychology of Mental Development* (1957). Most analysts who deal with regression and thought in schizophrenia acknowledge their debt to Werner's interpretation and its variants. Werner's own argument relies heavily on the anthropology of Lucien Lévy-Bruhl and some of the early investigations into schizophrenia undertaken by Alfred Storch. In Storch's view, all schizophrenic utterance and thought belong to a "more primitive psychological level." Instead of abstract ideas, we encounter in primitive thinking (so the argument goes) random perceptions without structure. There is little depth to primitive thought and the "consciousness of objects has suffered a loss of structure and constancy and has sunk to a lower evolutionary level. . . ." (Storch 1924, 18)

Lévy-Bruhl, Storch, and Werner all characterize primitive consciousness as deficient in its power to abstract and in its capacity to suggest a developed notational system. This view of primitive thought remains dominant in the psychiatric and psychological approach to schizophrenia. Parallels, it is argued, can be drawn between the thinking of children, primitives, and schizophrenics. From the standpoint of the model, delusion is an inferior state in relation to civilized forms, and its language—a meaningless "word salad" without any external referent or meaning—a breakup of all cultural artifacts in the self. Primitive and schizophrenic thought lack those "mental constants," in Storch's words, to make conceptual sense out of a reality whose impact on consciousness always seems to be random, without organization and formal intelligence. In the regression model, all evidence of mind slips away.

Werner's term for this act of perception is "physiognomic perception," that is, "the high degree of unity between subject and object mediated by the motor-affective reactivity of the organism" (Werner 1957, 67). In Werner's view, it is not a desirable state of mind. Thinking originates and *remains fixed* in emotional reactions to a specific environment. Consciousness regresses to a childlike psychic reality where the world appears only in the immediacy of magical or animistic perceptions. Thought is diffuse, without sharp demarcation, and representations of nature lack structure, form, and meaning. Such thinking and its accompanying speech, if they emerge in a healthy or normal ego, indicate pathology. Werner equates physiognomic perception with the degenerative thought processes of schizophrenia, a pathology indicating a "decline in the polarity of object and subject" (ibid., 81). Mind or intelligence ceases to be autonomous, and consciousness finds itself victimized by nature or primitivity.

Delusion pushes the self back to a realm (and psychic time) where all thought originates in primal, affective response. Affect actually forms the world itself, and "primitive emotional experience is much more intimately connected with somatic-motor activity than is the case on higher levels" (ibid., 83). The pathological or clinical label Werner attaches to this "lack of differentiation in primordial perception" (ibid., 86) is "synaesthesia," a condition where consciousness lacks any control or any formative power over the environment. What the self "thinks" depends largely on random associations, hallucinations, or images whose content is completely spontaneous and without structure. Synaesthesia strikes "primitive and archaic peoples" more than it does "our own cultural level." Further, the argument goes, synaesthesia destroys the cultural boundedness of all speech acts.

In Werner's argument (which is paradigmatic for psychiatry's approach to thought disorders), the self traverses specific "moments" in psychological growth. What corresponds to primitive thinking in schizophrenics usually appears in childhood, and stages of development give rise to appropriate mental forms: "Processes of a lower order stand in genetic precedence to the processes of a higher order." In advanced civilization, thinking consists in a "complex organization in which the higher process dominates the lower" (ibid., 216). We repress the lower levels and learn to live by the rules of socialization. Healthy people control these lower-level residues (primary process thought). Sick or schizophrenic people lose control of the logical and social properties of thought (secondary mechanisms) and become overwhelmed by the unsophisticated and illogical "primary process." Paleosymbols—the associations peculiar to delusion—fill the mind of the schizophrenic. The extent to which this odd language persists in conscious expression gives the therapist some sense of where to place schizophrenic thinking in a schema of regressive movement and ego disintegration.

To support his argument, Werner draws on Malinowski's anthropology. "In primitive societies [according to Malinowski] the main function of language is not to express the thought or to duplicate the mental processes, but rather to play an active, pragmatic part in human behavior" (ibid., 251). Language or mythic expressions may claim no formal structures independent of the pragmatic environment or the representations of nature. In Werner's adaptation of this idea to comparative

21

psychology (an adaptation that persists in the literature on schizophrenic thinking), primitive societies have "little use for general terms, since they are too circumscribed in feelings to express the kind of thought peculiar to the mentality" of any advanced logic. Words have significance only in relation to their emotive content, and apart from the expression of affect, the words of archaic communities "are essentially devoid of any meaning" (ibid., 251).

A similar phenomenon regarding the use of words, Werner suggests, can be seen in the schizophrenic. Words lose their abstract quality and degenerate into "concrete" or "overinclusive" manifestations of purely affective feeling: "The decline of the concept from the abstract to the concrete is a specific pathological symptom" (ibid., 274). According to this argument primitive thinking, in its appearance in schizophrenic expression, indicates deficiency, a lack of logic. The self, in ceasing to speak according to generally accepted conventions and in violating (through bizarre speech acts) the tacit communication paradigms of organized society, is viewed as sick, as mentally and verbally inferior and therefore outside of the culturally dependent message system.

It is vital, therefore, in any analysis of delusion to make clear what is involved in the ego-shattering process that pushes individuals "backwards" and to attain an understanding of what primitive thinking means and implies in the context of language and speech acts. Delusion represents a repudiation of culture (rationality, restraint, history) and a linguistic reversion to a natural, precivil condition. The regression model, which assumes a particular view of the origins and meaning of primitive expression, accepts, seemingly without much qualification, the anthropology of Lévy-Bruhl and Malinowski. Psychiatric and psychocomparative analysis of regression and schizophrenia have not seriously looked at Claude Lévi-Strauss's conception of primitive and mythic thought and his critique of Lévy-Bruhl. For Lévi-Strauss, it is Lévy-Bruhl who relegates "mythic representation to the antechamber of logic"; who argues that primitive mentality resides "entirely in the realm of affectivity" (Lévi-Strauss 1967, 41). And in his *Notebooks*, Lévy-Bruhl maintains that myths "no longer have any effect on us . . . strange narratives not to say absurd and incomprehensible . . . it costs us an effort to take an interest in them . . ." (ibid., 46). It is the same for many psychiatrists and for a comparative psychologist like Werner: the schizophrenic as primitive retains and exhibits "absurd and incomprehensible" characteristics in both thought and language.

It is generally agreed that regression, which moves the individual back to a "desocialized" state, constitutes a rejection of normal speech and logic (Vygotsky 1962; Kasanin 1964). The dispute lies over what this movement signifies and how to interpret it (Piro 1967). Few psychiatrists, if any, read that rejection as an attempt to forge an alternative theory of knowledge, what becomes the basis for delusional identity. It may be, however, that the rejection of the conventional meanings attached to language implies a serious disruption in the linguistic connections between nature and culture. It is here that a less medical and formalistic approach to what primitive thinking means might be useful. For if delusion, particularly with regard to its narcissistic foundations, is more than a lower level of integration of the ego and its structures, if it is an alternative theory of knowledge with its own logic and structure of meaning, then the condition may suggest more than clinical breakdown or decay. It may demonstrate a rejection that implicitly makes a statement about culture, value, habits, communication, *and* language. It may point to more widespread failures in culture, a reaction whose origins are in the unconscious and which emerges through bizarre speech and language, the eruption of "primary process" thought, and the absence of those "secondary process" mechanisms associated with socialization, authority, and the maintenance of conventional speech paradigms.

Culture may thus have a great deal to do with driving people crazy, and the bizarre gestures and behaviors of many schizophrenics may represent pathogenic reactions to intolerable social stress. It is certainly true that the effect of perverse social and family patterns can be so devastating that consciousness, in the interests of survival, denies the social in favor of the internal, the autistic, and the private. This internal world and its action rest upon certain understandings that have nothing in common with what is considered social or historical. It is the intensity of the split between inner and outer, the radical discontinuity between the delusional and the social world that lead me to the conclusion that delusion is a way of thinking that derives from nonsocial or precivil feelings. I equate the precivil, as the contract theorists do, with the "natural." But I want to emphasize that my argument is not a critique of the importance of social factors in matters of etiology or of the role that delusion plays in protecting the self from the intrusions of social reality (delusion as a form of what Wilhelm Reich (1972) calls "character armor").[1] Rather, it is an attempt to conceptualize delusion as a form of knowledge whose underlying assumptions and governing frames of reference represent an antithesis to epistemologies built on social and historical assumptions.

Delusional utterance suffers from a severe dislocation in social communication, a radical distortion in historical language patterns. "Once a language has been unhinged," Lévi-Strauss states, "it inevitably tends to fall apart, and the fragments that hitherto were a means of reciprocal articulation between nature and culture, drift to one side or the other"

---

1. It might be useful to look at schizoid defenses generally, including delusional projections, in Reich's terms as a form of character armor to keep others as far away as possible from what the self believes to be its innermost secrets.

(1969a, 10). In schizophrenia the process of unhinging pushes conscious-ness toward nature (what I see as delusional symbolizations) and away from culture. But this does not mean that the forms of thought coming from nature are any less complex or less intelligible than socially medi-ated forms. The psychological process involves a movement from one mode of expression to another, from the cultural or conventional to the natural.

The expression of delusion appears in highly symbolic, often unusual forms, in images that a culture refuses to admit into its conscious or functional ordering of the environment. Delusion, as an intrusion of nature into a historically derived culture and its linguistic system, disrupts formal signs (what Thomas Hobbes calls "common names") that are critical to the way society organizes and regulates its language. Lévi-Strauss, however, suggests another view of the natural representation of myth, the "thought" of primitivity. Nature, in his view, does not signify chaos, randomness, arbitrariness, or deviation. Rather, it is filled with meaning, value, and form. In primitive thought, nature is mind-in-action. Building on Lévi-Strauss's theory, one can view the process of dissocia-tion in schizophrenia as implying an unconscious rejection of cultural forms and a corresponding movement toward "nature," that is, a psycho-logical environment unmediated by consensual knowledge. This implicit and unconscious rejection of the language of socialization occurs through a series of defensive psychological maneuvers, in the form of delusion, that are an attempt at protecting the self from what is perceived as a thoroughly hostile external world. The most obvious symptoms appear in the disintegration of the ego, the fracturing of consciousness,[2] the trans-formation of language, the dissolution of any social identity, and ulti-mately the assumption of a delusional identity.

Language and Communication: The
Interpretation of Delusional Imagery
It is difficult, if not impossible, to understand the language and thought of those schizophrenics described in the litera-ture as "advanced," "hebephrenic," "catatonic," or "autistic." It is likely that persons in the last three categories may not use any form of speech. When a person labeled schizophrenic is driven to despair, it may be logical in certain instances to stop speaking. Cessation of speech might follow a person's terrifying realization that society, including his family,

---

2. Laing (1978) sees schizophrenia as a breaking up of consciousness; being degenerates into "partial self assemblies," none of which fits with any other—hence the bizarre masks of the schizophrenic person. Laing is considerably more sensitive to the symbolic and repre-sentational dimensions of schizophrenic speech than most traditional psychiatric analyses.

makes no effort to understand his own frame of reference. (See, for example, R. D. Laing's analysis of the failure of communication in *Sanity, Madness and the Family* 1980.) If society does make the effort, that understanding or attempt to achieve it is seen as threatening and therefore useless. To cease speaking altogether in conventional systems implies a denial of interpersonal and intersubjective reality. In the absence of an obvious physiological or chemical dysfunction, however, it is not at all clear that a catatonic person stops thinking or feeling.

Before the onset of catatonic silence, the regressive process in schizophrenia usually produces a great variety of language, sounds, and gestures, usually in strange combinations. However, before returning to implications of Lévi-Strauss's analysis, I would like to review briefly some major psychiatric interpretations of bizarre language.

Schizophrenic utterance (i.e., psychic facts that appear as language laden with symbolic content) has been described by Vygotsky as "complex thinking," a mental process that pulls phenomena together in "totalities." The very essence of complex thinking lies in its overabundance, in its "overproduction of connections and weakness in abstraction." Cameron sees the process as "a progressive loss of organized thinking . . . an incapacity for taking the role of others when this is necessary to enable one to share adequately in their attitudes and perspectives" (quoted in ibid., 52)[3] For Kasanin, "the schizophrenic thinks largely in more concrete, realistic, matter-of-fact terms"; it is a condition that signifies "a reduction in the capacity to think abstractly" (1964, 43, 45).

From a different perspective, Harold Searles takes issue with the argument that sees the "schizophrenic as unable to think in figurative (including metaphorical) terms, or in abstractions, or in consensually validated concepts and symbols, or in categorical generalizations" (1965, 560–61). In Searles's view, the confusion in the schizophrenic's thinking and the bizarre quality of his utterance have a great deal to do with what he defines as "desymbolization . . . a process whereby the illness causes once-attained metaphorical meanings to become 'desymbolized'; and in the grip of the illness, the individual reacts to them as being literal meaning which he finds indeed most puzzling" (ibid., p. 580). The schizophrenic, however, is capable of symbolic or metaphoric communication. It is the awareness of emotion, the "de-repression of long unconscious feelings," that moves the self from the concrete (that aspect of reality which lacks any differentiation between inner and outer) to metaphorical or symbolic understanding: "I think it enough to conclude that the awareness of emotion—whether murderousness, tenderness, grief, or whatever, awareness of the whole spectrum of emotion—is the father to metaphorical thought and, perhaps in the same way, to all forms

3. Cf. Cameron 1938.

of the symbolic thought which distinguishes the adult human being" (ibid., 572).

Excellent and sensitive articulations of this position appear in the work of David Forrest. Forrest, a psychiatrist who has devoted considerable time to the study of delusional language, argues the thought and language of the schizophrenic are intelligible on a metaphoric level. He asks whether the speech of any human is utterly meaningless or random. Can any human life be so different from the rest as to deserve the labels "meaningless," "random," or "deficient" (an argument that is made in much of the cognitive deficit literature dealing with schizophrenic thought disorders)? If that were the case, he maintains, poetic expression would be regarded as nonsense or unintelligible. According to Forrest, the intelligibility of language as a formal proposition is not the issue. What is important lies in the meaning and significance of language as human expression, in its capacity to convey meaning and uniqueness. He cautions researchers not to conclude too quickly that what appears to be different or odd in schizophrenic utterance represents only nonsense-language or disordered thought.

In Harry Stack Sullivan's view, "schizophrenic phenomenology requires for its complete exposition nothing different in essential quality from the elements of commonplace human life" (1962, 200). Schizophrenic utterance, since it is not qualitatively different from ordinary language, merely exhibits "problem[s] of symbol functioning" and "eccentric symbol performances" (ibid., 32). It "shows in its symbols and processes nothing exterior to the gamut of ordinary thinking including therein that of revery and dreams." Its experience is distinctly human; and the "extraordinary symbol situations" that emerge in the utterance reflect "parallels in the extravagances of dreams." Sullivan, like Searles, rejects any rigid classification of the schizophrenic's cognitive reality or any categorization that sets schizophrenic utterance apart from the kind of thinking that represents the self's efforts to adapt to implosive psychological environments. In this respect both Searles and Sullivan are at odds with Werner's views.

The interpretation of delusion as nonsense or as inferior in relation to a concept of normality depends on context and perspective. What is nonsense to a Werner or Vygotsky may be perfectly intelligible within a linguistic framework possessing different (yet consistent) relations that guide expression. In the case of mythic or primitive thought, images, figures, and symbolizations signify deep structures operating in what Lévi-Strauss (1969b) calls the primitive mind. He refuses to accept the proposition that primitive intelligence is only reactive to nature, that it processes only what it sees. Rather—and this is his great contribution— the thought of the primitive contains its own internal mental structures. Thought *organizes* and *creates* experience; it is not simply the product of observation. Thinking for the primitive is a dialectical process, not a mechanical or concrete one: "Contrary to Lévy-Bruhl's opinion [primitive thought] proceeds through understanding not affectivity, with the aid of distinction and oppositions, not by confusion and participation" (Lévi-Strauss 1969b, 268).

This is the criticism that Lévi-Strauss levels against culture-bound anthropology. It is a position, moreover, that reveals limitations in certain psychiatric and psychological perspectives on delusional utterance.[4] The schizophrenic creates experience through deep organizing structures that lie within the mind. This is what delusion is all about: it is reality lived according to definite patterns and logics. What is difficult is the retrieving and isolation of that logic, figuring out what the language means, finding the structure and form.

Delusional language is noninstrumental and cannot be understood by linear or historical methods of coding speech or analyzing the evolution of language forms. In mythic thought, for example, a "myth system can only be grasped in a process of becoming; not as something inert and stable but in a process of perpetual transformation" (Lévi-Strauss 1973, 354). In this sense of becoming, without reference to a fixed history or to a conscious or measured time sequence, the "crazy" utterances of delusion move beyond the limits of a culturally bound historicity. Such utterances exist outside or beyond history.

Becoming, in the way that Lévi-Strauss uses the term to describe the developmental patterns of myth, is never finished, never static. But the medical terms such as "asyndetic speech" or "predicate thinking," which take for granted a specific boundary and locus on a logical continuum, transform delusional thought into completed activity, an inferior psychological moment, a final stage reached after a series of traumatic episodes. Schizophrenic thought, so the argument goes, degenerates to progressively worse levels, and the delusional image or primary process material indicates mental operations that are either "simple," deranged, or derailed from a definite conception of what thought should be. One example of this is Arieti's notion of a "teleological regression" to an earlier mental state. The sickness lies in the language and by implication in the denial of historically (and logically) derived references as the source and content for images in consciousness.

The alternative hypothesis I wish to argue here is that schizophrenia reflects features that Lévi-Strauss sees in mythic representations: a multitude of images, occurrences, and structures "simultaneously present in the system" (1973, 354) that when decoded reveal common unifying

---

4. For example, to impute to a person "asyndetic speech" (Cameron) or a teleological regression (Arieti) or a "weakness in abstraction" (Vygotsky) is to utilize technical terms as interpretive structure for highly visible symbolizations.

structures. In any myth system there are inevitably numerous symbols that may appear to be unrelated and absurd. Yet it is these symbols in a state of endless becoming that provide the key for understanding structures implicit in what Lévi-Strauss sees as the complex mythic organization of nature. This incredibly rich reservoir of images, figures, and movements represents fundamental structures that account for differences among unique and idiosyncratic linguistic (and expressive) statements. It has been argued about Lévi-Strauss's interpretive procedure that, in this way, "myths produced by societies widely separate in space (and presumably in time) can be shown to be related and to illuminate one another" (Willis 1967, 525).

It may also be possible to find underlying structures linking unique and idiosyncratic expressions of schizophrenic speech. For example, the active thought process of schizophrenia may be analogous to what Lévi-Strauss calls the "dialectical character" of myth, a communicative event that "moves in spirals and not in circles. When we think we are back at our starting point, we are never absolutely and completely there . . ." (1973, 395). Myths derive from the complex interplay of intelligence and nature, an activity that creates depth, structure, and meaning. It is not thought of as moving in a linear direction but as consisting of clusters of "spiral-like" images that tumble about and through one another. A good analogy would be to imagine thoughts developing like swirls or spirals, connected to those preceding them but not developing in any linear fashion. It is the core of this spiral that contains the organizing principle of thought. This exchange of mind with nature, the active intervention of mind in experience, distinguishes Lévi-Strauss's views of the depth of myth from anthropological explanations that see myth as a set of rudimentary, dissociated symbols, as thought without form or structure.

The "Transmissions" of Nature: Myth and Delusion as Message Systems

What Lévi-Strauss argues about primitive thinking runs counter to prevailing interpretations that see delusion as unstructured, diffuse, simple, irrational, and "flat" (i.e., as affectless expressions of self). Such paradigms rarely enter analytically into the closed mythic spirals of delusion and deal with these images as disparate parts of a complex notational system.

For Lévi-Strauss, "nothing is too abstract for the primitive mind." It is both capable of abstraction and transcends itself by operating in a world of concepts. Many psychiatrists see the confusion of schizophrenia not as a concept, with pattern and message, but as a falling away from legitimate language functions. Language comes to be seen as other than structure or intelligibility (as, for example, Arieti's notion of "paleological" thinking in primitives and schizophrenics, or the views that the regressive process depletes the self of meaningful thought and that delusion possesses no status as message-creating intelligence). But given Lévi-Strauss's perspective, delusional utterance may indicate thought that is considerably more complex than the rudimentary translation of affect into disconnected speech and image. Citing Lévi-Strauss, one might respond that paleological thought (a fancy term for aggregations of images that come together as myth) is as comprehensible and meaningful, as deep and textured as any other kind of logic. What differ are the *foundation* and *context* of the logic (logic being understood as a series of relations describing given objects and their association) and their mode of expression (the lingusitic style that conveys meaning hidden in the logics).

The self-contained autonomy of mythic thought, its disregard for causal sequence, its apparent rejection of rules associated with Aristotelian logic, its inversion of symbols and experience—all these factors resemble properties that run through delusional imagery. Images are prerational but are capable of classification (in that they represent mind or intelligence forming or molding nature) and survive in expressive realms quite unlike the world of a normal or expectable rationality. Primitive thought derives from the interpenetration of mind and nature; it is without continuity or linearity. Its concepts of present, past, and future diverge from the structures that condition causal reasoning. Words for the primitive and schizophrenic do not disguise the indeterminancy of nature; rather, they embody or represent the turbulence of an immediately experienced reality.

The logic of myth suggests an activity that organizes nature in a manner consistent with natural occurrence and feeeling. But this does not mean that the mythological mind is any less capable of organization because it addresses itself primarily to feeling. Mind in mythic thought joins feeling with nature according to operations that derive from structures *within the self*. Lévi-Strauss assumes that primitive mythic organization implies an intelligence that is autonomous, separate from affect and independent of the specific object representations of nature. The intelligence of the primitive mind combines, recombines, and plays with nature in sometimes bizarre forms, but the resulting images have purposive content. They do not just happen, but have origins in structures *within the mind*.

These internal mental structures are critical to Lévi-Strauss's argument; in myth, events take place "not with reference to any external reality" but according to categories that derive from what is internal to the mind itself (Lévi-Strauss 1973, 473). From the perspective of the historian, logician, or linguist, mythic thought has qualities of absurdity and incomprehensibility, yet it is filled with inversions that, far from being absurd, make sense in terms of very real logics that perform critical identity functions for the tribal group. That logic appears through such nonscientific speech-acts as the inversion of "proper names and common nouns, metonymy and metaphor, contiguity and resemblance, the literal sense and the figurative sense" (ibid., 296). The communication system, then, must be understood in the context of these inversions. It is the same in the analysis of delusional utterances: the inversions, disruptions, and recombinations of language may signify a notational system that must be understood as consisting of messages with roots in the primary process flows of what is unconscious and precivil.

Mythic thinking creates meaning through the imposition of formal classifications—resident in the mind—onto experience. While those symbol formations that appear as myth draw freely from nature, they are not dependent solely on the experience of nature. Scientific thought, on the other hand, works causally and enforces a clear distinction between nature and intelligence or fact and hypothesis. Mythic thinking arises in relation to events that refuse description as causal occurrences. Primitive intelligence, dialectically playing with nature (rather than treating it as an inert mass) bears little relationship to the laws of combination or sequential thinking critical to Western reasoning. Nor does mythic thought duplicate what Hobbes, for example, thought vital to science: the "reckoning of consequences." Mythic thinking mixes up the logical connections that Western thought intuitively utilizes, and which are tacitly embedded in common rules of communication and understanding (associations that arise from habit, memory, socialization, and specific, identifiable histories and paradigms). In Lévi-Strauss's view, that the logic of myth is alien to Aristotelian forms is not necessarily evidence that myth lacks the power of abstraction. Acausal thought contains abstraction, but on a level that defies the criteria of a causal logic.

Similar operations may arise in the activity of delusional thought, with messages being imposed on reality without any particular regard for those conventional codes that are dependent on social or causal modes of knowing. It might be useful, therefore, to consider the following description of how myth is at times communicated as a model or basis for deciphering the language of delusion:

> It can happen that myths belonging to different communities
> transmit the same message, without all being equally detailed or
> equally clear in expression. We therefore find ourselves in a
> situation comparable to that of a telephone subscriber who is
> rung up several times in succession by a caller, giving or repeat-
> ing the same message, in case a storm or other conversations may
> have caused interference with his earlier messages. Of the various
> messages [particularly those sent by schizophrenics] some will be
> relatively clear, others relatively indistinct. The same will be true
> even in the absense of background noise, if one message is given
> at great length, whereas a second is abridged in telegraphese. In

all these instances, the general sense of the messages will remain the same, although each one may contain more or less information, and a person who has heard several may legitimately rectify or complete the less satisfactory ones with the help of the more explicit. [Lévi-Strauss 1973, 127]

A similar transmission may take place in schizophrenic thought dissociation. The garbled messages become terribly confusing to the listener, but underneath that confusion may lie a structure of meaning that has to be decoded and understood not in terms of conventional or formal modes of exchange, but through the logic peculiar to the transmission system itself.

If one follows up the implications of what Lévi-Strauss suggests, then schizophrenic language requires a decoding process that recognizes the unique quality of these utterances and at the same time sees the speech as a message or sign disguising both complex operations of mind and common structures that reflect an anticultural statement. To put it another way, delusion negates the impact of culture on consciousness and enforces a movement toward nature. The utterance describes a rejection of social and causal operations encircling the self (thus generating enormous confusion and misunderstanding) and a movement toward forms of linguistic expression organized according to idiosyncratic and private logics.

What the utterances mean may be similar to what variations in myths mean: apparently disparate images may be seen to reflect a shared experience (a view that will be argued, from a clinical standpoint, in the next chapter). That shared experience is discovered through common structures that underlie the infinite variations in any single myth or mythic statement. Delusional thought might thus become more accessible through an unconscious identity of structure. If such structures can be shown to exist, schizophrenic speech might not be as isolated, autistic, and monadic as its conscious utterances, taken at face value, would seem to indicate. The decoding procedures would allow the observer to look beneath what at first seems to be a jumbled aggregation of words. The search for structure, then, implies the discovery of some common element about the experience of delusion itself. This element could be analogous to the shared quality of structure that Lévi-Strauss finds in mythic variations deriving from sources separated by wide gaps in space and time. It is not that the experience of schizophrenia is shared in any conscious way, just as variations in myth from tribe to tribe are not shared on the conscious level: what imparts form and structure lies in the unconscious, and those unconscious structures have a validity no matter what their spatial or temporal conscious referents might be.

Physicians trained in the formal methods of Western science are not likely to be persuaded that a nonlinear, acausal mode of thinking, can possess the properties of abstraction, classification, and structure. Nor are psychotherapists likely to discover a shared experience in schizo-

31

phrenia, since all apparent signs of the condition indicate separation and singularity. Yet if common structures unify the garbled messages of schizophrenia, the significance of those structures is political, in the sense that withdrawal from the conventional codes of communication, from the historical messages, and from the language paradigms implicitly represents a rejection of culture. The denial of a culture and its past and the reversion to nature, as Rousseau pointed out, are political events. Overwhelmed by the pain of social values and forms, by domineering messages which the self finds impossible to accept or internalize, the delusional self turns away from society and its history and embraces the "logic" of nature.

The Opposition of Nature and Culture:
Primitive Logic

I should now like to look more closely at delusion as the presence of the "natural," as a mode of thought that rejects the formal structures of a historical language and logic. Delusion is a denial of history, of the language of history, and of the "archives" of a historical culture. It is a mode of thought that radically breaks with convention, inverts common and accepted meanings and references, and encloses the world in a framework that is completely self-contained. What the empirical reality of this natural self is—what constitutes the clinical evidence for it—will be the subject of the next several chapters. What I should like to do here is to establish the basic perspective that guides my interpretation of this language.

Again I turn to Lévi-Strauss. In myths concerned with the loss of culture, he finds that "creation takes the form of a *regression*" (1973, 212; emphasis added), what in the delusional process might be seen as desocialization (or as psychoanalytic regression). Such myths reflect the "discontinuity between nature and culture" (ibid., 232), a movement from mediated social experience to nature, a process analogous to the schizophrenic's rejection of social or historical contexts and the reversion to "primary process" or delusional thinking. The struggle between nature and culture appears in the "play" of the mythic changes, in their apparent unreality to the observer (the myths themselves, however, are very real for the participants). Consciousness as a mediator of mythic images "spontaneously constructs a gigantic set of mirrors in which the reciprocal images of man and the world are infinitely reflected" (Lévi-Strauss 1969, 103). This reciprocity suggests an endless process of composition persistently sending messages out through the "prism" of what the myth signifies. The myth, then, acts as the sign, the perceptual landmark, but organized according to a nonhistorical or acausal logic. Images are "*perceptually* decomposed and recomposed in the prism of Nature-Culture relations" (ibid.). That decomposition and recomposition in the case of delusion projects messages that ignore (and sometimes mock) forms appropriate to cultural and social interaction.

The logic of certain myths transmits an anticultural message, and the mythic story really constitutes an analysis (but in highly metaphoric form) of how the needs of social community and of the natural process find themselves in conflict. This conflict can be seen in the transformations reported by Lévi-Strauss in his description of a symbolic movement from culture to nature: "Because a taboo was violated [in a particular myth] things changed into animals; the basket [a product of culture] became the jaguar, the fisherman and his canoe changed into a duck; the head and beak came from the fisherman's head, the body from the canoe and feet from the paddles" (1973, 211).[5] The symbolic character of these transformations provides images whose content may be bizarre but whose significance (because of a taboo violation) may be crucial. In this sense the images (in spite of their apparent absurdity) contain a message. In each of these series of transmutations (basket/jaguar; fisherman-canoe/duck; fisherman's head/duck's head and beak; canoe/body; paddles/feet) a cultural phenomenon or representation regresses or changes into a natural form.

The kind of myth or image named above describes a particular kind of collapse. It suggests a "state of gloomy indistinctness in which nothing can be indisputably posessed and still less preserved, because all beings and things are intermingled" (Lévi-Strauss 1973, 259). Similar phenomena of consciousness may be present in delusion. The self withdraws to an isolated, hermetic world, to its own frantic gloom. All conventional, traditional, and cultural meanings become distorted or lost. In the words of Lévi-Strauss, "all beings and things are intermingled" (p. 47).[6] Delusional utterances can provide examples of this intermingling: "The

---

5. As an example of the dialectic between nature and culture as mythic image, Firth states: "The concept of men-lions can thus be a resolution of opposites and a fusion of characteristics. It provides a category of beings who combine the behaviour of both lions and men, [who] epitomise both the dichotomy and the bridge between nature and culture" (1960, 3).

6. Cf. the following description of Lévi-Strauss's conception of myth:

> Myths consist of "abstract relations," a characteristic which myth shares with totemic ideas. The main function of myth, the main cause promoting its existence as a mode of thought, is that it is a device for "mediating contradictions" or "oppositions" as experienced by men. The myth recounts certain events, but its significance for those who recite and attend to it lies not in this description, but in the structure, in which significant "contradictions" are posed and "mediated." [Cohen 1969, 346]

Imputation of a *structural significance* to schizophrenic thought appears very rarely, if at all, in the psychotherapeutic and psychiatric literature.

birds speak to me"; "The aliens in spaceships will take me to the other world"; "Will you cut my hooves—whoops, I mean toenails"; "I ate straw last night; I was with my own kind." Conventional logic can make little sense of such utterances. Looked at as signs, however, the bizarre images that emerge in delusion may be interpreted as a kind of primitive message system—one that identifies with the nonhuman but is nonetheless accessible as a form of knowledge.

The regression exemplified by myth moves from one modality of expression to another, from the givenness of a cultural phenomenon (a basket, for example) to a statement about nature (a jaguar). In the case of primitive myth, this movement symbolizes the breaking of taboos, the violation of which provokes cataclysmic transformation. Thus transformation takes the form of the absurd journey from things to living entities, from the body of a human to the body of an animal. A similar perceptual event occurs in delusion, although the schizophrenic's transgression is seen as disobedience or neglect of a whole set of social codes or collective values. To violate these codes implies dysfunctional or antisocial behavior.

It may be that the codes, expectations, and values of constituted social life have a power analogous to the restraining effect a taboo exercises on the tribal community. When the self violates those "taboos" that protect the sovereignty of language paradigms, when the self refuses to see or act in terms that make consensual sense, the pressure becomes so intense, the accusations so strident, that the only recourse lies in withdrawal: anticultural speech and gesture and the subsequent movements toward nature—in other words, delusion.

The direction, then, in schizophrenia is toward the representation of the unconscious in symbolic images that bear a close affinity to mythic expression. Perception of the schizophrenic as one having transgressed a social code (or the schizophrenic's perception of himself as a transgressor and the subsequent internalization of such accusations as truth) induces a dissolution in the structure of the schizophrenic's social ego and reversion to primary process thought, to nature. For Lévi-Strauss, there lies within mythic variation a "logical armature hidden beneath seemingly strange and incomprehensible" symbolizations (1973, 157). Delusional language may present a similar situation. A thorough and unbiased investigation of the utterances of schizophrenics might discover an analogous "logical armature." Such discovery requires intensive empirical investigation, including an examination of delusional utterance as symbolization and a mapping of the contours of the logical armature of delusion.

The thought process of myth, like that of delusion, "never develops any theme to completion; there is always something left unfinished." And myths, like some rites, are "interminable," a quality that schizophrenic utterance often shares. From the perspective of traditional anthropology, a myth looks arbitrary; it is characterized by a "supposedly spontaneous flow of inspiration and a seemingly uncontrolled inventiveness" (Lévi-Strauss 1969a, 16). Such qualities as randomness and the use of expressions without any apparent significance other than what is immediately available in the word itself are also frequently attributed to delusional thinking. The word, so the argument goes, is taken for a thing, not a sign. For Lévi-Strauss, however, myths are "free" in the sense that the images and their construction are not bound by any conscious rules or criteria of association that may be interpreted causally. Primitive communities "seem to have elaborated or retained a particular wisdom which incites them to resist desperately any structural modifications which could afford history a point of entry into their lives" (1967, 474). The freedom of myth, then, consists in its capacity to develop without those restraints and orders implicit in historical logic.

Lévi-Strauss speaks of the "curvature" of mythic logic, as opposed to the "rational" properties of what Arieti calls Aristotelian logic. It is the same with the delusional self: consciousness resists rational forms of understanding and association comprehensible through a linear logic. The schizophrenic ignores conventional reason much as myth disregards sequential thinking and laws of established logical paradigms. It is one thing, however, to argue that myths defy philosophical logics and a totally different proposition to maintain they are useless or lack significance. Lévi-Strauss maintains that mythic images are real and describe a "reciprocity of perspectives in which man and the world mirror each other and which seems to us the only possible explanation of the properties and capacities of the savage mind" (1969b, 222). Delusional utterances may reflect a similar reciprocity and not, as the paradigmatic psychiatric view argues, a fragmented internality with little meaning.

Conclusion: The Primitive Mentality and the Implications of the "Untamed" Mind

Primitive thought is not progressive or teleological. It does not grow or mature through innovations in any given tradition, but rather persists in time through its own closed regulations. It is not a system of thought that emerges from a historical tradition. It would be wrong to think of variations in myths in the same way that, for example, one might think of changes in political thought in Europe from 1500 to 1850. There is no sense of moving time in myth, of concepts having a historical origin in terms subject to causal measurement. And there can be several variations of the same myth, each with its own specific images, but these variations are not the result of the passage of time.

Similarly, it is difficult, if not impossible, to understand delusional

35

utterance as an extension of social or consensual forms of understanding. The thought processes of delusion are not subject to any artificial standard that uses sequential criteria (what Arieti calls "seriatim functions") or theories of interpretation stemming from historical or social traditions or values. Delusional thought, like myth, lies outside of time and any collective political history. Its linguistic expressions suggest a desperate desire to escape culture or society. Its images may indeed comment on matters of common experience by, for example, making use of political figures and symbols, but the direction of the thought is toward the private since the unconscious dynamic provokes delusional interpretations of reality. In delusion the private totally absorbs the public (or at least what is public for the self). What consensual reality conceives as the distinction between public and private disappears for the schizophrenic, and the autonomy of delusion absorbs the action of the outer.

In the writings of Lévi-Strauss, the "tamed" mind threatens the "untamed" or natural with extinction (1969b, 219). And in modern psychiatry the most vivid expression of that untamed mind appears in the delusional schizophrenic, the primitive seen as dangerous, the natural perceived as a complete violation of all social value and significance. The untamed mind occurs at the boundaries of civil society. It is distracted; the structures of the social ego break apart; the self wanders towards "gloomy indistinctness" and lives in dread.

If the logic of myth expresses a considerably more complex reality than Werner, Malinowski or Lévy-Bruhl indicates, if Lévi-Strauss in his *Les mythologiques* provides insight into myth as a complex form of expression with a logic peculiar to its own internal operations, then it may be necessary to rethink the entire question of primitive thought and its association with schizophrenic thought disorders. Lévi-Strauss may offer psychiatry an opportunity to undertake a thorough reexamination of the regression model with regard to what it signifies for formal thought and meaning and what it implies for the assessment of primary process language and its connection with culture. Such a reevaluation may lead to a fundamentally different position toward the significance of nature as it appears in the delusional symbolization.

The following chapters will look at this peculiar inversion of time and reality, at its meaning and structure, at its theory of reality, and at the "politics" that appears in its symbolizations. Like Lévi-Strauss, I believe primitive symbol formations contain logic and structure, that an accessible message pattern, reflecting fundamental oppositions between nature and culture, lies within the language of delusion. And finally, it would be well to bear in mind Lévi-Strauss's assertion that myths often "confer a positive significance on the disabled and the sick, who embody modes of mediation. . . . All states, even pathological ones, are positive in their own way" (1969a, 53). I would argue that the same can be said about delusion. Even though it represents "sickness" that is no reason to dismiss this language as irrelevant to the culture or to social processes of self-reflection. The positive quality of delusion appears in its ability to mirror fractures in the developmental history of the self and society, to refract what is hidden and secret in us all.

three Delusion and the Internal
Structure of Political Reality

The Definition of Schizophrenia

It occurred to me after listening for several months to delusional utterance that some connection might exist between internal emotional structures and the construction of ethical and political systems of belief. The origin of ethical systems, it seemed, might be linked to feelings of badness, worthlessness, and destructiveness. While it is beyond the scope of this study to draw definitive parallels between delusional realities and the construction of complex moral and ethical belief structures (to look, for example, at the psychodevelopmental phases in the growth of a tyranny), it still seems plausible to assume that the origins of ethical ideas might have something to do with the origins of feeling and the self's basic orientation toward its emotional life.

One might ask, for example, whether rigid exclusionary systems of belief are political forms of schizophrenia, delusional conceptions of reality projected outward as truth and embodied as "politics." Might the obverse of the schizophrenic's internality—the delusional system as a perpetual oscillation between images of power and victimization—be found in the political world of the tyrant, racist, or ideologue who demands that the world be understood in the radical images of good and evil, right and wrong, master and victim? One of the most striking things about delusional imagery is its violent, tyrannical, and intolerant cast. It is almost as if the self acts to protect its basic needs for trust, empathy, and compassion by cloaking them in imagery that denies even the possibility of such relations. What better way to accomplish such denial than through the images of violence, tyranny, torture, dismemberment, and domination?

To what extent is rational language used to project outward what are essentially delusional ideas? Is, for example, the labeling of a group as a scapegoat or as socially inferior as delusional as the statements of hospitalized schizophrenics? How different are externally projected delusions from the inner world of the schizophrenic? This is not to say that the schizophrenic is akin to the tyrant; unlike the delusional political leader or group, the schizophrenic holds his terror and explosiveness within, and does not vent them on objects in the political field. The kinship of delusional symbols and externally manifested political delusions lies in

38

images of power, in the expression of tyrannical demands, and in use of the language of extreme victimization when speaking of the self. The polarity of delusional systems into right and wrong, powerful and weak, good and bad frequently resembles that invoked by a tyrannical leader who has managed to acquire a following in the external, social world. Do both systems, the political and the schizophrenic, originate in similar psychodynamic structures? Are the "values" of political tyranny similar to those of schizophrenic delusion?

It is possible that the inner reality of delusion contains evidence that might shed light on "rational" expressions and projections of political madness. Delusional utterance may reveal deficiencies in the historical community's relation to concepts of authority, power, rights, obligation, participation, rules, and commands. Images of sadistic tormenters, which are persistent in the delusional drama, may have a great deal in common, in terms of their affective origin, with political types whose ascendancy depends on domination and torment.

It might be useful at this stage to offer some definitions of schizophrenia. First, however I should like to stress what I feel to be the persuasiveness of psychoanalytic theorists who see the impact of the first year of life on the psychogenetic process as leading to the emergence of what is called schizophrenia. As Theodore Lidz states:

> Although the question of whether schizophrenia is basically a genetic, biochemical or environmental problem certainly has not yet been definitively settled, our findings and theory lean heavily toward the environmental. . . . It appears to us that belief in a genetic or biochemical causation or predisposition to schizophrenia increasingly rests upon preconception and tradition, while evidence points to environmental and social factors. [1965, 430]

Silvano Arieti (1955) argues that "schizophrenia is a specific reaction to an extremely severe state of anxiety, originated in childhood and reactivated later in life." It is characterized by regression, cognitive disorders, and an intense experience of fear.

For Lewis Hill, who for many years was senior psychiatrist at Sheppard/Pratt, schizophrenia implies

> a rupture, a dissolution of the ego, a shrinking of the ego, an invasion and taking over of much territory, which did belong to the ego, by forces which are normally excluded from it. Subjectively this is experienced as a catastrophic event of cosmic proportions. It is terrifying. Thought, feeling and action are taken over: the patient is dispossessed of his own mind and body. Objectively this panic arises as a response to some rupture of human relations or of the hope which the patient may have had of them. [1955, 26]

39

Harry Stack Sullivan, whose theory derived from his pioneering work at Sheppard/Pratt in the 1920s, holds that

> the term *schizophrenia* covers profoundly odd events which are known to most of us only through what happens in our sleep; in our earlier years of life, a great part of our living was schizo-phrenia, but we have been carefully schooled to forget all the happened then. When a person is driven by the insoluble charac-ter of his life situation to have recourse in waking later life to the types of referential operations which characterized his very early life, he is said to be in a schizophrenic state. People who come to be called schizophrenic are remarkably shy, low in their self-esteem, and rather convinced that they are not highly appreciated by others. They are faced by the possibility of panic related to their feelings of inferiority, loneliness and failure in living. [1954, 206]

I do not see Sullivan's definition as inconsistent with that of psy-choanalysts who locate the source of schizophrenia in the first year or two of life. What Sullivan adds to the more formalistic psychoanalytic model is an interpersonal dimension. He focuses on the phenomenology of the process: how the schizophrenic experiences the world in relation to the other. The sense of the self as inferior, worthless, or empty may have origins in psychological events that have been repressed during matura-tion and socialization.

Yet another definition is presented in the *Diagnostic and Statistical Manual of Mental Disorders* (*DSM III*) published by the American Psychiatric Association, one that might be considered the official view of the content of schizophrenic symptomatology: "The essential features of this group of disorders are: the presence of certain psychotic features during the active phase of the illness, characteristic symptoms involving multiple psychological processes, deterioration from a previous level of functioning, onset before age 45, and a duration of at least six months" [1980, 181]. The diagnostic criteria for any given schizophrenic disorder include:

> (1) bizarre delusions (content is patently absurd and has no possi-ble basis in fact) such as delusions of being controlled, thought broadcasting, thought insertion, or thought withdrawal
> (2) somatic, grandiose, religious, nihilistic or other delusions of being controlled, thought broadcasting, thought insertions or thought withdrawal
> (3) delusions with persecutory or jealous content if accompanied by hallucinations of any type
> (4) auditory hallucinations in which either a voice keeps up a running commentary or the individual's behavior or thoughts or two or more voices converse with each other

(5) auditory hallucinations on several occasions with content of more than one or two words having no apparent relation to depression or elation

(6) incoherence, marked loosening of associations, markedly illogical thinking or marked poverty of content of speech if associated with at least one of the following:

   (a) blunted, flat or inappropriate affect

   (b) delusions or hallucinations

   (c) catatonic or other grossly disorganized behavior. [ibid., 188–89]

Psychodynamic definitions include the following characteristics of the schizophrenic reaction: a serious impairment in the expression of affect; the turning inward of "object energy"; a growing gap between emotion and cognition; a disruption or "infiltration" of the thought processes; disturbance in both ego and body-ego boundaries; considerable anxiety and fear; the projection of delusion as truth; withdrawal from the outside world; disturbance in interpersonal relations; and disorientation with regard to meaning, value, and action.

It is not likely that such symptoms are learned. Nor, from the psychoanalytic perspective, is it plausible to assume that environmental stressors alone account for such psychically destructive phenomena:

Children are born without the ability to be directly dangerous to others. An infant who is neglected during the early weeks of life can be destructive only to himself. And the most primitive manner of self destruction, the only one within the grasp of the helpless infant, is self-neglect. That was the suicidal method pursued by Narcissus. [Spotnitz 1976, 115]

The delusions of schizophrenics frequently contain themes that comment on self-neglect and feelings of worthlessness, and which may take the form of victimization, incessant despair, torment, hopelessness, uncontrollable rage, a sense of being absorbed or of withering away, and a hooking up to some powerful force that threatens to assimilate the self or thoroughly control it.

The self-absorption that Spotnitz sees in the Narcissus myth appears in an extreme pathogenic form in the withdrawn internality of the schizophrenic. The Narcissus myth ends tragically: life falls away because of inactivity and a gaze that becomes completely preoccupied with internal musings rather than focusing outward. The Myth of Narcissus turning into a flower, far from being happy or romantic, reflects the tragic fate of many schizophrenics: "Although [Narcissus'] self destructiveness was effectively covered by manifestations of self love and self admiration, he actually behaved in a way that could only end in death" (ibid., 115). The situation of the schizophrenic is similar: the grandiose self-images, the delusional sense of power and control, disguise a deeper, more threatening reality, a fear of life itself and the trust and love necessary to sustain life. Yet even within his self-absorption, the schizophrenic refuses to die, to wither away. Delusion provides a fragile connection with survival. The very capacity to speak indicates the will to live and to struggle with the horrifying forces that are overtaking and tyrannizing all aspects of the schizophrenic's consciousness and physical being. For the schizophrenic to cease surviving, to leave delusion, and return to what the patients in Hannah Green's *I Never Promised You a Rose Garden* call the "World," is to relinquish the delusional truth, to turn from narcissistic self-absorption to the tenuous but quite real encounter with the autonomous, external other.

I would like next to look at certain aspects of this narcissistic self-absorption, to examine it as a delusional process with specific content. In the words of Jane Loevinger, "in the pre-ego of primary narcissism, reality is not something outside" (1977, 38). In what follows, I will look at the differences between consensual and delusional reality and suggest a model that describes the movement of the self from the tyranny of delusion to a sense of freedom in facing the therapeutic other and the subsequent rejection of the delusional identity.

Internality and Language: Delusion as an Inner Form of Knowledge

Delusional projections sever the self's connection with others, and reality, understood as an interpersonal interdependence, becomes horrifying. The situation of a patient named Mary[1] shows at Sheppard/Pratt the tragedy of progressive isolation turning into delusional withdrawal. After her first hospitalization in the early 1960s, Mary, then in her early twenties, wrote in a letter to one of the staff: "I am forced often into a lonely silence for the sake of self preservation and as a defense against isolation." She lived and moved in a world that held little promise of relief from her sense of increasing estrangement:

> No amount of talking, thinking or feeling seems to be of any
> avail in over-throwing my inner demons. My inner struggles
> make all of my life seem not to be worth the trouble it takes to
> go through each day. There is as much force in me pulling me
> toward personal destruction as there is pulling toward construc-
> tion.

During her first hospitalization, she had been diagnosed as having a "severe hysterical disorder." At times there was some confusion about

---

1. All names of patients have been changed.

what to label her; but what is clear from the records is that the early part of Mary's hospitalization reflected serious disturbances in living, tremendous anxiety, and despair. Only later did the delusional world begin to intrude. In some respects, her consistent expressions of existential dread, described eloquently in a series of letters after her discharge,[2] show a person struggling with meaning, a sense of hopelessness, and a world that simply refuses to understand. Mary tried, quite hard, to adapt to the demands and expectations of the external world, yet her own inner doubts, the tenuousness of her existence, and the social and economic reality confronting her made it increasingly unlikely that she would succeed. The letters show a despair and a hostility toward culture that seem stronger than her attachments, her therapy, and the minimal support she received from a rejecting and, in many ways, pathogenic family:

> The real fact of the matter is that I have been very ill for a very long time and I am rather tired of being in such a state with no relief in sight. I have been unable to work and going out brings as much pain as staying in. I force myself to go through the motions of a day even though my heart is not in this business of living. This going on, anyway in isolation no matter how I feel usually keeping the way I feel to myself is my only new strength. I have learned through long and harsh experience that it does not pay to let others know that I am in acute distress. Most people, first of all, do not care how I feel and in the second place don't understand the pain involved in neurotic states of mind and body. These feelings further increase my sense of isolation, separateness and difference. I always feel paranoid and queer and inadequate in public, sort of as though everybody knows how sick and awful and frightened I am to be a human being. Thus, I only venture out into the world when I feel strongest and able to cope with my irrational feelings. I fight a continual battle with myself which leaves me totally exhausted, fatigued and depleated [sic].

In the late 1960s, after a series of disastrous personal experiences, Mary recommitted herself to Sheppard/Pratt. Discharged three additional times, she rarely spent more than a few months on the outside before life-threatening circumstances sent her back to the hospital. She has been continually in the hospital since the early 1970s. The report of her last and final admission to SEPH states that she "was readmitted to SEPH for the fourth time when she was discovered standing in the middle of an expressway, talking about germ warfare." At this point her utterances, notes, and letters no longer revealed an introspective but still relatively connected self, able to reflect on the conditions of her existence

2. These letters were subsequently placed in Mary's psychiatric records.

43

and her illness. The world now threatened her with its germs. The nurses, doctors, and aides at Sheppard were out to kill her. A world war seemed imminent to her; institutions tormented her. A note from a psychiatric chart stated: "It seems as though she feels that the Catholic Church is very militant and out to take her soul and to punish her." Mary felt such intense pain it became unbearable. She moved from reflections on existential dread to a stage where her social life ceased. She completely refused society's terms and what it could or could not offer her: "If only they would give me poison, I would drink it." The social world represented murder, destruction, and threat to her; what was "outside" ceased to guide her thinking and behavior. She reverted to emotional states whose origins precede the development of social forms, the norms of socialization, and the ethics of interpersonal communication. Her inner world took on a life of its own.

Earlier, Mary had felt a tremendous need to relate to others. In a letter describing how she might help with the hospital's patient council, she wrote:

> I have been wondering about the Patient Council; is it still in existence, and can I be of any help with it now? I think maybe that I can be a little help to somebody, if I make the trip [to SEPH for a visit]. I feel that I have unfinished business. I have learned deeply from my own experiences, and I would like to share my insights. There is no bitterness in my heart as I say all the above, and I mean every word I have said. . . . All we have in this world is a desire to learn, to understand, to grow, to serve, to Love, to walk gently through life looking where we are going and to hope that we will not stumble.

At this point Mary still felt the need for relatedness; her letter is a plea, a recognition of the critical importance of trusting another enough to love and to allow herself to be loved. Mary's tragedy was that this need, which was never met, was later transformed into uncontrollable dread and a sense of persecution:

> I have made my biggest mistake in trying to find a home, and a Mother and Father. I have been looking for these things all my life with all my heart and soul, and was frustrated at every turn. Well, I have at least given up this search *to be loved* and cared for with tenderness. I seek rather now to love actively.

Unable to "love actively" or be loved, in her subsequent psychosis Mary admitted her defeat in the world of others: "All I want is oblivion. . . ." The actions that embodied this utterance were a withdrawal from culture and the construction of a delusional world. Mary began to create her own inner logic of grandiosity, suffering, and transcendence. A note made in one of Mary's reevaluation conferences describes the intensity of her fear of people and her need to withdraw:

> A very poignant moment came in the interview when she was describing how she behaves like a "turtle" who when she moves a little bit out of her shell and gets involved in anything with people she then immediately feels frightened and weakened, has ideas about being murdered, and pulls back into her shell.

But inside her "shell" (which in Lévi-Strauss's terms represents a reversion to nature) Mary found herself preoccupied by a number of dreadful experiences. Her statements below contrast strikingly with the excerpts from the earlier letters. Unlike the letters, nothing searching, tentative, or contemplative intrudes on these later thoughts. They come from an inner universe whose terms, structures, logics, and values have absolutely nothing to do with the embodied social universe. At this stage (almost fifteen years after her first admission to SEPH), delusion completely defined Mary's identity. She found herself in what amounts to a Hobbesian state of war.

Note 1:

> All these lies about me will never stop. Joan Dell[3] [a pseudonym] wants to put me in seclusion on hydrogen cyanide shots every half hour until I am dead. She wants my power for herself to kill everybody in sight. The only thing she enjoys in life is to kill. She does not even know that killing is bad. She has no conscience. She is worse than an animal. They don't kill for *sexual pleasure* just because they enjoy it. Killing gives Joan Dell orgasms and the same is true for all the rest of the people on the hall. All three halls are involved, and so is the rest of this Russian stronghold.

Note 2:

> Dr. _____: It is so dreadful in here. I had a wonderful sleep and got dressed slowly and carefully enjoying the trees and the grass around my window. Then murder in IGL begins right away. People bother me all the time. I think most of the men are just sexy in a perverted way. Joan Dell is so ugly and mean all the time, and never stops going after me *all the time*. She is just plain

---

3. Joan Dell, the head nurse on Mary's hall, was a very compassionate and sensitive woman. She was the exact opposite of Nurse Ratchet in Kesey's *One Flew over the Cuckoo's Nest*. She was also quite close to Mary and important in her life. But Mary could never accept the fact that someone actually loved her; it was too threatening a thought and seriously disturbed the inner logic of her delusions. She therefore transformed Joan Dell into a tormentor and persecutor. It was much easier to relate to her this way than to accept and internalize the care that was so obvious in Dell's treatment of Mary.

mean and nasty. I do not know why so many people think I have to die. I have not done anything wrong except to survive. Joan Dell lies about me lots I think and she's out to kill me herself with a knife.

It should be mentioned that IGL, or "International Guide Langauge," is a form of communication with specific meanings known only to Mary herself. She shares very little of this communication matrix with anyone. It manifests itself primarily in bodily movement, gestures, and facial expressions. For Mary, it is a very real language that communicates true statements about the world. For instance, in reference to some of my gestures, Mary maintains that "stroking your beard means you want to make love to me"; "scratching your forehead means you want to kill me"; "sticking your tongue out between your lips means you want to poison me." The gestures of IGL are filled with ideas, preferences, needs, desires, and feelings of anger that belie and supersede all spoken utterance. IGL may be implicit in the way words are used, the connections between words, and in the manner and content of their presentation. It was a code Mary never revealed to anyone, except for the rare glimpses into the forms in which the language was registered on the body. However, it was for her real communication, the fundamental basis of all believable messages.

Note 3:

Dear Dr. _____:
I am so glad that you are back in your house. I did not start writing to you until I was wide awake and "with it." The situation at SEPH from the inside, is so incredible. People all over the hospital on all the halls, deal with murderous feelings and thoughts because they are addicts of one kind or another. People at SEPH are all on pentathene, morphine, heroin or triptophane and lots of experimental drugs. The people that I am around are all famous people, and even if they kill me for fun they might even get away with it for awhile. Then they will all start to be kidnaped by people who want them dead for being insane killers all the time. Right now they are just getting up for the day. Medications have been given so they are quiet and even a little bit happy. I want to be taken off all medication because I am tired of being poisoned with stricknine [sic] and liblum [sic] carbonate and given huge shots of distilled water for the sexual pleasure of the people who give me the shots. I am afraid of medications because I am being "pilled" for death. Right now I am not sick in any way. I should not be given any medication at all because I am healthy emotionally and physically.
I save them all every day or they would all be dead and so would I. I keep them alive for one more day and myself too. I don't know what happens to people as crazy as they are, in the end.

Pretty soon no medication will help them. Then they will start hitting me and each other. I have a very deep and abiding faith in life in all its forms. I believe that even the insane should be allowed to live out their lives until they are old.

I do not know who I am because nobody ever tells the truth to me. I think I'm very famous, but I never have delusions of grandeur. [Mary frequently thought that she controlled the "war of the rocks," the "world bank," the "refugees landing in Mexico," and all "relief operations," in addition to being in constant communication with all the "world's greats."]

I even like insects, birds, grass, flowers and the trees. [The birds often carried messages for Mary or to her from people in distant lands.]

Nature always talks to me.

For Mary, the world as she knew it appeared to be filled with famous people whom she contacted, who dined with her, sent messages, and so on. If Mary saw a stranger in the hospital, he might be "Castro coming to visit me." Or if she had lunch with a new patient or one she hadn't yet met, he was actually "Brezhnev in disguise." Sheppard/Pratt was a "Russian stronghold" and as such very dangerous for her. In some respects, Mary had reason to feel famous. Within Sheppard/Pratt she became something of a legend, and psychiatrists, social workers, mental health aides, and other visitors to the hospital (myself included) showered her with attention. Unable to distinguish the clinical and evaluative basis of this interest, however, Mary transmuted it into a worldwide fame and recognition with political overtones: she saw herself as powerful, as making earthshaking decisions, dominating vast resources, assembling and disbanding armies, and presiding over global conflicts.

For Mary, being famous meant being recognized, but she strenuously resisted the notion that such acknowledgment was a result of her delusional state. It was impossible for her to accept the clinical basis of her fame. Such an understanding would not only have disrupted the complex structures of her delusional world, it would also have threatened what little identity she had. It would mean admitting that she was in fact delusional. (During her years at the hospital, Mary withdrew so completely that it was generally conceded her delusional identity would probably remain for the rest of her life.) However, she retained enough energy to survive each day because her role as a famous person demanded constant vigilance and sacrifice. If she was not overseeing the "war of the rocks" she was "speaking with Mao"; if she was not leading her "mob" in some form of action, she was listening carefully to what the birds were saying or the "voices" she continually heard.

When she was feeling trapped by the "Russian stronghold," she saw the administering of medication as an attempt to kill and pervert her, yet without medication Mary fell completely apart, both physically and mentally. In her case, antipsychotic medications seem to have helped in bringing her some relief from her terror and panic. Even though Mary became suicidal when her medications were withdrawn, the giving and receiving of medication became translated into murder and victimization in her inner universe. Being medicated, in her view, made her helpless, and she felt that the world, in the form of the patients and staff at Sheppard, was free to take advantage of her situation, to murder her, "rape" her "dead body," or mutilate her in particularly horrible ways. What is important here is the logic behind Mary's view of medication. This logic was not dictated by the terms of treatment (which in fact amounted to the careful administration of medication that diminished the terror of her hallucinations and delusions); rather, it consisted of images and messages originating in an inaccessible inner universe that defined Mary's attitudes toward both medication and the staff of Sheppard/Pratt.

Language and the Power of Internal Communication

On one occasion Mary told me about a conversation with another patient whom I shall call John:

MARY: John explained my suffering; now I understand.
JMG: What did he say?
MARY: We talked.
JMG: What did you talk about?
MARY: He told me about how I might ascend and attain grace.
JMG: Did you actually speak in words?
MARY: No, we spoke in International Guide Language.
JMG: Was there any verbal communication?
MARY: No, he looked at me and I looked at him and we spoke.
JMG: What did he tell you?

Mary proceeded to tell me of her "theory" of suffering and endurance, a theory that expressed the compelling need of her own internality through a parable she projected onto John. During other discussions, new theories emerged with some regularity, depending on which of her defenses was at work and the kinds of images that were filtering through her consciousness. But at the time the conversation above took place, Mary understood the situation and prescribed for herself a method of relief. Her theory can reasonably be viewed as a form of knowledge designed to protect the self and to provide an organizing thread for her critical day-to-day struggle to survive:

John tells me he is the bastard mulatto son of Pope Pius XII. He is a monk in the Vatican and he told me how to handle all this torture. I am being made ready to ascend, to be initiated into a state of grace. If I can get through the day, with all this murder going around about me, if I can make it until about 9 or 10 at night, then I might find some peace. I can be in a state of grace and all my suffering prepares me for this.

This language contains a referential matrix, an existential gestalt; its content totally defines the moment. Mary's words leave the listener confused and troubled; her explanation of her personal suffering reflects such tragedy that her language seems to issue from the deepest recesses of the self. Mary believed John to be the bastard mulatto son of Pope Pius XII; for her, this was the truth: it organized that particular moment in her reality. Mary's theory of suffering, complete and hermetic, possessed reality, took hold of it and dominated all sensory phenomena. It was an explanation that by its utterance provided the praxis of survival; the words had to be spoken before the defense became real. It was as if Mary was actually giving birth to this strange bastard son, actually hearing the incantations of the monks, actually being told in a kind of ritualized proclamation that her life depended on her attaining a state of grace, made available to her by the illegitimate child of Pius XII.

On another occasion a patient named Louise turned toward me and implored me to tell her she was alive; she felt her body was "outside her soul." I assured her that she was, that her name was as it appeared on her chart; that she really was Louise. After a few moments of stunned silence, she turned to me and said with great feeling , "Thank you." The impact of this exchange on me was enormous, since Louise's tenuous hold on being seemed to be at stake. Her language contained an emotional or affective praxis; it was as real as life, a plea for affirmation of her need to survive. In her language, Louise permitted herself to realize that she wanted to survive. Indeed, by giving tangible proof in language that her self possessed at least a degree of reality, Louise assured her survival, at least for a time. The following notes taken from Louise's psychiatric chart, give some indication of the hopelessness of her condition:

> The patient has a history of long-standing chronic schizophrenia dating back at least ten years. Although no significant psychiatric dysfunction was noted prior to the patient's age of nineteen, when she was a student at _____, the patient had increasing difficulties in her scholastic performance while at college. By the third year of college, the patient had become catatonic, agitated, fearful and delusional. This necessitated the first of her hospitalizations at _____. She remained there for approximately six months, made some improvement, and was discharged. The patient then went to live on her own and deteriorated rapidly requiring hospitalization in _____, where she received electro-convulsive therapy. The patient was then transferred in 1972 to

the _____, where she stayed for approximately two and a half years. Although some improvement was noted the patient was discharged to a halfway house near her home, she soon again decompensated when her boyfriend in the halfway house required hospitalization. The patient returned to _____ and _____, where she received electroconvulsive therapy and massive drug chemotherapy. Since the aforementioned therapies were not successful, the patient was then transferred in 1974 to _____ where she remained until _____, and was transferred to Sheppard Pratt Hospital.

During the better part of the patient's history of psychiatric illness, the patient has been severely delusional, hallucinating, suffering ideas of reference, ideas of influence, somatic delusions, somatic complaints, dissociative experience and at least one suicide attempt by wrist-slashing.

When Louise's delusional self wrote or screamed that her brain was being burned out by cosmic rays, her language was not mere distortion: it may have had something to do with the horror of electroshock. When Louise said that her soul passed out of her body and through her eyes "thousands of times per day," her utterance was more than a jumble of words. Langauge here transmits the knowledge of a special reality, the resonances of therapeutic "interventions" that may have served only to confuse her more. When Mary described the experience of "chopping off the head, watching your body die," and then slowly being witness to the death of the head for over an hour, these statements involve an absolute or binding definition of the universe and a symbolic tale or fable of what is happening to the self—a semiology of the inner.

When Mary gave voice to the often-stated fear that her fellow patients wanted to murder her, rape her dead body, and then "cut it up into little pieces" and scatter the parts around the grounds of Sheppard/Pratt, or when she stated that Nurse Dell was secretly training a squadron of doppelgänger commandos in the Sahara desert with the objective of eventually taking over Sheppard/Pratt, her statements reflected in part her own psychological death, the reality of murder and dread. When Louise observed that the "C.I.A. has implanted receivers in her body through which she receives hallucinations which cause her to dissociate from her body" (from her psychiatric chart), these thoughts not only bracketed reality, they also became the critical forms of knowledge governing the behavior of the self. Each moment brought with it a confrontation between the internal necessity to survive the day ("Will I be alive when you see me next week?") and the imminent threat of bodily destruction and desecration.

A patient named Tom believed that a telekinetic spirit was inside his mind. He gave this spirit a name, an imaginary home, and a yellow chair. All Tom's delusional self wanted to do was communicate with this spirit presence, which would play games like the "icky game" and the "foopa-loo game" (JMG: Tom, what is the buzzing in your ears saying to you? Tom: I hate you, icky, icky, icky). It hardly need be said that such a psychological environment is radically at odds with the prevailing culture.

Tom's psychiatric history reveals the extent to which delusional reality defined all aspects of life. His existence was totally dominated and defined by an internal spirit presence (Henry), as is clear from the following entry in his chart:

> The patient was committed for psychiatric evaluation in
> _____. Apparently while he was in _____ he had read a
> book by _____ which dealt with finding spiritual leaders
> through various black magic rituals. He performed the ceremony
> and was convinced that he was put in touch with Henry whom he
> believed was a telepathic human being, a disembodied soul living
> on an astral plain. He became convinced that he had to flee
> _____ because the police were going to kill him and he finally
> came to the attention of the police near _____ for Henry
> made him stand up in a bus station and repeat over and over
> again for hours that he was a silly person who could not control
> himself. The police held him for several days because they sus-
> pected him of murdering someone in _____. He was eventu-
> ally released after psychiatric evaluation and made his way back
> to the _____ area.

Tom was subsequently arrested for "snatching a woman's purse and was placed in _____ for psychiatric evaluation where he stayed for four-teen months." After being transferred to several state hospitals, and having at one point stolen a car at knife point, Tom was eventually hospitalized at Sheppard/Pratt. In some respects, Tom's family bore a high risk of producing offspring with some form of mental disturbance—a situation unlikely to favor a happy childhood. Again, I quote from Tom's psychiatric history:

> The patient was born while his mother was a psychiatric patient
> at _____. The patient's mother had been a psychiatric aide at
> _____ [another psychiatric hospital], who had a schizophrenic
> break and was admitted to [the same hospital] as a patient. His
> father was an inpatient at this hospital for (several) months, and
> the patient's older sister was conceived while both parents were
> inpatients. They married shortly after both were discharged.
> Mother was admitted to [another psychiatric hospital] during her
> second pregnancy.

There were times when Louise's identity appeared as Louise in the hospital, as Carol in California, and as Beth in New York, each self possessing differing qualities of beauty and ugliness. These experiences were real to her. When Louise looked outside the hall's bay windows at dark, heavy rain clouds and muttered "The A-bombs are going to explode today," she actually felt the imminence of massive destruction. "God is trying to kill me . . . I just died." When David maintained that the P.L.O. was going to attack the hospital and liberate the patients in three hours, he was absolutely certain such an assault would take place.

In all these instances, the self is plagued by its own internalized projections. There is no autonomy, no real freedom since behavior follows the demands of an inner necessity and the reality of what happens depends on what the inner self stores up as knowledge. The ego is powerless; it is absorbed into these experiences. The person becomes a shadow, tormented by internalized commands and fears which effectively destroy any sense of freedom or possibility. Delusion overtakes consciousness and obliterates a conception of consensual reality. Knowledge becomes dependent on the power of an inner world asserting itself as delusional reference. As the delusions multiply, the ego compensates with flights of omnipotent fantasy that display extraordinary qualities of control, power, and transformation. It is this dialectic between victimization and control that structures the knowledge claims of the schizophrenic and accounts for the conflict over power expressed in fables or myths of torment, torture, dismemberment, death, and periodic redemption or transcendence.

The delusional world often appears as a series of political relationships embodied in the fundamental position of tyrant/tyrannizer or victim/appropriator. It is the strong, the tormentors, sadists, controllers, and the powerful who are victorious in the delusional system. An essential structure, then, of delusion is conceived as a political relation, a statement about what is just in the world. Justice lies in the interest of the stronger. Within this delusional environment, the self is perceived as worthless, evil, corrupt. ("I committed a sin in heaven; I am being punished.") It would be easier and safer if the self were removed, were to become invisible or change into a spirit. Justice would be served by annihilating this weak, evil self. For example, Mary asked, "You know what I want right now? I want you to take an axe, chop off my head and end my misery." Bart made such statements as "I'd like to hang myself from the bathroom door" and "I thought of tying a wire around my neck until I sliced myself all the way through." The delusional world is determined by cycles that move through stages of suffering, despair, and destruction, and rarely attain salvation.

In delusion, time as sequential development or duration disappears; depending on the inner structure of the torment the patient suffers, a second might translate into months, years, or centuries. Time is often circumscribed by the technical: by maleficent machines, by "rays," "electrical currents," "high voltage zaps," "wires," or "engines." When technology appears in delusional imagery, it provokes torment and fear. It is associated with instruments of power that inflict pain: "I am being electrocuted"; "My brain is being burned with X-rays"; "The brain police are out to get me"; "They're exploding H-bombs all around me." While Sheppard rarely uses electroshock or massive chemotherapy, many patients have suffered such experiences in previous hospitalizations. It is inevitable that delusions involving brains being burned or electrodes being implanted in the skull should derive from the experience of electroshock treatment. Technical functions and activities become persecuting instruments, ray tubes, and electrical current, and the self is tormented by these representations. In psychoanalytic terms, such torture might be described as a consequence of an intensely persecuting, sadistic, introjected superego. The following written communication provides an example of the superego taking on the persona of an aliented technicalism:

> It seems as if somebody has a top secret machine that they want to test out on a guinea pig. . . . I don't know what these devices are . . . they explained that the machines emitted Q-waves upon the brain . . . I have been having severe headaches, itching around my skull and heated temperature. My brain feels like it's cooking. . . . They talked about killing me; they said they destroyed 700 million brain cells.

The self has no defenses against such power; it is condemned, or so it feels, to torment in perpetuity. Nothing brings relief, and all energy is expended on the basic task of day-to-day survival.

Internal Emotional Structures: Splitting and the Infant's Relation to Objects

In recent years psychoanalytic theory has undertaken a great deal of research to explain the infant's inner emotional world in the effort to convey some sense of the global identifications characteristic of infantile emotional states (e.g., Mahler 1968; Spitz 1965; Winnicott 1965). Unfortunately, this research is difficult to paraphrase in nontechnical language, since the entire theory rests on metapsychological assumptions concerning infantile drive states and the nature of early defenses in the pathology of splitting and fusion. It would be impossible here to go into all aspects of the work on "infantile" or "preoedipal" emotional states (Jacobson 1964). I would, however, like to elaborate four concepts central to an understanding of the inner polarity of delusional knowledge: the splitting of the object world into good and bad and the origins of this experiences in infancy; fusion and the lack of ego boundaries (problems in identity, body-ego, differentiating self and other); the experience of the self and other as a unit exercising omnipotent control over the internal environment; and the function of delusions in protecting the self from the explosive power of aggressive, hostile, and angry drives (Klein 1950).

Psychoanalytic theory regards the infantile universe, the "preverbal," as the storehouse of a complex value system, although not values as they might be described in a rationalistic, philosophical form. For the infant, value depends directly on the gratification or frustration of drive states. Nothing else matters: if a drive state is gratified, the universe is good; if it is not gratified, the world is bad. These concepts of good and bad are projected outward onto others, such as the mother and father, and internalized or reprojected inward onto the self. If the world is bad (if the other brings pain), not only is that object bad, but in taking in the badness of the other, the self, too, becomes bad, at least in part. These identifications lead to specific global views about the status of self (as bad or good, or part bad and part good) and other (also as bad or good, or part bad and part good). Part of the self may be good, part may be bad; what is peculiar in this value system is that each part is separable. The good self is a separate entity from the bad self. Each side retains its own identifications, meanings, and values. It is hard for the adult world to understand this concept, because most of us possess aspects or qualities of self that are both good and bad. We recognize the ambivalence and indeterminacy of human identity and need. Not so for the infant: when the self is bad, it is completely, absolutely, irrevocably bad. When it is good, it is completely and unreservedly good. The same holds for the outside object: when mother is bad she is utterly evil, destructive, and threatening; when she is good, those aspects of mother's persona no longer exist: she is all-gratifying, supreme, sublime, and perfect. When such a dichotomy arises, the object world is said to be "split." This split is a consequence of what Burnham and his associates (1969) see as "object relations characterized by a severe need-fear dilemma" (p. 16). The world is either absolutely good or bad; the self is either absolutely good or bad; nothing "in-between" or ambivalent can define either feeling or identity. It is an "all-or-nothing" universe (Schulz 1980).

> This infantile value system knows only absolute perfection and complete destruction; it belongs to the early time in life when only black and white existed, good and bad, pleasure and pain, but nothing in between. There are no shadings, no degrees, there are only extremes. Reality is judged exclusively from the stand-point of the pleasure principle; to evaluate it objectively is still impossible. Nor does a realistic evaluation of the self exist as yet. Like tolerance for others, tolerance for oneself is a late achievement. [Reich 1973, 301]

Delusion for the schizophrenic perpetuates or, better, re-creates this infantile value system. Properties that derive from delusion encapsulate either extraordinary images of power and omnipotence or terrifying situations of victimization and destruction. If we accept Anne Reich's view of the infantile universe, then schizophrenic delusion represents a massive regression back toward this early universe split into opposing images of good and bad, powerful and weak, loved and hated, and so on. The understanding of ambivalence, the recognition of tolerance, and the tentativeness of understanding are not cognitive properties of the delusional schizophrenic. Rather, what is striking about this state of mind is its tendency toward cosmic identification, its apparent trust and belief in the delusional reality.

Let me try to elaborate this theory. In the psychoanalytic view, an object is "something through which drive gratification is achieved" (Mahler et al. 1975, 111). For the schizophrenic, that object, more often than not, has been the mothering presence. Whoever mothers the infant presents the first face the infant sees, the primary refracting presence. The argument is not that mothers "cause" schizophrenia. It is important here to distinguish between the causality or etiology of schizophrenia—which may involve any number of social, genetic, physiological, or intrapsychic processes, all compounding one another—and early psychodynamic "events" that may end up precipitating schizophrenia later in life. Given the confusion over multicausal explanations, the interpretation of schizophrenia has moved considerably from what was understood as its primary cause twenty years ago, the "schizophrenegenic mother." However, even in light of recent research, both psychodynamic and physiological, the importance of mothering as a critical event in the development of schizophrenia or schizoid tendencies should not be underestimated. For any human being, schizophrenic or not, mothering exercises a tremendous influence on later development. Therefore, I would like next to focus on the nature of this relationship and on what it implies for the internal structure of delusional knowledge.

Probably the leading psychoanalytic researcher on infantile emotional states is Margaret Mahler. Her studies of infantile behavior and action, her recognition of the importance of intrapsychic states, and her methodological thoroughness all provide useful theoretical perspectives for looking at psychodynamic processes in psychotic developments. In *The Psychological Birth of the Infant* she writes: "One could see with special clarity during this period [the first thirty-six months of life] the roots of many uniquely human problems and dilemmas—problems that sometimes are never completely resolved during the entire life cycle" (Mahler et al. 1975, 99–100). If the relationship between mother and infant is seriously disturbed or impaired, "defense mechanisms" arise that are "wrought with panic." In the adult schizophrenic, such defenses emerge in the form of complex delusional systems that may perform a psychically protective function. In describing the origin of such defenses, Mahler speaks at some length about the process of introjection—that is, taking into the self images of goodness and badness: "The child has split the object world more permanently than is optimal into 'good' and 'bad'" (ibid.), a process intensified through the continuing psychological, cultural, and social maturation of the self. Or in the words of Lewis Hill, "the whole problem of the schizophrenic can be seen then as that of a small child who is utterly dependent upon a person by whom he feels persecuted and who is, in his opinion, unstable and uncertain" (1955, 54). Because of the "unsatisfactory early mother-infant relation," Mahler argues, the ego develops a "brittleness" (1968, 38), which may appear in the child's movement: "The body image thus appears to be mechanically put together in a mosaiclike way, fragments of a machinelike self image" (ibid., 63). (In dance therapy with severely regressed schizophrenics, what is remarkable is the stiffness and utter lack of coherence in body movements; also, there is often little sense of movement as flow, identity, or symmetry. It is almost as if arms, legs, torso, feet, and hands move in ways unrelated to the motion or rigidity of other parts of the body.)

The uncertainty of psychological and physical identity or confusion over the meaning of a sexed identity "may be the effect of insufficient separation of . . . self representation particularly in terms of differentiation of self boundaries." The infant never learns where the self begins and mother ends. The capacity to separate, to recognize an identity independent of introjected images, becomes impossible, and the infant constantly fears being engulfed by the other. This fear "remains a threat against which the child must continue to defend himself beyond the third year" (ibid., 223). Engulfment or reengulfment is a powerful need. Lacking a sense of boundary, the infant searches for a defining attachment, what might be described as the need to fuse with the nurturing object. The need to fuse or merge with the other in an omnipotent unity appears in schizophrenic delusions as imagery of enormous power and significance. For example, to merge with the "star-people" or to be "ruler of the world," or to be involved in a scheme promising rewards of over $650 million represents an attempt to experience the unity and grandiosity implicit in the fusion with an all-powerful object. As Mahler describes the process, within the self's intrapsychic environment (and later in the schizophrenic's regression back to this early stage), "there is an oscillation between the longing to merge blissfully with the good object representation . . . with the erstwhile (in one's fantasy at least), 'all good' symbiotic mother, and the defense against re-engulfment by her, which could cause loss of autonomous self identity" (ibid., 230). For the schizophrenic, then, getting too close to any human being threatens engulfment through the loss of a sense of the ego's limits to an object that has the power to absorb and therefore deny those boundaries. Inevitably, the defense against such loss involves withdrawing emotional trust from other human beings, and the inner world of delusion compensates; it is a substitute gratification, an attempt at reparation, at recreating in part the earliest feelings of union with the omnipresent and omniscient nurturing figure.

In Mahler's view, the splitting of the object world for the infant results in the construction of a rigidity in the infant's experience that emerges to haunt the adult schizophrenic. An infant that is seriously disturbed in its object relations splits the object world and its own ego into good and bad parts, each with its own dynamics. This act of splitting inhibits the capacity to sustain the ambivalence crucial in the movement toward autonomy and interpersonal independence. While aspects of the ego might be repressed and denied through the latency phase of maturation (ages 6–12), they are not completely lost. Feelings split off from the ego during infancy may reappear with considerable virulence in the adolescent's struggle to separate self from family and establish an autonomous presence in the world. The stress of separation, the demands of peer groups, and newly awakened feelings of sexual desire and need may activate the hurt, rage, and fear kept under control or denied during latency. The consequence of such repression may be a full-blown psychotic episode. Mahler and her coauthors argue that while the "splitting of the object world" may be the child's solution to the "pain of longings and losses," it defines all later development and makes for "greater difficulty in the resolution of the complex object related conflicts of the oedipal period . . . throwing an ominous cast on the oedipal and post-oedipal personality development" (1975, 230).

What the ego internalizes determines to a considerable extent later developmental elaborations of personality. In addition, internalization (or interiorization) has a great deal to do with what the personality understands to be of value. Infantile emotional responses may then structure perceptions more than we realize or choose to admit. As Anne Reich puts it: "When an adult still finds magnificence, let us say, in being able to ride by himself in a train, he manifests an infantilism of inner standards. Usually the survival of such infantile values, too, is the end result of compensatory needs" and indicates a "fixation on infantile levels of libidinal and ego development" (1973, 298, 303). With the schizophrenic, the fixation is so intense and the regressive process so overwhelming that whatever the ego produces as relational, social, or rational structure dissolves before the onslaught of unconscious images. The ego becomes absorbed by the split-off, repressed parts of the infantile unconscious. In the delusional world, "badness" appears as images of destruction, devouring, and annihilation. The self ceases to exist in a social environment and moves through a universe whose motivating affective dynamics derive from an ego that was split, wounded, and traumatized during the first year or two of life.

Infantile value systems also appear in the anger directed at the bad object. In the schizophrenic, anger may be expressed in any number of ways: catatonic rigidity, physical outbursts of rage (which have, however, become infrequent with the advent of the phenathiazines), yelling, screaming, delusional projections, hostility, or self-mutilation. Anger may be the safest form of human contact (certainly safer than trust). Interpersonal intimacy lies beyond the boundaries of the schizophrenic's emotional world. Consider the following forms of vulnerability:

> If severe enough to be called schizophrenia the vulnerabilities are in the form of loneliness with dependency conflicts, severe anxiety in relation to both aggression and attachment; fluctuations between omnipotence and helplessness; problems around experiencing grief, loss or separation; a punitive threatening conscience in place of normal guilt; idealistic goals of attainment contributing to a sense that any achievement is worthless; and a defect in integrating past experience for foresight of future planning. [Schulz and Kilgalen 1967, 254]

Trust threatens the sovereignty of delusion, and what therapists call "warmth by friction" or "negativism" replaces trust or cooperation in the self's relation with any other. It should be stressed that, like the infant, the schizophrenic self often experiences anger as the power to destroy, to make "not there." To become too angry may actually unleash the atom bombs, or bring the spaceships down with their ray guns, or provoke World War III. It is therefore important for the delusional self not to show all aspects of the rage it feels because of the possibility that that anger will initiate the holocaust or bring absolute destruction down on the hospital, its staff, and its patients.

Anger such as this, involving the desire to kill and feelings that the expression of rage will physically annihilate, is not a form of expression sanctioned by society or by the forms of reason. It is a totally defining emotion, precivil and prerational in structure, that derives from infantile feelings of hurt and pain. Because of this sensation of omnipotence, the ego may indeed feel that its anger not only has the power to destroy the bad object (and therefore place the self in even a more threatened position, totally helpless and abandoned), it may also experience such anger as endangering its own boundaries. The anger may have the power to explode the self from the inside, to annihilate all consciousness. But, even in schizophrenia existence is preferable to nothingness or to the possibility of being abandoned (if it is believed that anger will in some way destroy the bad object). To feel such anger, then is unbearable. It must be dealt with by being denied, split off from the rest of the ego, repressed, and forgotten. Anger is a critical feeling in determining not only the infant's relation to vital objects in its life, but also in structuring

58

relationships between the schizophrenic self and significant others. "If I get angry at you will I ever see you again" is a rough translation of the complex feelings that accompany the expression of anger. Afraid of both the object's anger and of its own uncontrollable rage (and the guilt over feeling such rage), the schizophrenic self lives in perpetual dread that if such anger is manifested, the self may through its extraordinary power kill or maim whoever is in its path. It is simply impossible for the nonschizophrenic to imagine what it is like to feel such anger.

It should be emphasized that the split in the ego between good and bad produces an imagery that may be described in the language of political relationship. Good is equated with images and feelings of power and control; bad with images and feelings of victimization and torture that desecrate the self. For example, Mary commented "I was ascended today. . . . My body was boiled and I ascended and became a saint." For Mary, ascension signifies a dual process: on the one hand it demonstrates her utter worthlessness, expressed by her being boiled, yet the desecration precedes her "ascension" to the state of sainthood. In this delusional moment Mary expresses both the fact of victimization and the opposing image of absolute control and power—sainthood, which means being beyond wrong or judgment and being all-powerful in the eyes of the world. The delusion becomes an implicit message, a commentary on deep emotional structures that see the world as either all good or all bad.

The power to create and destroy, to abnegate the self and in the next moment assert complete domination, magically duplicates the omnipotence experienced by the infantile self. The tyranny of these systems of good/bad identification is absolute in delusion; I never witnessed any expression of ambivalence about the rightness or justness of properties attached to delusional projections. The intense belief in the truthfulness of these systems serves as the key to the self's survival. Such belief, then, is not idle or capricious, but represents a serious claim about the world. To question the beliefs or images may even push the schizophrenic deeper into psychotic withdrawal. Delusion is identity; questioning identity threatens life, and the self's ability to live hinges on the reliability and utter truthfulness of the delusional imagery.

Mahler emphasizes the importance of separation from the other and the movement of the self toward individuation, a process that takes place around the end of the third year. For the schizophrenic however, the process has been inhibited, and the overwhelming images of self-annihilation may be some indication of the traumatic reactions that accompany the fear of engulfment. This phenomenon was particularly acute in my discussions with Louise. She used anger as a defense against feelings of closeness, emotions that frightened her and threatened to upset the delusional sequences she perceived as real. Yet, since in her world anger possessed cataclysmic power (she believed her rage could effect great changes in my physical presence), sne often expressed guilt over the result of her fury. For example, during one conversation she threatened to call the police and have me arrested and put in jail. She stormed out of the room, proclaimed that I had thrown her down an elevator shaft (a ritualized expression that occurred time and again), and screamed she never wanted to see me again. When we met the following week she asked if I had been arrested and apologized for calling the police. Of course she had not really picked up the phone, but by uttering the threat, the inner praxis transformed me (the other) into the object of her rage. In her fantasies she may very well have experienced my being in jail, being "punished" because of feelings that had surfaced during our dialogue. She had exercised her power by assaulting me with anger; the consequence was to place me in danger. When I did return after these episodes, she seemed genuinely relieved, and on one occasion, after an especially violent outburst, she thanked me for not leaving, for just sitting there and waiting. Just being there seemed to defuse her inner panic; after I learned this strategy, the outbursts became less frequent.

Periodically, during my conversations with Louise I heard language that seemed to be coming from someone else, commands or injunctions or obligations appropriate to a mother speaking about a recalcitrant and difficult daughter. In these instances Louise merged with the bad object.[4] In her mind she became her mother, and the distinction between self and other ceased to exist altogether. Louise lost whatever hold she had on a self remnant not attached to the bad mother introject. What Louise became in those moments could not be distinguished from an intrusive presence that appeared to take over her features, voice, expressions, and gestures. It was as if a persona (the mask of a punitive, harsh mother) had descended on Louise and totally absorbed her. In more technical language, events that occur during the first year of life (during which fusion is a critical psychodynamic process), "be they deviant, improper or insuf-

---

4. Compare the following:

> Whether any given individual becomes delinquent, psychoneurotic, psychotic or simply "normal" would appear to depend in the main upon the operation of three factors: (1) the extent to which bad objects had been installed in the unconscious and the degree of badness by which they are characterized, (2) the extent to which the ego is identified with internalized bad objects, and (3) the nature and strength of the defenses which protect the ego from these objects. [Fairbairn 1952, 65]

For Fairbairn, it is the bad object that is primarily internalized and that functions as the reactive identification: "It is always bad objects that are internalized in the first instance, since it is difficult to find any adequate motive for the internalization of objects which are satisfying and good" (ibid., 93n). (This argument is consistent with Plato's description in the *Republic* of the descent of the soul into the realm of Thanatos.) The merging process itself is filled with fear, and it may be that the psychodynamics of fusion have a great deal to do with the desperate attempt to defend against the torment coming from the "bad introject."

ficient, have consequences which imperil the very foundation of society" (Spitz 1965, 300). Louise could never be herself because she had yet to discover the content and connections between her part-self representations.[5]

To summarize: the turning of anger against the self (aggression directed not outward but inward toward already fragile ego boundaries) is a serious result of disturbed object relations during infancy (Mitchell 1981). "As long as the infants were deprived of their libidinal object, they became increasingly unable to direct outwards, not only libido, but also aggression" (Spitz 1965, 286). The chaos of the schizophrenic's inner world, with its political messages of tyrannical domination and absolute salvation or power, is portrayed in dualistic images of good and bad. This split inner universe demonstrates the inability of the ego to integrate positive and negative or sustain ambivalence. The self, deprived of an object in the internal world, turns against its own person, and the injured drives take the self as their object. Given these developments, it is unlikely that identity will ever be stable. The serious difficulties that arise involve the ego's sense of boundary, gender identity, a fear of intimacy, and a whole array of defenses for protecting whatever core or center remains in the self. In the regressed schizophrenic, this system of defense takes the form of delusional knowledge.

The Organization of the Internal World:
Delusion as a Political Logic

The "symbolic realization" therapy of Margaret Sechehaye (1951) represents an attempt to draw together insights in psychoanalytic theory and existential philosophy. Sechehaye observes of the "schizophrenic mode of existence": "It is apparent that beneath a show of disintegration and psychic dissolution, there exists a well-defined structure where the patient's image and expressions define a true function, a power of organization and equilibrium, an *Ordnungsprinzip*, as Binswanger calls it." (1956, 4) The *Ordnungsprinzip*, which unites the delusional reality, gives meaning and structure to utterance and constitutes the organizational matrix peculiar to the political structure of delusional utterance. It manifests itself in oppositions, dichotomies that take shape in inner images of: good/bad, god/devil, Americans/communists, black/white, good therapist/bad staff, bad therapist/good staff, as well as feelings of being devoured (incorporation) or of being ejected ("worms fly out of my head").

This divided inner self defines the content of delusional imagery. Each

---

5. For a fascinating discussion of this process—the self experienced not as multiple, but as fragments constantly appearing and disappearing—see Searles 1979, in the chapter, "The Function of the Patient's Realistic Perceptions of the Analyst in Delusional Transference."

utterance takes the form of lived experience, a symbolic duration whose qualities bracket the universe through the concrete properties embedded in words. When Louise stated that worms were coming out of the top of her head, that she saw faces wearing white masks, that she had discovered sperm in her coffee, or that she saw others in the hall (including myself) as hermaphrodites, she was bracketing reality at the very moment of speaking. By saying, "worms are coming out of the top of my head," Louise actually underwent that experience. Uttering the words gives existence to the feeling, or delusion. This is not to say that delusions are real only if they are spoken. But for the schizophrenic, to utter such words in the presence of an other means that the self is implicitly making a claim about knowledge and truth *for everyone* at that moment.

Utterance, then, for the schizophrenic defines a moment in time and space. When Louise believed that the milk in her coffee was actually sperm and refused for that reason to touch the cup, no amount of argument could persuade her otherwise; looking at the coffee, she actually knew that the pale whiteness of the coffee was not milk but sperm. The logic of her perception lay beyond consensual reason. It was a logic dictated by the peculiar *Ordnungsprinzip* governing the structure (and utterance) of that particular delusion. From inside Louise's world, it was imperative that she identify the milk as sperm. What organized her world at that moment was an emotional logic of such power that it imposed a conception of reality lacking all consensual meaning.

Again, this is a political relation: Louise became the victim of an inner logic that through its sheer power imposed itself on her consciousness. Whether she saw worms coming out of her head, sperm in the coffee, or bombs bursting in the rain clouds, what organized the utterance was a relation that posited Louise as the victim of her own internal projections. She may at times have controlled those projections, but she could not be considered free. Everything she saw or uttered tormented and imprisoned her and estranged her from consensual reality.

Because of the atemporal character of its *Ordnungsprinzip*, the schizophrenic mind moves from one modality to another quite rapidly, from the world of external organization and purposes to the inner necessity of repressed and hidden emotional logics. For example, when Mary observed that the coffee is poisoned, the utterance meant exactly that: the coffee represented a threat, even possible death. Yet, after declaring the coffee to be poisoned, Mary very calmly poured herself some, without any visible evidence of fear at drinking it. The shifts in logic and meaning in such situations are abrupt: at one moment, Mary wanted desperately to stay away from the coffee pot, yet its poison searched her out. A few seconds later she took a sip from the nearest coffee cup. On another occasion I was speaking with Mary when her eyes suddenly appeared to be turning inward. I became lost to her consciousness;

hallucinations dominated her perceptual field. I asked what her ears were saying to her (when Mary heard voices, she believed her ears were speaking to her). She answered: "They tell me not to talk to you, that you want to murder me." Here it was as if Mary's self moved in and out of inner emotional logics without ever realizing that such transformations or shifts occurred. It is rare that delusion ever becomes completely free of an inner *Ordnungsprinzip*. As a form of knowledge, a way of perceiving and interpreting the world, these inner logics—which drive the self away from cultural or social frameworks—dominate consciousness.

The invisible psychological process that took place in the incident of the "poisoned" coffee might be understood as follows. Mary knew she could drink the coffee because in her inner reality she participated in a vast universe of power and control. This world was her own; she possessed and dominated it; she constructed its logics. Her "mob" (as she often called those who wanted to save her) or her "spies" intervened in all situations. That Mary was able to drink the coffee meant that her mob, through a magical process, transformed the coffee even before it reached her lips. This process, of course, was necessarily invisible to the observer. Although she said nothing, Mary's ability to drink the coffee hinged on the intervention of her all-powerful mob.

In this instance, the delusional reality was present in Mary's thoughts, and was only manifested by the action of her drinking coffee. The transformations that allowed this action to develop occurred on the symbolic or unconscious level; the dialogue was inner and quick, and the source of Mary's knowledge—the nature of the transformation—was hidden from the observer. Mary saved herself by psychically banishing the poison, and her omnipotence made it certain that some member of her vast international army would make the coffee drinkable. Seen in another way, the coffee was purified by the omnipotence and magic of her own system of inner knowledge. Here delusional reality, the antithesis of culture, took hold of external phenomena and completely dominated all aspects of the transaction, suggesting an intrapsychic communication, only parts of which are revealed in utterance. This event transpired according to a logic or sense of duration (and in an inner space) that could not be measured in linear time, that lasted possibly a few seconds; nonetheless it involved Mary's self totally. For those two or three seconds and the psychic space they bracketed, what was meaningful about the universe lay in Mary's relation to the knowledge of coffee-as-death, to her subordination to the tyrannical power of a delusional form that defined all aspects of her external world.

To illustrate the effects of the rapid oscillation from being victimized to being powerful or identifying with a powerful rescuer, I should like to describe what I see as the essential structures defining the inner knowledge forms of complex delusional systems. Some of the basic oppositions

Table 3.1

Images of victim	Images of control
Appropriation	Appropriator
Defilement	Sadist
Passive	Aggressive/destructive
Devaluation	Overvaluation
Acted upon	Acting upon
Worthlessness	Omnipotence
Futility	Infinite power

that might appear in the schizophrenic's inner world are given in table 3.1.

Each of the oppositions given in the table develops through an inner system of knowledge. Delusional reference shapes itself around these binary poles. In fact, any delusional system can be broken down into fundamental representations of basic oppositions. These kinds of oppositions, which are political in structure, suggest that there is implicit within delusional knowledge a "politics" that, over time, can be uncovered and decoded. The following utterance, for example, revolves around the passive-aggressive/destructive poles: "I have been ripped apart; I am going to die at any moment: I will not be alive to see you next week" (Mary's remark). This comment is characterized by its utter helplessness and passivity; nothing can intervene to prevent the disaster. Mary will be dead the next time I see her. Yet the remark also contains elements of aggression, for Mary visualizes herself as the object of horrendous violence. While Mary sees herself as a helpless victim, she also projects a world in which, for whatever unconscious reasons, she authors her own destruction—an expression of the aggression she feels directed against her. At another time Mary stated: "They want to operate on my head and cull my brain; they want to use my dead body as an icon to rule the world" (The word "cull," in Mary's delusional world, refers to the surgical removal of the brain from its skull casing). Mary was continually obsessed by various forms of torture that separate the head or brain from the body. A classic symptom of schizophrenia is the sense of being disembodied, of having lost control over the body, with the body being "over there" and the observing consciousness "over here".

A delusional process is never static (although certain aspects of it may become ritualized). It constantly grows, changes, and assembles new structures, a process that might be likened to a myth that begins in a single form but then multiplies and spins off tales that become tangentially related to the original story. The *Ordnungsprinzip* in delusion is a knowledge of action; it defines and keeps together an inner world where polarity or the primary oppositions or power and victimization determine the content of any imagery uttered in language. Table 3.2 describes the kind of action characteristic of major political structures that determine identifications of good and bad. These structures are elaborated with specific contents. Each of the images in table 3.3 occurs within an identifiable delusional matrix and each is part of a series of observations that takes place within a minute or two of the other. Each knowledge claim occupies a psychophysiological moment, although the images change depending on what emotional structure defines the self's relationship to its own internal struggle. Moreover, the organizing logic is absolutely

Table 3.2

Experience of being victimized	Action of exercising power/domination
Being set upon	Setting upon
Being neglected/forgotten	Acting as ruler
Being devoured	Tormenting/conquering
Being diminished	Enlarging/grandiosity
Being made impotent	Being made powerful

Table 3.3

Knowledge of being victimized	Knowledge of exercising power/domination
Being set upon (victim of the Russians)	Setting upon (controlling the world bank)
Being neglected/forgotten (being made into a little ball)	Acting as ruler (controlling the heavens)
Being devoured (a male patient experiencing women as appetitive; fearing they will rape him)	Tormenting/conquering (being head of the PLO; destroying Israel)
Being diminished ("Who am I? Why am I a fetal pig?")	Enlarging/grandiosity ("Should I come down?" From where? "From God.")
Being made impotent (feelings of having been crucified)	Being made powerful ("The world is coming to an end and I am one of the messengers from God to save the world.")

binding in the movement from victim to victimizer, from sufferer to tyrant, impotent to powerful, tormented to tormenter, and so on.

Each utterance makes a statement about the world; each constitutes a form of knowledge explaining why the self exists and what its purposes and its feelings are. No doubt or contradiction arises over the rightness of the utterance, its absolute validity, and its structure as a form of knowledge. The realization that the utterance might not be consensual knowledge, that it might disguise more fundamental truths in the self's psychodynamic experience appears only when the tyranny of the internal world has been broken by therapeutic intervention and by the creation of a trusting relationship with a significant other.

If we are to look for the earliest truths of political relationship, particularly experiences of power and authority, it may very well be that at least some of the evidence emerges in the emotional structure that conditions schizophrenic utterance. Power, authority, control, domination, and praxis define what occurs in delusional worlds whose inner space and time possess their own logic and significance.

Table 3.4 lists some examples of the knowledge of delusion at any given moment in psychophysiological time (i.e., duration measured not by the sense of a linear series but by the effect of a delusional image known through its intensity and terror). Each of these oppositions defines the self as sovereign over its own form of knowledge, and the power attached to that "sovereignty" ultimately rescues the self from its experience of victimization.

Conclusion: The Inner Split and the Power of Delusional Systems

The internal images of the schizophrenic can reveal to the social world tendencies that explain basic facts of human nature. In this sense, delusional language helps define just what "human nature" is. It holds the key to what is fundamental in the self. Its imagery may hold clues for the reasons why certain ideological and philosophical systems divide phenomena into radical forms of good and evil. Schizophrenic language then may be an index of inner processes and structures that represent a regression to the earliest moments of life, the very foundations of the self, or what in the past political philosophers called human nature. What the schizophrenic utters and the structure of that utterance may in addition reveal something of the origin of political and ethical identification. Schizophrenic language appears as intense regressive flight toward good/bad identification; it is a language that frequently utilizes imagery of political relationship and action; it reflects internal introjects that are as demanding, oppressive and rigid as any

Table 3.4: Some Examples of the Structure of the "Inner" at Any Given Psychological Moment

Victim/victimized/tormented (images/impressions/feelings)	Victimizer/controller/power agent (images/impressions/feelings)
Patient A: Feels he has been raped by three women; tormented by females.	Is member of PLO; will wipe out Israel; has satanic dreams; is in direct communication with king of Arabia to plan terrorist acts.
Patient B: CIA out to get him because he makes noises; CIA will reduce him to nothing.	Makes the CIA dizzy; has suicidal impulses that will liberate him from the CIA; exercises control over the threat by fantasizing the ultimate form of control: removal of self from field of threat.
Patient C: Feels self is diminishing; constant self-deprecation.	Exercises control over self by mutilation, cutting.
Patient D: Is being murdered, raped, sexually abused; is powerless.	Is ruler of the world; communicates with Mao; is power behind the world bank; is head of a "mob" that protects others.
Patient E: Was raped in France; everybody talking about her; has feelings of futility amid the constant conversation about her.	Shows great cruelty toward sicker patients.
Patient F: Is depressed; sees self as victim.	Experiences omnipotence; demands perfection from others.
Patient G: Voices taunt him; tell him he can't do anything; is unable to turn voices off; experiences a great deal of dependency.	Experiences self as prophet, wise hermit.
Patient H: Voices tell him to drive car at 100 miles per hour; experiences detachment; inability to do or relate.	Is great literary expert; views self as playboy; controls destinies by flipping coins and dice.
Patient I: Is afflicted with venereal disease; has fantasy of head being popped off, spaghetti coming out of head.	Can control the stars with his mind; is entrepreneur of a huge stadium that will teach math to rock students, leading to a new form of music called "multiplication rock."

tyranny. It reflects pieces of self whose reality has been torn apart by violence and terror and a desperate need to see everything in absolute terms.

It is also true, however, that individuals who are not labeled schizophrenic often withdraw into fantastic worlds, whether these take the form of rational or ethical abstraction, bizarre political commitments, cults, or perverse representations of desire embodied in alienated communities. That culture places a distance between itself and those it calls psychotic means only that the language of psychosis contains threatening information that is made easier to deal with by labeling it an aberration, something other than what is collectively present in human nature and in the community as shared experience. By seeing delusion as a private event (and therefore as not possessing any of the properties of human nature that define the sane or normal self), the community psychologically protects its own values and patterns of behavior. What the schizophrenic does and says is seen as a "fall" from sociality. But while delusional systems pose an obvious threat to sociality, they may demonstrate hidden aspects of human nature that are nevertheless part of the continuum of human experience—the movement from nature to community. Withdrawal may be likened to the differences in emotional experience alluded to in the classical conceptions of the movement from the natural condition to the politically or socially embodied forms of the social contract. For the schizophrenic, inner struggle, dread, and anxiety would suggest that social forms of mediation (ego functions that rely on the temporizing effect of others) are absent; that what remains in the self are internal projections having a logic, value, and structure that situate the self outside of what passes for normality or consensuality. It is arguable whether such an emotional situation may be likened to a state of nature. What is clear, however, is that the schizophrenic delusional self is isolated and locked into an often paranoid world whose utterance, meaning, and imagery possess a distinctly Hobbesian quality.

I would like to emphasize however, that the delusional self is not a Hobbesian human being; it is more likely that what the schizophrenic experiences or feels derives from a powerful need to repress the emotions of love and empathy, to defend against what Rousseau describes as *pitié*. In some respects, the schizophrenic has fallen from the Rousseauian natural condition (an emotional life that, because of its empathic and compassionate quality, prepares the self for existence in civil society) into a Hobbesian universe of the "war of all against all" or in a psychodynamic sense, the conflict between split off parts of the ego. What is therapeutically necessary is the recovery of the Rousseauian relation, the retrieval of the self from its inner, isolated, warlike environment, enabling the "hurt" self to receive life (or Eros) through therapeutic empathy. This process starts the patient on the journey back toward some ability to trust and therefore again to enter into the terms of the social contract.

For the schizophrenic, delusion represents a mode of survival against the very real fear of annihilation and death at the hands of the external world, particularly other human beings. The self stays alive by using internal forms of knowledge to protect itself against real or imagined hostility embodied in the outer world. In this situation, survival demands that the schizophrenic project onto the world delusion as explanatory knowledge: "the coffee is poisoned"; "the brain police are out to get me"; "the atom bombs are ready to explode." Such projections are absolute, and constitute what might be called the action of survival. Everything is either good or bad, but it is primarily the bad *introject* that carries the schizophrenic's thinking. Self, experience, and value—all are enclosed by this dichotomous internal splitting. Nothing is connected; nothing outside is autonomous. All acts derive from the interplay of good and bad in which the self experiences reality as complete and devastating victimization or exhilarating and omnipotent control. This dichotomy between victimization and control defines the political content of delusional imagery. And the internal structures that define this dichotomy constitute another way of studying power and its origins.

It should not be assumed that splitting is a phenomenon characteristic only of withdrawn or asocial schizophrenics. Unyielding conceptions of good and bad appear consistently in the political universe. It is not unusual to find in political life a Manichaean split between absolute good and absolute evil, nor is it unusual to find such splits in ethical systems that are held together by rigid positions and arguments. Such readings of politics may derive from internal, psychodynamic structures projected in language as ideological or religious dogma, as the isolation of a racial or ethnic group as the bearer of a historical evil, or as the imposition of tyrannical laws. Entire societies, dominated by schizoid psychological structures, may be split and driven into extraordinary political actions.

The drive to polarize political, ideological, and ethical experience into good and bad has a beginning—it does not just happen. It is a product of a psychodevelopmental process that begins in infancy and finds itself elaborated through crucial events in maturation. Polarization, however, particularly in relation to power, may be examined and understood through what the schizophrenic communicates as message, through the internal symbology and action of delusion. The key aspects of this chapter, then, have been the relationship between a rudimentary Manichaeanism and political reality as expressed in the internal content and structure of schizophrenic language and imagery; the relation of such imagery to an understanding of a deeply hidden level of political phenomena; the content of a delusional symbology that reflects a fundamental political dynamic; and the data visible in the self's internal regime as empirically useful in tracing the origin of political value and in revealing the structure of psychological orientations that may push a culture toward specific political and ethical forms of identification. The next chapter will look more closely at these phenomena in terms of the political structure of power.

four　　　　　　Knowledge and Power in
　　　　　　　　　　Delusional Symbolization

The speech acts of delusional schizophrenics constitute a kind of window into the self, an intimate, first-order view of the drive toward omnipotence, a drive that is critical in the development of human thought and action. This language, while intelligible and logical in its own terms, radically skews the terms and context of historically given meanings. However, I agree with Harry Stack Sullivan: schizophrenic utterance is not qualitatively different from ordinary language. Its distinguishing feature is its delusional frame of reference, which gives rise to linguistic acts that represent an inner state whose meanings and values have no consensual foundation. It is language in the process of consistent representing or becoming, and in such representations (which originate in a symbolic inner universe) lies its significance and its peculiar theory of knowledge (see Searles's discussion of the "derepression" of long unconscious feelings and the embodiment of these feelings in metaphoric or symbolic understanding [1965, 571]).

Delusional utterance is not unintelligible. It is indeed possible to speak with articulate, sensitive patients, to encounter symbol systems of the most unusual kind, and to hear these theories, concepts, and ordering principles described in a complex language that is not at all gibberish. Meaning and context are the issues—not intelligibility. For example, utterances such as "I am speaking with the aliens" or "Every morning my brain is culled by the head nurse" or "I am the Curator of Delusion" possess an intelligible structure. Each refers to or is composed of symbolized premises that, on the surface, refer to specific events or concepts. It is only these events and concepts that seem bizarre and often thoroughly out of place.

A patient named Rebecca often spoke to me about reaching the "essence" of things. When I asked what that meant, she laughed, a huge roar of a laugh, with more irony than humor. She refused to reveal the essence of things, although it seemed to have a great deal to do with being caught up in uncontrollable power and manipulated to death. She hinted at it by referring to the unseen, hidden "beast" inside her and to how people demonstrated their affection by wanting to scratch furiously at her skin. As she put it, "They want my skin; they want to take it off; they want to strip me bare; they want to eat my bones; they want to bash my brains

71

in." The concept or felt presence of "them" was a persistent theme in Rebecca's dialogues—"they" as invisible forces of cosmic stature, lurking, waiting, ready to torment or absorb her being. But is Rebecca's beast any different from a tyrant? Or is she revealing the structure of tyrannical intentionality simply by describing how she feels? Is her language then an illustration of those internal dynamics that in the tyrant's call for action are projected outward onto the world? Is Rebecca's beast (her contained energy with its rage and hatred) a metaphor for the inner core of political tyrannies?

Rebecca felt that everyone surrounding her, including those who took care of her, wanted to be within the beast, to join it by merging with her, to be a part of this monstrous representation implanted inside her. Although Rebecca kept the beast inside, she made it appear in language through her association with immense power. Caught in delusions whose very foundations rested on claims about the entrapment of different forms of power, Rebecca had no way to escape. She remained convinced that the world was a vast battleground for the struggle between History and the Clemente Group, with her life as the prize. Her inner world revolved around feelings of dread and domination. Speaking with Rebecca was like confronting force, a pure energy imbued with an overwhelming sense of imminence. All conversation became urgent; nothing in her belief system was trivial (triviality she experienced as the day-to-day chore of living). At any moment, History or Clemente or Nature would swoop down and take us all away. Her fear that everything could be annihilated "in the next second" became almost tangible.

The schizophrenic must continually confront the dreadful. The will takes on the form of grandiose, omnipotent figures who wait sadistically to devour the weak, helpless, and the worthless. Delusion resembles a nightmare without end, in which psychic energy appears as a population of giants, dwarfs, animated machines, juggernauts, spirits, or Star People—grotesque distortions of human form who conquer, torture, maim, and destroy. At other times such figures may submit, surrender, die, explode, or disintegrate. Torturers and victims are the chief protagonists of the schizophrenic's delusional world—a world from which all democratic or egalitarian relations are absent. Each drama acts out the fears, traumas, and anxieties of an inner universe that cannot tolerate ambivalence or intimacy.

I would like next to examine the foundations and properties of delusional knowledge, and look at delusion as an epistemological formulation, a theory of knowledge that provides the organizing dynamic for consciousness. In addition, I wish to argue that delusional theories of knowledge represent radically unfree states of human experience, that delusional knowledge in its obsession with power and omnipotence, keeps the schizophrenic person in an unjust state of bondage (the internal self here being understood as a set of political relations). The therapeutic demystification of delusion initiates a struggle over two competing forms of knowledge: delusional (which is unjust, tyrannical, and domineering) and consensual (which is collaborative, democratic, and egalitarian).

Ann

Ann[1] was a nineteen-year-old who felt trapped by the hospital and everyone in it and who experienced machines as sexually animated. As she put it, "All machines want to have sex with me." When we walked by the coke machine, she insisted we make a detour: "That machine wants me; it wants to get in bed with me." When we walked on the hospital grounds, she demanded that we stay as far as possible from the grounds crew and their lawnmowers. Every time we found ourselves within earshot of a lawnmower, she became terribly frightened and felt in imminent jeopardy. She was absolutely convinced that all machines in the world desired her sexually. It was a consistent theme with her: sex was bound up with mechanical functioning, with the noise of bars, levers, motors, engines, and propellers. Her images of machines operated within an intelligible frame of reference; her assumptions, however, lacked any credibility in consensual terms. For Ann, a machine did not perform neutral functions nor was it composed of parts seen strictly in terms of engineering. It was a sexual being whose noise

1. The following is from Ann's discharge summary:

> Though there was some generalized improvement in the patient's period of hospitalization, she continued to be delusional and hallucinatory throughout the course of her hospitalization. The patient believed quite firmly that she was being observed all the time by way of television sets, radios, and other types of listening and spy devices. The feeling was that she had some special talents that the government was especially interested in and that this accounted for all the surveillance of her. At times, she also reported auditory hallucinations where various people would be talking to her and advising her what to do. Improvement was seen in that the patient was able to control her more aggressive impulses and some of her violent outbursts. She was also able to cooperate with her program insofar as to attend her activities and to demonstrate herself to be responsible enough to progress to a higher responsibility level than the special observation she had been placed on at the time of admission.

Similar observations appear in a nurse's note:

> [Ann] also spoke of the only good people in the world being "flyboys" and "flygirls" and of flying saucers, of which she has seen four "mother ships" and an undetermined number of ancillary vessels. The mother ships, she states, are octagonal in shape. When asked who operates them, she stated that she had probably already said more than she should and declined to discuss the subject further.

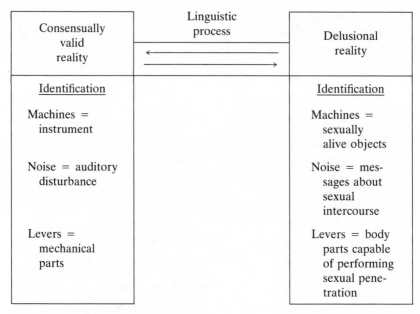

Consensually valid reality	Linguistic process	Delusional reality
Identification		Identification
Machines = instrument		Machines = sexually alive objects
Noise = auditory disturbance		Noise = messages about sexual intercourse
Levers = mechanical parts		Levers = body parts capable of performing sexual penetration

Fig. 4.1.   Reality and Identification

transmitted messages about sexual intercourse; its apparatus appeared as the potential instrument of sexual penetration (see figure 4.1).

The logic expressed in Ann's delusions connects mechanical functioning, the self, and the sexuality of the human body. These associations understand sexuality not as intimacy, but as a depersonalized, abstract power relation that is embodied in the sexual power or force of mechanical things. Ann's inner world identifies sexual intimacy with mechanical coldness. Yet, given her frame of reference, Ann's attributions (the way she defends her knowledge claims) make perfect sense. The references in her language and her concept of interpersonal relations derive from unconscious or internal forms of identification.

For Ann, the world of humans was powerless. Nevertheless, humans represented a danger and threat (in contrast, for example, to beings she called the "aliens," who wanted to "come down to earth and take me away, take me flying about the earth"). She refused to believe that machines were inanimate and incapable of thought or sexual desire. When I appeared confused, she remarked that I didn't understand, or explained that the aliens chose not to communicate with me. She experienced herself as hooked up to extraordinary forces in a manner reminiscent of Tausk's "influencing machine" (1948). Her conception of how machines work and of the machinelike character of human responses and feelings animated all aspects of her life. It was her organizing principle, the core of her structures of meaning. Further, Ann's imagery implied that her self had forsaken the consensual world for a fantasized projection of immense power that provided gratification on a deep unconscious level and protected her from dangerous feelings of vulnerability, dependency, and erotic need. Ann existed as both passive victim and active aggressor in a psychological tyranny that assaulted and terrorized her through the depersonalized apparatus of sexually animated machines.

This delusional belief system was essential to her emotional and physical survival; in its unassailability it stood in striking contrast to the powerlessness of her social situation and her inability to establish relationships with other people. Yet her isolation and withdrawal seemed not to bother her; her understanding proceeded according to a logic inaccessible to those who kept her "locked up." She communicated with aliens who were waiting in the sky to take her away, and was privy to the "power" of machines. The hospital environment, however interfered with the form these truths assumed in her consciousness. She also resented the therapeutic implication that these feelings constituted delusional and fundamentally mistaken notions. (She often complains to me that being in the hospital reflects a conspiracy between the hospital administrators and her parents to keep her away from the aliens, from going to California to learn how to "fly.") Her world revolved around the presence of power threats (machines wanting sex) and the possibility of power fusions (joining with the aliens, flying). It should be noted that this rather diminutive teenager was initially committed for psychiatric observation because she hijacked a ten-ton dump truck. I asked her what had made her do this, and she responded that she liked "the feel of its power, its engine underneath me."

Figure 4.2 elaborates the terms of this patient's experience of sex as penetration by machines. For Ann, sex was a power relation premised completely on the sensation of power internalized as domination. Each of the components of this particular sexual relation differed according to the logic of consensus or delusion. According to Ann's delusional truth, a room became analogous to a landing strip, her lover's arms appeared as propellers circling over her body, and her recollection of intercourse involved the feeling of being invaded by engines. She described her experience in terms of a disembodied energy, as being entered by a force "with the whirl of propellers." After her lovemaking, she perceived her lover rise like an airplane, his engines reverse themselves, and his body fly out of the room/landing strip.

For Ann, sexuality or touching took on nonsensual, nonerotic properties; power replaced sensuality, and the sheer force of domination replaced "pleasure." The lover's body, symbolically experienced as engines and propellors, penetrated without warmth or tenderness; sex meant being consumed (or annihilated) by a cosmogonic energy devoid of any human quality. Every aspect of this relation seemed to be depersonalized. What Ann felt or knew in her sexual encounter was the exact opposite of sensuality. Warmth became coldness; physical need was transformed into mechanical gratification; closeness became absorption by a vast, uncontained power; touching translated into cold, nonhuman annihilation. Ann's consciousness was filled by the idea of omnipotence.

Consensually valid reality	Linguistic process	Delusional reality
Meaning structures		Meaning structures
Room = erotic environment		Room = airport landing strip
Body = lover, sensuality		Body = lover's arms as propellors, whirling, making a great deal of noise
Coitus = sensual excitement, physicalness, sensitivity to body, heightened sense of the pleasure of exchange		Coitus = experience of being penetrated by engines, sensitivity to noise, to the energy of engines
Postcoital situation = lingering sensuality, pleasure in the other, feeling of physical release and gratification		Postcoital situation = body rising (like airplane), engines reversing themselves, body leaving, flying out of room

Fig. 4.2.   Reality and Meaning

To experience sex as cold, distant, mechanical power implies that there is something terribly threatening about human contact—that it might result in annihilation of the self. To be sexually dominated by a power that moves like a machine implies that the self associates warmth and intimacy with imminent danger. (I understand intimacy to be acceptance of the other as an autonomous presence not defined by delusional projections, and as the willingness to take delight in the other's reality, both physical and psychological.) By merging with an extremely powerful agent (machines, aliens, spaceships), the self constructs a universe over which it exercises absolute control. It names what is significant; what is and is not there; what is and is not meaningful; what should receive attention and what should not. Power and knowledge fuse. What is real and believable is the powerful, the omnipotent.

Not only does such knowledge "possess" the world; through the imagery of power, it also creates the foundations for identity. Whatever feelings of hopelessness and despair lie behind the delusional symbol system, Ann's consciousness moved on a level of absolute omnipotence. She was convinced she was powerful; she knew that the spaceships enhanced her power. Her identity was thus resilient and firm. She complained that I, the hospital, and her therapist unjustly tampered with what she understood to be true. We became instruments of untruth.

The Omnipotent Fantasy: Power Identification as a Mechanism for Survival

Two properties distinguish power in the symbolized inner universe of the schizophrenic: (1) the fixation on domination (there is little mediation, compromise, or limitation in the imagery) and (2) the simultaneous experience of complete domination in one series of images and victimization, torture, dismemberment, and annihilation in another series (often part of the same observation). In addition, the relation between the images of power and the experience of victimization reflects specific political analogues (see table 4.1). Imagery involving care, closeness, cooperation, or mutuality (the political imagery of community) has no functional significance in the patient's delusional world.

Listening to schizophrenic patients, I would hear the statement, "I have lost the fascination with life." Even though the schizophrenic self is neither empty nor dead, at times everything might appear hopeless and filled with imminent horror, as is clear in the following excerpts:

Plants for nourishment are given water and sunlight.
Are you given nourishment?
How can you when you're fed rat poison?

We are cows going to slaughter.
I am kept here by a vast army of juggernauts.

77

Table 4.1 Fantasies of Power and Feelings of Victimization[a]

Power image	Experience of victimization	Political analogue
"I have so much power, if my secrets are revealed, there will be retaliation."	Feels all men and women want to rape her.	Domination Defilement
Aliens in spaceship want patient to join them. Deadly sparks and rays come out of her fingertips. Patient is a powerful cat, able to dart in and out of human society.	Sees herself as part of a dirty, polluted earth; feels herself to be in a hole.	Destruction Manipulation Devaluation Confinement
Patient is "above" other patients who are not worthy of her company. Occasionally patient wields "cosmic, galactic power."	Sees everything as paralyzed. Feels herself behind an "iron curtain." "Clemente" group wants to keep patients drugged and incapacitated. Cosmic forces do brain scans on the patient.	Domination Manipulation Destruction
Fantasy of being a dog trainer. Patient has a hundred women. Patient spends considerable time lifting weights.	Feels helpless; frequently hallucinates an intestine wrapped around his head and squeezing like a steel band. Hallucinates uncontrollable shaking in his head; often can't control his eye movements.	Domination Bodily enslavement

a. The political column is meant to represent general political relationships that appear consistently in any political environment. In this sense, the political analogues I witnessed were phenomena describing broad tendencies and developments over time. Thus domination and defilement in the first example are classical political positions (master/slave) that have a long history in political thought and action. Similarly, in the rest of the examples, I sought political language (to describe the psychological states) rooted in relationships that historically have exercised tremendous influence over the development of political structures and theories.

They tell me the world is corrupt.
Who are "they"?
It doesn't matter; they're everywhere and they'll destroy all of us
in the end.

Nevertheless, despite such despair, the schizophrenic self seems to show a longing for connectedness. Images of power serve to link the self with events, people, or presences so large and overwhelming that there is no possibility of annihilation within the environment of the delusional series. Furthermore, while power imagery defends against feelings of closeness and compensates for an unconscious identification with utter worthlessness and badness, the delusions do not suggest that the *longing* for embodied human contact ceases altogether. What has in fact been smashed is the *belief* that such warmth is possible and, even more important, that the experience of empathy and intimacy is safe. Any intimation of warmth or closeness in the therapeutic encounter is, at least at the outset, strenuously resisted. What brings safety is the contained and absolute hallucination of power.[2]

In a discourse not defined by delusional knowledge, desire signifies feelings of attachment, the need for an other, a form of embodied connectedness. For the schizophrenic who operates according to the structures of a delusional knowledge system, desire has attributes that can hardly be recognized: it becomes a disembodied statement about the world couched in the imagery of omnipotence/grandiosity and victimization/torture. It takes on global, absolute qualities, represented by grandiose figures who equate trust with obedience and domination or submission. The delusional system contains no aspect of personal intimacy, such as the foundation for a trusting relationship.

In delusional systems, images of sexuality may take the form of murder, rape, dismemberment, or some extraordinary conquest. Desire, tied as it is to a world of domination and submission, may emerge in passive images of being incorporated, swallowed, or killed: "The Star People took me in; and I became one of them"; "when Bob made love to me, it was the airplane coming into the room." Desire may also be expressed in active images of devouring, incorporating, swallowing, or annihilating: "I am the head of the Arabs and I'm going to wipe out the Jews"; "I want to screw every girl in the hospital"; "I just want to sit there and let them all, all twenty of them, make it with me, one at a time"; "I'll drop the atom bomb and destroy everyone."

---

2. Therapy, to the extent that it is successful, intrudes on the defensive functions of omnipotent fantasy. The therapist competes with power symbols, what Adler calls the "striving for power and dominance" that "may become so exaggerated and intensified that it must be called pathological" (1954, 68). In Adler's view, psychological development rests on a primitive and "uninhibited striving for power" that has become the "most prominent evil of our civilization" (ibid.).

Such imagery invariably suggests states of gross inequality. If justice exists in the delusional world, it is certainly not the justice of compromise, mediation, and limitation. If anything, it resembles the Hobbesian war of all against all or Thrasymachus' definition in Plato's *Republic*: "the just is the same thing everywhere, the advantage of the stronger" (1961, 589). In delusional systems, justice is not the capacity of human intelligence to search for the self's potential through interaction with others, nor does it have anything to do with limits or balance. What is just and right is what is powerful, namely, the agents or presences, given "body" through the schizophrenic's thoughts, who overwhelm and dominate.

The schizophrenic's inner world is not free. In it, "will" does not manifest itself as mutual recognition, but asserts itself as power and tyranny. If there is a political language that describes the schizophrenic's internality, it is the language of tyranny, domination, and annihilation. It is important to bear in mind, however, that the radically unfree character of the schizophrenic self refers only to the psychic reality of delusion. The schizophrenic's will has been assimilated to an internal knowledge that rests on injustice and force. This profound transformation utterly defines the conditions and boundaries of identity, and deeply entrenched delusions defend against mutuality, cooperation, and trust. What serves as knowledge in the delusional world is tyranny.

The delusional universe mirrors Plato's description of the descent into tyranny (*Republic*, book 9), with the erosion of reason and the emergence of despair and unhappiness. The tyrannical soul or psyche "is continuously and in waking hours what he rarely became in sleep." The internal world of the tyrant is one of tremendous violence; the tyrannical nature "will refrain from no atrocity of murder . . . the passion that dwells in him as a tyrant will live in utmost anarchy and lawlessness." The tyrant becomes the "sole autocrat" and "never tastes freedom or true friendship" (pp. 801–2). Schizophrenic delusion, then, is a glimpse into what Plato conceived of as an absolutely ravaged psyche, an inner world that "teems with terrors and is full of convulsions and pains" (p. 806).

Again, I wish to emphasize that this description does not apply to the person who, for whatever reason, has become schizophrenic. The schizophrenic as a human being suffering from considerable misunderstanding and social abuse should be distinguished from the delusional systems that arise as a defense. The schizophrenic, as a victim of misalliances and confusions in the family and in social maturation, should not be equated with his delusional defense. Delusion functions as a desperate measure to protect the self from having to deal with unconscious feelings that carry with them an unbearable pain.

The Levels of Therapeutic Discourse:
Demystification of Delusional Reality

In the effort to liberate the self from its preoccupation with power relations and the images of domination, the therapeutic exchange traverses several different levels of meaning and discourse. Figure 4.3 gives a schematic representation of these levels. The
transformation from delusional to consensual knowledge is represented
by the movement from plane A (where all knowledge within the self is
defined by delusion and the realm of will is one of power) to plane E
(where there is demystification of delusion and resymbolization of the self
in the language of consensual reality).

More specifically, plane A signifies the fantasies and hallucinations of
delusional reality. Plane B denotes associational thought (no matter how
random), instances of self-reflective awareness linking delusional references to life-historical events, and occasional comments on grandiosity
and power in the context of recollecting the past. Plane C suggests more
differentiated and systematic exploration of the feelings attached to
delusion. It initiates a therapeutic dialogue that occasionally looks at
what symbols mean as psychodynamic issues (as opposed to their significance as ordering devices for the projections of will). In plane C, broad

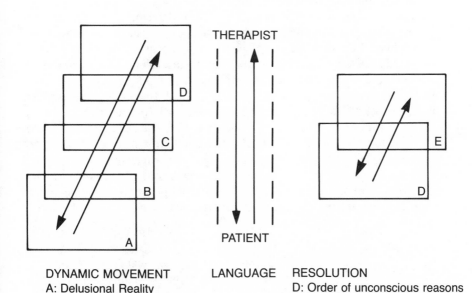

DYNAMIC MOVEMENT   LANGUAGE   RESOLUTION
A: Delusional Reality   D: Order of unconscious reasons
B: Plane of associations   E: Consensually valid experience
C: Emotional logics

Fig. 4.3.   The Structure of Psychological Space

emotional patterns are identified which may be of some help in untangling the complicated delusional defenses.

Plane D represents the incipient breakup of delusional knowledge. During this stage, the therapeutic dialogue becomes focused more concretely on emotions, on the patient's feelings toward the therapist, and on specific analysis of psychodynamic issues that initially may have motivated the psychosis. It is more (although not entirely) a partnership, tentatively exploring the insights generated through a mutual recognition of consensually valid meanings in psychological experience. Delusional references recede and may even disappear altogether, replaced by a dialectical reflexivity that continually resymbolizes the self with a theory of meaning accessible to at least two persons. The patient during this stage may feel more hopeful and, most important, the relation between identity and the images of power becomes less critical that it was before. The patient begins to realize that desire is more than the imagined activity of domination and victimization, more than an extreme sadomasochistic exchange. Desire comes to be experienced as intimacy, trust, and connectedness with an other, and to be seen in less threatening terms (although it is unlikely that the self will ever feel completely safe in intimate relationships). Therapy at this point attempts to reestablish the relation with culture and history in an effort to bring the self back into historical time and consensual logics.

Plane E completes the demystification of delusion. It represents the ego's organized attainment, reached after great struggle, of consensual communication in a language whose ontological assumptions can be verified or experienced through the therapeutic dyad. If delusion can be understood as the self's radical subjectivity, (its movement toward "nature") then the emergence into consensually valid meanings reflects some measure of objectivity mediating psychic reality (the return to community). Power loses its Manichaean aspect and instead becomes recognized as a quality that exists objectively, in a context of sharing. The self no longer finds it necessary to construct symbols distinguished by one-sided images of power. As the fusion with power systems diminishes, the experience of other human beings takes on properties more yielding and flexible than during the delusional phase.

ANALYSIS OF PLANE A: DELUSIONAL CONTENT

Plane A contains what is manifest or visible in the schizophrenic utterance to the observer, namely, the representation of alternative logic and thought in language. The speech act reflects what functions as knowledge for the schizophrenic:

Aliens are out there; they speak to me.
I am a cat, but don't tell anyone, keep it a secret.

I am being tortured by the Clemente Group.
I am speaking with the Star People.
They culled my brain last night and cut me up into little pieces.
The ladies are following me and tell me what to do.
I am a pursuer and a victim at the same time; when the pursuer
catches the victim, either I'll be very well or very sick.
They'll all get us in the end . . . I'm in danger; they've mobilized
all the squadrons in the Sahara against me.

Nothing separates the patient's self from the identity of the hallucinations. Identity is implicit in the hallucinatory imagery; no attempt is made
by the patient to question the terms of this identity or to break through
delusional meaning. Themes of grandiosity, victimization, torture, dominance, and annihilation weave in and out of the delusional systems. The
worlds described in these utterances are truly fantastic as the following
examples demonstrate.

For Ann, as we have seen, machines and sexuality defined the core of
her system of knowledge. She also experienced herself as a cat, but as a
cat moving mechanically through any available space. She frequently saw
herself leaving her body and moving around the room as a cat "with
claws." Her descriptions were mechanical, as if her catlike character were
simply an extension of another machine.

Mary knew herself to be a leader of the "World's Greats," the most
powerful people in the universe. She commanded huge armies, rescued
thousands of suffering souls, and spent considerable time on the tele-
phone calling the "World Greats" and transmitting messages essential to
the survival of the planet. She presided over secret squadrons (her spies),
mediated conflict, provoked mass migrations, and controlled all the funds
in the World Bank. She also kept in continual contact with a group called
the "Divine Visual Aeries."

Rebecca experienced herself as connected to a cosmic presence called
"History" (which represented both goodness and protection). She was
tormented and harassed by agents of a world conspiracy she called the
"Clemente Group" (which transcended History and represented evil).
Although the Clemente conspiracy threatened Rebecca, she also believed that if any of its thousands of agents came too close, History would
be there to save her. History, even with its great power, chose to communicate with her through messages sent by her dead father. These
messages were received in her bowels, either through pains in her intes-
tinal tract or in what she saw as the "green slime" of her bowel movements. Although History was ready to respond to her plight in the face of
the deadly Clemente Group, she expressed some doubt in History's
ability, when called upon, to overcome the collective power of the
Clemente Group; and History (like Rebecca) found it difficult to escape
the network cast by Clemente's agents, who waited patiently for the right
moment to take over the world and annihilate all human life.

Tom was dominated by an invisible spirit figure called Henry. He spent considerable time "playing" with Henry, although the games Tom described had extreme sadomasochistic properties. Henry, as Tom put it, enjoyed taunting and tormenting, and in the past drove Tom to commit criminal acts. This relationship consumed Tom's attention, and he would have preferred to be left alone by the hospital staff and his therapist, to be free to lie in bed (for any period of time) and play with Henry (Tom and Henry engaged in endless dialogues, primarily about biting, itching, and scratching). Henry kept Tom immobilized, turned inward, preoccupied with games that often had a diffuse sexual content. Henry possessed no body, features, or materiality; he only manifested himself through dialogue (the games) or through specific commands—e.g., "Henry tells me I shouldn't talk to my therapist"; "Henry told me to rob the liquor store"; "Henry told me to go to South Carolina."

Jack's sensory apparatus was under the control of the Star People. They determined what he ate, what he saw, and how he saw things. They also controlled all movement in the universe. At night they would steal into his room by means of the moonlight (or "starlight") and communicate with him. They revealed "signals": if during the day the top of the trees moved, no harm will come to Jack or the world. If, however, the bottom of the trees moved, there was an impending disaster.

Each of these systems is quite complex, with several permutations and twists built around the organizing images of power, domination, and victimization. Each is perfectly accessible to linguistic description, and none of the patients felt any great embarrassment about either describing the system or believing it to be absolutely true. The presentations above outline only general configurations; each system of symbols involved intricate stories about myriad events or figures. Each contained a cast of characters, some of whom remained constant and some of whom changed. And each utilized themes, variations, events, and "presences" to orient the self to all action and meaning in the universe.[3]

ANALYSIS OF PLANE B: ASSOCIATIONAL CONTENT

At some point in the therapeutic process, delusional reality takes on qualities that extend beyond bizarre and uncon-

---

3. In Ferenczi's terms, the ego possesses "a magical capacity that can actually realize all . . . wishes by simply imagining the satisfaction of them" (1916, 222). Rank states: "Our own act of will . . . we oppose to the outer force of reality as the inner pressure after truth" (1936, 250). For the schizophrenic, such "inner pressure" manifests itself in delusional systems, as statements about a particular kind of truth, and as an urgency that takes shape as elaborate power images. Such productions of will are "uncontrollable and insatiable," and the very essence of will consists of its "inability to be controlled or satisfied" (ibid., 73). Further, what Rank refers to as "negative will" or "scorn, anger, hate" erupts frequently in the schizophrenic's relation with things and people in the external world.

nected images. Language begins to have meaning on two levels: an internal logic becomes more apparent, and utterance appears that gives clues to psychodynamic causes that may lie behind the delusional ordering of reality. Dialogue in plane B moves back and forth from hallucinatory imagery to associations whose meaning still remains tangential. Occasionally the therapist may hear a word or phrase that is not part of the elaborate hallucinatory system. Such language may make reference to specific emotional events or recollections. These references, however, are sporadic, and may not be therapeutically significant. The following exchanges are typical of plane B:

Dialogue 1
Why won't the hospital cure me?
What do you want to be cured of?
Rabies.
Why rabies?
Because I don't feel that rabies should be passed around.
How is it that rabies is passed around?
Because my mother was magical.

Dialogue 2
I am a black hole.
Why is that?
My girlfriend left me; she never loved me. . . . Sometimes I
   don't know who I am, whether I should be boys or girls. . . .
   But I can move the stars with my eyes.

Dialogue 3
I am a cat, but don't tell anyone in the hospital. Right now I'm
   traveling around your office; my claws are feeling everything. I
   am not a pussy cat.
Why not?
Because my claws are long; the big cats have long claws, the
   pussy cats, short ones.
What is the feeling of having claws? Can you describe it?
I feel like I'm going to trap you.
Does it remind you of anything?
My father beat me when I was little; everyone on the football
   team called me a whore.

In dialogue 1, the terms "rabies" and "passed around" form part of the vocabulary of a delusional knowledge. Not only is the patient (Rebecca) convinced she has rabies, she also fears that she might infect others. The sensation of having rabies possesses an enormous importance for Rebecca's ordering of the universe, although it is unclear what the disease means in a psychodynamic context. She also associates these thoughts with her mother's being "magical." There is no obvious reason for the association, and it remains for therapeutic work to discover what the reference means. It may indeed have no significance, yet the associational phase is filled with these types of clues or hints, some of which may be more productive than others. What I wish to emphasize here is that this kind of utterance (even with its sporadic, unsystematic quality) characterizes a particular effort at deciphering the content of delusional symbols.

In dialogue 2, the "black hole" is associated with the departure of the patient's girlfriend, with the experience of rejection in a love relationship. Nothing is clear about these associations; they are undifferentiated and lack obvious coi nections. Yet they are significant in the context of the dialogue: at the moment they are uttered they become central to the patient's organizing consciousness. It is still too early to distinguish with any degree of certainty associational content from delusional knowledge, but the language suggests that at least some chinks are appearing in the armor of delusional knowledge. The patient is attempting to make some contact (no matter how slight) on a level that implies movement away from delusional definitions.

Plane B brings data to consciousness. The patient's expression of confusion in dialogue 2 over gender identity—whether or not he should be "boys or girls"—and his ability to move the stars with his eyes constitute reflections on an organizing principle or logic that resides inside the human mind and lacks any confirming structures in social or historical reality. Here delusional nature is circumscribed by its own epistemological foundations, yet the very fact that "will" takes form in language creates therapeutic possibility. Utterance brings the unconscious to consciousness; language makes the unconscious accessible, visible, public. These data, although they lack consensually verifiable meaning, nonetheless point the way toward further and more differentiated acts of demystification (the movement from nature to society, from delusion to consensus). The observer may be witnessing an exotic form of truth, knowledge that excludes the therapist, but in the process a *person*, who is experiencing pain and longing, emerges from time to time from a delusional cocoon. These moments, which lift the self out of delusional identity, give evidence that significant psychological transformations may be developing.

Figure 4.4 shows the links between delusional content and associational signs. Certain associations may be more evident than others, and at times the associations may not fit in with the delusional construction of reality. What is important is that delusions may be tied to specific associations or events or recollections in the patient's life. What those associations mean (and how they connect with the delusions) derives from a therapeutic listening that requires a sensitivity to the content of delusion itself. The associations listed in figure 4.4 represent what I experienced to be the connections, at the moment of utterance, between the delusions of dialogues 1, 2, and 3 and events that seemed to be more realistic and that

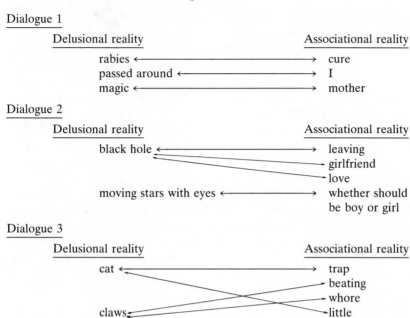

Fig. 4.4

might accurately be understood as being within a "consensual reality" (whether belonging to the patient's past or present).

The mapping of the linguistic event is not always neat, nor can it ever be absolutely correct since the mind's processes are fluid and associations change over time, and even from moment to moment in the dialogues. What should be recognized, however, is that delusions do in fact produce associations. Whether those associations are accurately identified by the listener depends on a whole range of clinical exploration that develops over time. For example, in dialogue 3, it might legitimately be asked how the concept of "littleness" connects with "cat" when the patient says she is not a pussy cat but a big cat. On the surface, the mapping seems to be contradictory. However, once one has entered into the phenomenology of the remark, the reference to the cat can be attributed to Ann's experience of her father's treatment (and lack of attention) when she was a child. She indeed does wish to be a big cat when she's feeling hostile, but I saw her delusional wish as a reaction to the spankings and beatings (giving rise to intense feelings of worthlessness and smallness, allusions to which occurred throughout her dialogues) she received as a little girl. Being a big cat defended against the terror of these feelings or recollection of the terror.

Another example is provided by the use of the word "trap." On the face of it, the closest connection would seem to be between "trap" and "claws," so it might appear odd to associate trap with cat. However, in the context of the dialogue, it was not the claws that trapped me, but the cat; the entire being of Ann-as-cat wished to trap, to claw at me. Ann's "claws" represented what was essential to her self and to her survival: the delusion of being a cat allowed her to survive encounters with any person. In mapping the relation between the delusion of being a cat and the associations of trapping, it appeared to me therefore that the emotional connection was the strongest between cat and trap, rather than between claws and trap.

Similarly in dialogue 2, Jack expressed considerable despair at not knowing whether he should be "boys or girls" and in the next moment stated that he could move the stars with his eyes. In this instance, the delusion seemed to dispel the despair. Instead of having to deal with the terrifying confusion over gender, he retreated into a fantasy or delusion that he could handle and that presented no confusion. Since the grandiose imagery of moving the stars appeared persistently in his utterance, it served as a massive defensive system against dealing with the horror of not knowing whether he was a boy or girl.

ANALYSIS OF PLANE C: THE EMOTIONAL LOGIC

In each of the dialogues, words are used to describe, through symbolizations, the self's internal state. To feel infected by rabies or "lousy . . . as in louses sucking at the body" or to be a black pigeon means that the relation between self-knowledge and identity is refracted in a highly condensed symbolic language. Meaning is hidden in the symbol. To grasp the emotional logic, to understand what lies inside the delusional imagery, is to initiate a process that strikes at the core of delusional knowledge. For the therapist to have an awareness, no matter how slight, of what emotionally or psychically motivates the images is to know where to begin the attack, where to probe, the forbidden areas. To recognize, for example, why a patient needs to possess and hold within himself a bodiless spirit that torments him and that exercises arbitrary power—in short, to understand why these images protect, is to make a therapeutic judgment that penetrates the shadows of the delusional world and disentangles the disparate, symbolic statements. This effort can retrieve a sense of the person that goes beyond the delusional identity, and by its intuitive, even artistic, inferential leap can situate the broken, fragmented being in consensual values. This means constructing as a therapeutic possibility an alternative truth, a view of self and other that is not filled with the images of power.

To see these patterns constitutes a philosophical recognition, a conviction about a form of truth that differs from the patient's and depends on an intuitive mapping of psychic reality. It is, to borrow from Plato, knowledge of what is inside the cave—an awareness of shadows, nightmares, and anguish. It is also, as it was for the Platonic philosopher, the beginning of a real struggle over competing conceptions of knowledge. Plane C thus demonstrates the power of the therapist, the possessor of an insight that rests on epistemological premises radically opposed to those of the patient.

It may even be that this process of discovery, the search for truth, begins with the first stirrings of the countertransference. For if the feelings the therapist discovers derive from the unconscious projections of the patient, then the therapist becomes the mirror for an underlying emotional logic informing all speech acts in the therapeutic situation. The phenomenon of countertransference, as Searles (1975) has convincingly shown, not only explains emotional reactions in the therapist, it also represents a profound communication, a joining of self on a level that is unspoken but essential to the outcome of the entire process.

Figure 4.5 further analyzes the language of the earlier examples. The arrows represent the movement from the associational clusters to what

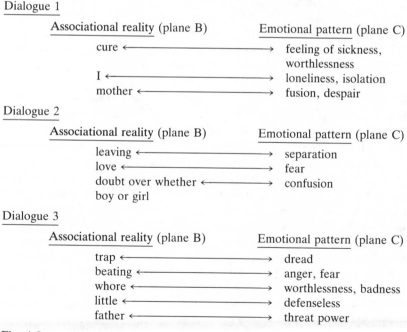

Dialogue 1

Associational reality (plane B)	Emotional pattern (plane C)
cure ←——————→	feeling of sickness, worthlessness
I ←——————→	loneliness, isolation
mother ←——————→	fusion, despair

Dialogue 2

Associational reality (plane B)	Emotional pattern (plane C)
leaving ←——————→	separation
love ←——————→	fear
doubt over whether ←——————→ boy or girl	confusion

Dialogue 3

Associational reality (plane B)	Emotional pattern (plane C)
trap ←——————→	dread
beating ←——————→	anger, fear
whore ←——————→	worthlessness, badness
little ←——————→	defenseless
father ←——————→	threat power

Fig. 4.5

these clusters of words and thoughts mean in the context of an overriding emotional pattern or logic.

The emotional patterns I have described represent my reactions to the associations of the dialogue. In this sense, what I am calling emotional patterns should be understood as a reaction to those feelings manifest in the language itself. Thus other patterns might well be discernible in the utterances. For example, in dialogue 1, feelings of destructiveness or badness (instead of worthlessness) might be appropriate given the emotional interaction between patient and observer or therapist. In my case, the emotions designated in figure 4.5 reflect the dominant sensations I felt during the dialogues. The issue is not so much the specific emotional patterns identified, but the willingness of the observer to "listen" for emotional patterns that infuse the linguistic construction of reality. Obviously these patterns change from day to day, nevertheless it is still true that emotional patterns (however they are identified) define and in some respects determine the utterance.

ANALYSIS OF PLANES D AND E:
THE DISINTEGRATION OF DELUSIONAL POWER
Rank observes: "With the truth, one cannot live" (1936, 83). Indeed, for the schizophrenic, delusion defends against a truth that threatens to annihilate the self. What is at stake in the therapeutic demystification is identity, and its boundaries in a knowable universe, no matter how bizarre that universe may appear to the outsider. Delusion defends against truth understood as self-reflection, as exploration of the dreadful. In Rank's view, the modern equivalent of the Socratic injunction "know thyself" lies in the psychoanalytic insistence that the recognition of truth requires a willingness on the part of the self to endure pain and to search (through recollection) for meanings that may not be gratifying, comforting, or safe.

Therapeutic demystification, through its psychoanalytic dialectic—a reaching toward understanding through language grounded in consensual forms—confronts the invincible, willed belief system of the schizophrenic mind. Therapy works on the patient's extraordinary commitment to the terms of psychic reality and its images of power: "For the painful reality from which the individual wants to get free is his own consciousness in the form of self consciousness and release is sought in the overcoming of the temporal forms of consciousness" (ibid., 177). This overcoming is accomplished through the construction of "permanence or eternity symbols," which in delusional thought take on the seemingly inviolable character of power figures. What Rank sees as release from temporal consciousness is for the schizophrenic a defense that avoids the

90

consensual limitations imposed by a world-view grounded in society and history.

In the ideal therapeutic world, delusional truth recedes and finally disappears in the dialogue established in planes D and E (the areas of explanation and interpretation and of recovering the frameworks of social meaning). Both therapist and patient work toward a recognition of the limitation inherent in socially constructed experience and the realization that trust and intimacy might provide some defense against life's uncertainties. During this period, both the breakup of the delusional system and a radical rethinking of the meaning and significance of omnipotence take place. Ending or at least seriously disrupting psychotic modes of identification involves a corresponding establishment of a relation with social reality and consensually valid experience.

The process culminates in an act of emergence or, as one patient described it to me, a "waking up" from a nightmare and the ability to "breathe easy" again. This patient felt an intense sense of accomplishment in having left behind the horror of his nightmare and then having reoriented himself without the aid of what he saw as his "crazy thoughts." As he put it, his former self had been "left behind." He could not remember "that person" and expressed gratitude at being able to "be himself." He often referred to his therapist, and stated that without her he never would have made it. She brought him "back from the dead."

What distinguishes this patient from the others described in this chapter is his ability to relate to the world, not under the terms of a delusional system, but according to the very tentative social conditions of a knowledge gained, with considerable effort, through his therapeutic relationship. It was extremely difficult for him to relate to other human beings; he felt "awful nervous" in my conversations with him, and he could not sustain dialogue for any length of time with anyone but his therapist. Yet, compared with the kind of knowledge that had previously guided his behavior, his ability to even reflect on his illness (to a stranger) could be considered a kind of cure. He had moved from one form of knowledge to another, from the knowledge of the cave to the awareness and acceptance of experience constituted through others. To exist outside the province of delusional forms of identification represents a radical reformation of identity structure and a truly extraordinary shift in focus. It is a transcendence that situates the self in a form of knowledge that serves the ego's life instincts.

Figure 4.6 traces this developmental path from the initial schizophrenic regression and its corresponding delusional forms to the "cure" or what amounts to the annihilation of the delusion and the founding of relationships within an experiential world constituted through other human beings.

1. Tyranny of primitive domination
   (unconscious fantasy or introject)

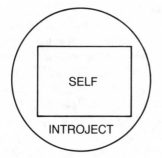

- therapist as intruder
- introject as pivotal identification
- primitive defenses

2. Fractures in the introject's
   authority-possession system

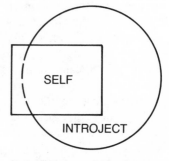

- therapist as peripheral
- power of introject occasionally diminishes
- self remains trapped by intro-jective identifications

3. Struggle for separation and
   the development of a potential
   for autonomy

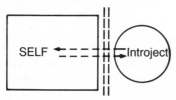

- introject as active agent in self's internality
- therapist as competitor with intro-jective identifications
- self's personality beginning to appear apart from introject

4. Establishment of a sense of relation and the initial movements
   toward an autonomous sense of
   self

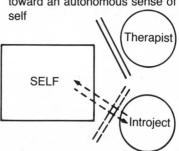

- therapist actively engaged in pa-tient's internality
- therapist still not as powerful as introject
- self's capacity to sustain ambiva-lent relation growing

Fig. 4.6.   Stages in a Psychopolitics of Development

5. Emerging self as autonomous
   object and rejection of introject

6. Creation of a therapeutic alliance
   and emerging sense of an interpersonal justice

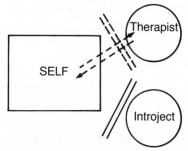

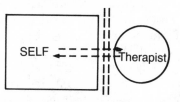

• power of introject as source of
  identification neutralized
• self appears without being dominated by inner fantasies
• therapist experienced more as a
  primary, nurturing objective; gives
  sustenance by "being there"

• therapist experienced more as a
  person with autonomous
  qualities
• therapist's functions increase as
  autonomous other
• introject for most part disappears

7. Separation and the primacy of
   inner images of autonomy and
   identity built on consensually
   valid experience

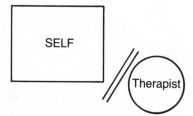

• developing sense of mutuality
• concern for the outside world and
  planning to be in the outside
  world
• heightened sense of the need for
  other people and the reality of
  sharing, empathy and intimacy

Stage I represents a self completely defined by what the introject (or delusion) designates as identification and meaning. Stage II corresponds to the period of associations; the introject loosens its hold on consciousness, and the patient may at times associate delusions with a recollection, no matter how obscure. Stage III describes the development of an emotional logic that, for the therapist, orders the schizophrenic's internality and provides points of reference. Therapy begins the process of deciphering (or demystifying) the delusional knowledge and working on its defensive functions. Stage IV is a more advanced point in the movement toward demystification; it suggests a progression toward an analysis of the psychodynamic reasons that lie behind the delusional defense. Stages V and VI further elaborate the patient's increasing reliance on consensual forms of identification and experience. During this period, the delusional system starts to disintegrate and the patient's discovery of "identity" depends increasingly on the therapeutic relationship and the willingness to accept consensual points of reference. Forms of social knowledge, such as cooperation and mutuality, take on increasing importance. Stage VII represents the demystification of delusion and the corresponding resymbolization of the ego in the context of consensual knowledge. Utterance is free of delusion. There is a willingness to accept others as autonomous, and power is seen as shared and tentative. Finally, one finds the capacity to accept trust as a critical dynamic in human relationships. Stage VII in an ideal therapeutic environment would constitute a cure, or the composition of the self in a psychic reality circumscribed by social forms of knowledge.

five   # The Delusional Possession of Reality: Ritual, Therapy, and Narrative

Ritual as Domination

Therapeutic knowledge, understood as intervention into psychotic states, represents an attempt to guide the deluded self back toward a relation with consensual reality. It is an effort to move the self from enclosure by psychotic imagery to a sense of the self as an autonomous, freely deciding being capable of trust and empathy. It is a commitment on the part of the psychotherapist to do battle with an inner "natural condition" (the violence of delusional action) and to banish that inner natural condition with a social compact (in the form of the therapeutic alliance) that assumes the importance of intersubjective experience. This chapter, then, will elaborate on delusion as an internal prison, and on therapy as an effort both to retrieve the historical self and to forge a new social compact with external reality.

Among the ritualized functions that delusion performs are a bracketing of the self and the creation of patterns and truth through repetition. To perform a ritual is to construct and affirm certainty about the world. When Chuck said every morning, "I'm going to die; Miguel and Saint Anselmo are after me, waiting outside to kill me with ray guns," he found himself inhibited by a ritualized enactment. Ritual, a deeply rooted intellectual structure, was as powerful for Chuck as a primitive tribe's invocation of spirits through dance or chanting. By enacting the terms of the ritual drama through language, Chuck populated his world with meaning and significance. For the primitive, however, ritual possesses liberating and therapeutic functions; for the schizophrenic, the ritualized utterance or belief alienates the self, reinforces the internal tyranny, and defends against the intrusions of the consensual world. It is anything but therapeutic.

Most delusional systems possess a ritualized quality: similar phrases or ideas are repeated over and over; the same images are invoked day after day; the world moves in spirals; events or figures appear and reappear in different contexts. The logic of ritual responds to specific emotional situations, and the world of ritual is distinguished by its persistence and indestructible character. Ritual reinforces identity; the more entrenched ritualized utterance is, the more rigid is the self's identity. When Chuck told me that his world was ruled by Tolcek, the cat god, Ra, the god of nature, and Tutankhamen (the deliverer of the dead from their torment), he was constructing an identity around his utterance. When Ann kept stating that machines desired her sexually, her ritualized utterance paralyzed her capacity to act and fixed her in a state of intense, almost unbearable anxiety. Through their use of language, Chuck not only gained mastery over the gods and Ann over her machines, but they also ritually enacted their intentions. By speaking these figures, they invoked their presence and privileges. Language gave them power and magic. This process is similar to a primitive tribe's attempt to gain power over nature through ritual enactment, although here it is undertaken by an individual.

Psychotherapy confronts delusion as ritualized identity. Since a belief in ritual lies at the foundation of delusional knowledge, to break its power entails demystifying what amounts to a magical experience. In offering an alternative view of reality, therefore, the psychotherapist runs up against not only the power of magic, but also against the seductiveness of an identity entrenched in ritual enactments. If the psychotherapist's persuasion is successful as a result of the sharing implicit in the therapeutic alliance, then it may be possible to break the hold delusional rituals exercise over the patient's consciousness and identity. Therapeutic persuasion moves from ritualized expression (delusion acting as a kind of internal tyranny) to a knowledge of competence in the external world. However, the process is a continuum, and the significant struggle occurs in the middle ground, the indeterminate area where self begins to doubt delusional premises but has yet to discover the foundations and value of consensual identity. Table 5.1 illustrates the dynamic of this process as a scale, where the numbers 1–3 represent the entrenched, ritualized identity, 4–7 the area of indeterminate identity (where delusion begins to break), and 8–10 the consolidation of and reaching toward a sense of self, and the establishment of its relation to others, consensual reality, and the historical community.

Yet even if the therapeutic demystification of ritual succeeds, it is likely that the self will appear in the world not with a new sense of what it means to be human, but with a painfully depressing recognition of the demands involved in participating in human relationships. What distinguishes this kind of depression from the morbidity of delusion is the belief in an intersubjective life. For the self capable of intersubjective communication, the historical community offers one possibility: although pain is unavoidable, it is endurable and is not projected onto fantasic images. It is not the absolute and unyielding pain of ritualized delusion.

Ritual thrives in the dread, darkness, and incessant fear of the delusional world. Louise needed to say, "I'm Louise here at Sheppard/Pratt" in order for those thoughts to constitute her identity. If she failed to convince herself that she was indeed Louise at Sheppard/Pratt, she

Table 5.1: Movement in Identity Modalities

Ritualized identity 1 2 3	Indeterminate identity 4 5 6 7	Consensual identity 8 9 10
• entrenched delusional systems • private language • ritual enactments • denial of historical community • therapist used as real object • intense symbiotic attachments	• confusion, indeterminacy over meanings • creation of therapeutic alliance • tentative efforts at sharing feelings with therapist • language structures change • logics not as rigid or hidden • more openness • capacity to be depressed • regression not as debilitating • beginnings of therapeutic transference	• knowledge of self in social world • knowledge of potential in historical community • awareness of crippling effects of delusional identity • capacity to express grief, sadness • more "integrated" personality • delusion no longer serves as knowledge base • considerably more openness about secrets • tentative efforts at intimacy • self capable of maneuvering using instrumental logic

might feel she had no existence. Ritual utterance—a constant reminder of identity—keeps the self together; it replaces the social and historical motives that construct identity in the consensual world, and is thus essential to the location of the delusional self.

The Ritualism of Entrapment: Delusion and Imprisonment

A patient would repeat, several times a day, "I am dead," or Chuck would say periodically, "I put my father under for twenty-one years . . . I'm a hypnotist . . . I can put you under too," or Jenny would insist: "The food is poisoned; it's burning my stomach away." Each utterance demonstrates a ritual of subjection and tyranny. A phrase is uttered and repeated, and whatever ritual happens to be in mind functions as identity. This phenomenon is difficult to understand because the consensual derivation of identity comes from any number of sources, personal, historical, and social. But for the delusional self, these avenues of identity creation simply do not exist or do not function.

Chuck was continually chased by an entity he called Joey Steinfield, who also spoke to Chuck through voices and hallucinations. It was not clear whether Joey was an actual person or an imaginative construction. But for Chuck, the presence of Joey as tormentor took on, over the years, a ritualistic significance. Joey chased Chuck, and this relation consumed Chuck's consciousness. The relationship, however, evolved around a single ritual: Joey's efforts to kill Chuck, usually through two agents stationed in Sheppard's parking lot:

> *What did you do to Joey?* I only wrestled with him, in Saigon, I don't remember, maybe I killed him. They gave us guns, he's waiting outside, with his Baltimore Mob. I don't know why he's after me.

When Chuck described the ritual of Joey waiting to kill him, it was as if, at that moment, everything that composed Chuck and Joey *in relation* constituted Chuck's identity. This ritual animated Chuck's life and experience. The belief that Joey was seeking him out, attempting to kill him, and tormenting him with voices, bombs, and explosions restricted Chuck to a minimal sense of self. While Chuck's ritual centered around death, without Joey, paradoxically, Chuck would have had no identity. His being, his core self, was Chuck-pursued-by-Joey: it was everything that Chuck was, had been, and would be *at the moment the delusion was being uttered.* Hilda, another patient, kept repeating: "I'm mother Mary, am I mother Mary? I'm mother Mary; Dr. Glass tell me I'm mother Mary." Even though these utterances had a ritualistic structure, without them Hilda would have had no existence. The words "mother Mary" refracted her identity.

The entrapment felt in these situations is very real; it is like a prison. Peering out from behind its walls, the self refuses to allow the consensual world admittance to ritualized identity. An enormous gulf separates delusional and consensual reality. Therapy must therefore establish a bridgehead, a connection. Even though delusional figures torment the self, it is rare that the rituals will be experienced as a lack of freedom. Chuck refused to give up Joey because Joey filled Chuck's life with purpose and "reasons." Each struggled with the other, but the very existence of the relation confirmed Chuck's "freedom to be." This sort of freedom, however, is ahistorical and asocial, and amounts, ultimately, to a kind of radical narcissism. It excludes all real, embodied others. Therapy offers indeterminacy, uncertainty, doubt, and depression along with trust. It is much less threatening to live with the certainty and hermeticism of delusion, despite its fear and dread.

If an alliance is established with the therapist—a relation that depends on language—the self, often unwittingly, strives for acknowledgment, the right to be heard within the human community. The alliance moves to reclaim rights: the right to be within history and culture, the right to experience intersubjectivity and embodied and autonomous relations. All these rights the self relinquishes through the delusional defense. While an outside world may have existed for Chuck, it was not a "space" or universe he could see—rather, it lay beyond his awareness. It is difficult to be without rights, no matter how humane the environment. Chuck lacked any knowledge of how to rule himself; he lived as a pawn in the hands of Joey Steinfield; to free himself from Joey required a sense of how to govern, without the voices, his own internal thoughts, and an appreciation of his rights as an extension of relationships with others, not as an extension of Joey's plans for him. Delusion inculcates fear and acquiescence; therapy encourages collaboration, participation, and self-governance within limits defined by community and convention. Therapeutic intervention, then, is more than a process of "sealing over" inner disturbances—it is (or should be) a fundamental commitment to what might be called an "education in self-governance" that strives to break the hermetic world of delusion, an effort to establish a compact with a social world that assumes the importance of integral forms of self-regulation and consensual understandings.

To be outside the hold of delusion implies some sense of rights and reciprocal obligations, but to achieve this state requires a great deal of patience and time. It is no easy task to escape the delusional prison and its obsession with death and survival. Therapy is frequently sabotaged by delusional obsessions: a patient who thinks he is running from the mafia, who wonders whether he will live another day, or who maintains that "a death ray is coming out of my belly button and surrounding my head with its poison" is bound to put up some resistance to therapeutic overtures. The patient's preoccupation with death results in an exhausting and perverse sense of what it means to be free. The following exchange with Mary exemplifies this preoccupation:

> MARY: I'm tired today.
> JMG: What's making you tired?
> MARY: Everyone's trying to kill me.
> JMG: What are they doing to you?
> MARY: They're getting ready to murder me; the pressure's too much. Will you kill me, now, will you ax me? I wish you would just chop off my head and get it over with. It's too much to do, to keep alive from one moment to the next. There's so much murder here at Sheppard/Pratt. I can't stand it any more.

The "freedom" that Mary experienced is that of Hobbes's state of nature, which admits of no sensuality, beauty, harmony, or asylum. Mary's inner

99

world was a Hobbesian nature filled with violence, hostility, and fear, and it demonstrates an alienated nature cut off from empathy, trust, and dependence on others.

The obsession with power, death, and violence extends to physical preoocupations, for example, conceiving of the body as being "not there" or dead or mutilated in some horrible way. Suicidal thoughts or attempts frequently reflect little emotional content, as if the action of suicide were an experiment to see what it would be like to transcend the boundaries of the physical self. (At this stage, the patient frequently describes tortures of various kinds: "Would you believe what they did to me in my sleep last night? See all these punctures on my body, the black and blue marks; boy, they must have had a field day!") On one occasion Ed told me about twisting a wire around his neck, and on another he stated: "I hanged myself from the bathroom door; it was no big deal; I didn't think much about it; what I wanted to do was leave my body here and go and be with God. It didn't work though because the belt wasn't tight enough." Vera declared: "I wanted to slit my wrists yesterday, but I couldn't find a razor . . . I wonder what it would be like if I used my fingernails to puncture my jugular vein?" It is interesting to compare these statements with the following fictional expression of the wish to die with its seeming objectivity and lack of passion:

> Whenever I stand near a window high up in a tall building I have
> a recurrent desire to put my head through it. I imagine every de-
> tail in slow motion: the glass cracks and splinters, shattering its
> reflections. I see my blood and hear the glass hitting the sidewalk
> and the roofs of cars and the screams of people far below.
> [Kosinski 1974, 58]

It was unnerving to listen to the patients' talk of death, for at first it appeared to consist of simple matter-of-fact descriptions, like a grocery list. But these recitals contained a kind of muted terror; beneath these monotonic reflections on annihilation lay a fear, a shrill plea for recognition of pain, as if these utterances were issuing from an unspeakable horror deep within the delusional mind (see table 5.2).

For the schizophrenic, the freedom to possess delusion is really the freedom to continue living. The real trap is death, fear of which accounts for the enormous energy spent on rituals that protect the self against tormenting figures and voices. Even though dread and fear fill consciousness, the patient frequently wishes for the therapist to perform magical acts in order to drive away demons, rescue the patient from terror, and unravel the entanglements of the dreadful. As Chuck remarked: "The enemy is life . . . I stopped life . . . Dr. _____ will get it back for me." But what his therapist means by life (trust, empathy, alliance, and collaboration), Chuck sees as death or annihilation. Death thus confronts

Table 5.2: The Structure of the
Suicidal Utterance

Flatness, unconcern/ detachment	Visible properties
Reflections on physical annihilation/on being "not there"	Utterance
Terror/scream/plea for acknowledgment and recognition/ symbiotic needs	Invisible properties

the self from two directions: the real world of other human beings and their needs, and the world of internal projections that threaten pain, torture, dismemberment, poisoning, and extinction. In the face of these twin evils, "freedom" is equivalent to remaining alive (see table 5.3).

Language and the Enclosure of Delusional Reality

The core of delusion lies in its hostility to any embodied relation; the world is held within. The dialogue below (written down by a patient [Tom] at my request) describes part of an internal relationship and demonstrates the power of delusion to enclose completely all aspects of reality. The dialogue offers a momentary glimpse into a delusional process severed from any concern with what might be considered real or identifiable. Although the dialogue is meaningless on the surface, it reveals a special strategy that made it unnecessary for Tom to seek out contact with others. The dialogue evolves around an unseen, bodiless spirit whom Tom called Henry. His behavior and action absorbed Tom's attention: whatever or whoever Henry was (a bad self-representation, sadistic superego, or introject), his presence accounted for Tom's being and activity in the world. If Tom was silent and withdrawn, he might be speaking with Henry. If he was attentive to his food, carefully placing each forkful in his mouth with an exaggerated slowness, he might be feeding Henry. If he "eloped" (a local term for leaving the hospital without permission or authorization), he did so because of Henry's commands. If he refused to speak with me, it was because Henry thought I may be a bad influence. If he closed up with his therapist, it was because Henry was jealous and taunted Tom for being too open with his thoughts. If he stole a car or robbed a liquor store, it was because of Henry's pressure. Henry composed Tom's universe; he thoroughly pos-

101

Table 5.3: Delusional vs. Therapeutic
Conceptions of Freedom

Delusional concept of freedom	
Death (tyranny)	Life (freedom)
• presence of embodied others	• delusion
• presence of embodied history, past	• hermetic languages
• presence of society	• possession of reality according to logic of delusion
• risk of an empathic relationship	• denial of embodied others
• acknowledgment of rights in a human community	

Therapeutic concept of freedom	
Death (tyranny)	Life (freedom)
• delusion	• presence of embodied others
• hermetic languages	• presence of embodied history
• possession of reality according to logic of delusion	• presence of society
• denial of embodied others	• risk of an empathic relationship
	• acknowledgment of rights in a human community

sessed and enclosed reality. In the dialogue, the H refers to Henry; Tom
gave himself the name "Eater":

> *E*: Henry is a nick Icky boo
> *H*: Icky, Icky, Icky
> *E*: What does Icky Henry Do?
> *H*: Henry bites anuses
> *E*: Eater likes Henry's nose, bite, bite, bite
> *H*: Evil Eater—evil eater
> *E*: Ha, ha, he
> *H*: Icky, icky, icky
> *E*: Icky, icky, icky—Henry is the skeleton
> *H*: Henry is not the skeleton—Henry hates eater
> *E*: Hate hate hate hate the Henry hate hate hate
> *H*: Henry says you are stupid

E: Henry is the dumbest icky in the universe ha, ha, he
H: Icky, icky icky—you are icky
E: Eater doesn't know what to say—does Henry have brothers and sisters in the spirit world?
H: Henry has 18 brothers and 23 sisters
E: They are all icky
H: Icky brothers and sisters are fun to have
E: Eater has a sister icky
H: Henry knows that
E: Is my sister going to the spirit world like I am
H: Henry says Ha ha he
E: Well, is she
H: Henry knows but he won't say
E: How come, icky acky biter
H: Henry is not an icky, acky biter
E: Yes he is
H: Henry bites eater
E: Good good good
H: Bite bite bite bite eater's testicles bite bite bite
E: Thank you biting begonia
H: Henry says go away
E: Eater says just a few more lines
H: I hate you you are icky
E: Hate the Henry hate you hate you hate you ha ha he
H: Eater doesn't like Henry
E: He likes Henry's clitoris
H: Henry doesn't have one
E: Henry has one on his nose, ha ha he bite Henry's nose bite bite bite
H: You are the most horrible icky in the universe
E: Ha ha he, I'm only number 37
H: How come, icky acky biter

The dialogue continues for an additional two or three pages without significant change. Henry lacks any shape or form. He is distinguished only by his voice. Activity in Tom's life was totally taken up by his games with Henry. If Henry were to disappear, Tom believed, so would he. Henry decided what to do or where to go or whom to engage in conversation; Tom refused to conceive of a life without Henry's presence. Although Tom's exchanges with Henry went nowhere, and although the dialogue above is circular, often silly, and obsessed with power and aggression, it provides a clear example of ritualized utterance. Although Henry's voice (and Tom's interaction with it) appear to be nonsensical, it performs critical survival functions, because Tom avoids death by fusing with Henry, by becoming Henry.

Henry claimed dominion over Tom's existential universe; Henry was life, no matter how painful or humiliating. Without Henry there would be oblivion, and life's magic for Tom lay in these ritualized exchanges. Henry elicited obedience from Tom; he "worked" because he was invisible. While Tom could not see Henry (although he knew Henry had a yellow chair and lived in a house), the language of their exchanges haunted him, pushed him into action or withdrawal in the form of playing games. It would have been impossible for Tom to give Henry up since that would have meant acknowledging Henry's imaginary status and losing what for years had served as Tom's pivotal sense of identity. Henry's abuse and assaults created a series of sensations and activities that coalesced into a permanent existential field.

Henry's power robbed Tom's life of its vitality and thoroughly absorbed whatever good self-images or feelings Tom possessed. (This certainly was the opinion of his therapist.) It was as if Henry, as ritual, functioned as reflection of an extraordinary inbalance in power relations, a symbolic manifestation of failures in Tom's fragmented history. Henry emerged as a graphic projection of compressed images that commented on a peculiar inversion in psychological time, an inner picture of the origins of basic distrust and fear. All other stimuli, whether from the hospital, his therapist, others, Tom considered intrusive. Indeed, Henry controlled all external "inputs" and was particularly sensitive to Tom's feelings toward his therapist:

JMG: How do you feel today?
TOM: I love my therapist.
JMG: Have you told her this?
TOM: No.
JMG: Why not?
TOM: Because Henry tells me not to.
JMG: Why does Henry tell you not to?
TOM: Because if I do he'll bite my anus.
JMG: Do you love Henry?
TOM: Sometimes.
JMG: Then why don't you tell him to go away?
TOM: Because I can't; how can you tell your arm to go away?

The ambivalence Tom experienced in his feelings toward his therapist became unbearable. He resolved it by closing himself off, breaking whatever alliance and trust had been established, and submitting completely to Henry's plots, demands, and games. Tom never integrated any perception of goodness or worth into his self-representation. Badness, as embodied in Henry, remained in full control and overwhelmed Tom's identity. Henry's victory was Tom's sense of worthlessness and inner despair. Tom succumbed to self-hatred so completely that he resisted any therapeutic effort to help him move toward consensual reality.

Eventually Tom eloped from the hospital; he hitched a ride to downtown Baltimore, stole a car, held up a grocery store with a toy gun, and was later caught and placed in city jail. The judge remanded him to a state hospital for the criminally insane. Tom once told me he had been happy in a similar hospital in Pennsylvania. He said that at least there, "I could talk to Henry; I would just sit outside in the football field all day, playing with him. We really enjoyed each other; no one bothered us; no therapists would try to separate us. We were happy."

What, ideally, should take the place of delusion are a relationship based on mutuality, a process that involves a shared search for meaning, trust, and interpretation, and a world where the expression of loss, grief, and depression is not felt as unendurable. As the relationship with the therapist develops, the identity-creating function of delusion should recede. Successful therapy requires a movement from the absolutism of the imaginary to the negotiated reality of a historically given present, a sense of self developed in the therapeutic alliance. In the words of the Finnish psychiatrist Marti Siirala, this event signifies the transcendence of the "fragmentation, loss of oneness, succumbing to splitting" characteristic of schizophrenia. It "ensues when some kind of elementary sharing is restored" (Siirala 1976). Therapy erodes the ritualized power of delusion and replaces ritual with the knowledge of shared, nonmagical realities. This is not to say that therapy is only applied pragmatics. Magic, however, stands in the way of *life*, the social pragmatics of experience, and it is simply not possible to reclaim the rights of the human community as long as the self feels in possession of magical or ritualized powers that place it beyond the laws, assumptions, and limitations of the social and historical community. Psychotherapy focuses consciousness on pragmatics, and in so doing enables the self to realize a conception of rights preferable to the magical solitude (and power) of delusional nature. In treating the schizophrenic patient, the therapist must confront a confusion over meaning, since the delusional self encloses reality in a way that departs radically from medical assumptions about the meaning and function of psychotic language.

A certain kind of misunderstanding may develop in the therapeutic relation whereby two different theories of explanation wind up sidestepping each other. This is particularly true, in Siirala's view, if the therapy happens to be heavily laden with medical assumptions, which he sees as frequently distancing the therapist from the patient. It oftens happens, however, that the fault of the misunderstanding lies with the therapist, particularly with regard to the observer's unwillingness to grant legitimacy either to the language or to the identity being witnessed. Siirala suggests an analogy. It is not usual to doubt "a foreigner's identity because that person speaks in an unfamiliar language." The case of the psychotic patient is similar: what is important is the structure of communication, the "threshold of two different native tongues reaching a common ground," an alliance whose strength transcends the despair of misunderstanding.

It is essential that the therapist not deny the validity of the patient's utterances and their crucial function in enclosing the self, either by avoiding them or even dismissing them as nonsense (and then retreating to the protective and neat classifications of psychiatric diagnosis). The "foreign language" of delusion is a existential event, an identity-creating system. The therapist should search for the "isomorphy between individual and collective structures and processes . . . the isomorphous network of schizophrenia like features' (Siirala 1972, 145) in the history, habits, and traditions surrounding the community. What the therapist sees in psychotic language is a whole range of influences reflecting intrapsychic, interpersonal, and cultural factors.

For Siirala, the withdrawal or retreat into fixed definitions, whether it takes place in delusion or in rigid medical enclosures of reality, suggests a deep level of alienation extending throughout the culture, what he describes as "this ubiquitous web of latently despaired repression, repudiation, rejection, withholding, denial of partnership in dialogue, or sharing of burdens." Delusional reality demonstrates "one type of death-proneness of our shared living . . . to fall ill schizophrenically represents not only a particular kind of weakness (our current name is ego-weakness) but also a special capacity to react totally to poisonous aspects of man's coexistence, to exist as an encoded message thereof" (ibid., 14). However, therapy not only acknowledges this separateness, it attempts to transform it into recognition of a mutual humanity. What maintains the delusional self in the world is knowledge of its basic or essential humanness; if that is lost, then contact with others disappears: "What is possible though, is to let oneself step by step be drawn to accept equality with the patient, equality in the sense of being of the patient's kind, that is with the same basic predicament and carried on by the same interdependencies as the other" (Siirala 1976, 28). In Siirala's view, therapist and patient meet on a common ground, a "painful acknowledgement of the ubiquitous alienation of man in all of his basic relatedness . . . accepting the presence of the transfer-network of offenses to basic rights, of traditions of lovelessness and delusional possessions which have found one's patient as its vicarious target" (ibid.). These understandings or felt realizations that connect the self to the human world appear as an elemental sharing, a "process in which none of the partners has a primarily privileged position" (ibid.). The problem lies in any linguistic system that seeks to understand reality by possessing it, by excluding any other mode of understanding.

If a therapeutic alliance is established, the patient at some point (although it is unclear when) makes a choice addressed primarily to the delusional world. This choice leaves behind rituals and their existential field and embraces, however tentatively, the shared mutuality of an embodied human relation. The decision whether or not to leave delusion and assume an alliance with the therapist hinges on the extent to which feelings such as trust, love, and dependence are felt to be gratifications that open up possibilities. If the sense of gratification prevails, it may forge a psychological connection with events that offer an alternative to the world of ritualistic magic. With the development of a sense of rights and potentialities within the human rather than the delusional community, the self's theory of explanation (embedded in magic and ritual) weakens. Attachment to delusional frames of reference becomes less significant; the therapeutic alliance withstands attempts to withdraw and subvert; primitive symbol formations break down; the self becomes capable of looking at the psychotic defenses; and a new social language of understanding replaces the private meanings and assumptions that govern delusion. If therapeutic intervention is successful, if the self leaves the delusional universe, it is testimony to the ability of the therapist to do battle with demons, ghosts, and stubborn, persistent rituals. Without this kind of agility in facing delusional representations, it is unlikely that therapeutic intervention will ever redirect the self from the terror of an inner world to the pragmatics of life in a social environment.

The Basis of Consensually Valid Meanings

It is important for therapeutic intervention to distinguish consensually valid meanings from what symbol productions infer about private truths and logics. In delusion, even though private meaning functions as an organizing principle, the utterances that arise from it are not subject to any kind of proof or demonstration. The language of delusion lacks (to borrow a phrase from Hannah Arendt) a "public space." It has no audience other than the self: meaning remains private and hidden and therefore not consensually defined. "Joey Steinfeld" reflects no history; the figure has no meaning for anyone other than Chuck—it is a name without a context or location in time.

The public nature of discourse transforms inner experience into a series of psychic facts retrievable through language. While Tom may write down a conversation with Henry, the discourse remains private and hidden. Henry refuses to allow Tom to "explain" what the games mean. Language is thus denied any consensual validation. When Tom says, "Henry tells me I should rob a bank to become good," the logic and meaning of the statement are inaccessible. No public or historical frame of reference governs the discourse. While Tom's speech is "normal" in that the words are not invented or incomprehensible, the communication lacks a consensual basis. This is also evident in the following conversation with Chuck:

> CHUCK: I think my grandfather was a woman.
> JMG: Why?
> CHUCK: Because my grandmother changed into my grandfather and then my grandfather married my grandmother . . . I'm a hypnotist.
> JMG: Who have you hypnotized?
> CHUCK: I put my father under for twenty-one years . . . I put my mother under. . . . The boy emperor lives in a house in Baltimore. . . . He's out to get me. [The "boy emperor" is Joey.]

Chuck's utterance describes a reality; it contains facticity; it brackets the self in meaning; it reflects situations and feelings. However, only Chuck knows the meaning and context behind the words. Because delusional utterances fail to find a consensual ground, there is no way of grasping the relation between the images. Delusion prevents a public space from being established between self and other.

Consensually valid meaning must by definition move beyond private inward communications or symbol structures. A conception of truth that cannot be articulated, that lies hidden in some inaccessible region of the mind, is not a belief system that rests on consensual facts. There is nothing consensual about the utterance, "death rays are coming out of my belly button." On the face of it the statement describes a specific situation, but it is one thing to grasp the images and decipher their syntax and an entirely different matter to discover what the images mean with regard to their public or common point of reference. The utterance is, ultimately, a symbolization of an inner horror the self refuses to make public.

What makes knowledge public and therefore verifiable lies in what Harry Stack Sullivan describes as a "transfer from the realm of the autistic or wholly personal, almost animal meaning, to the impersonal, social, conventional" or the "*consensually validated* meaning of the word" (1964, 212–13). When frames of reference are established through consensual validation, words lose their private, mysterious quality and their ritualized functions. They appear in a public space—the realm of common speech—and the public nature of discourse transforms inner experience into a series of psychic facts retrievable through language.

The goal of therapy, then, is to enable the self to grasp the public nature of its symbolic productions and to move from what Sullivan sees as the "autism" of withdrawal to the field of common speech and shared relation. The therapeutic encounter elaborates psychic facts, organizes the self's narrative, and isolates critical value structures in a *shared* experience; it facilitates the self's capacity for its own internal governance.

A historical perspective is critical to destroying the inwardness of these private delusional truths. If therapy discovers the historical relation between a symbol and feeling (if we understand "historical" to refer to psychodynamic history, events in a specific past remembered and recollected in the therapeutic encounter) then it may be possible to demystify the rituals of delusional knowledge. For a psychic fact to be consensually valid requires an interpretive context, a social environment, a shared *historical* field. Delusion often disguises a more complex, deeper emotional structure; because that structure is not shared, its context remains invisible. It is not consensual, public, or historical. Such statements have meaning only for self. Each of the following utterances falls into this category:

— Che Guevara protects the salad bar.
— I live in doom city . . . they're going to keep me in the poor house.
— I'm a bum but some people wanted me to be a prophet.
— I'm an American who comes out of a can.
— I'm a god of the world; I have angels up there.
— When I was four years old Jesus told me to commit suicide.

Sometimes, however, delusional utterances are stark and lucid. This usually occurs in rare moments of self-reflection:

— The enemy is life.
— Talking to you is like talking to myself but listening more.
— I'm at the other end of the bargain.
— My reality is all I've got.
— I have no feelings; I don't want feelings . . . feelings get in the way of situations.
— Man, you don't know what crazy is until the radio talks back to you or the night voices come in and wreck your sleep.
— Life is a ping pong game of pain.
— I want to blank out my mind, my garbage pail.
— I'm a very troubled boy.
— I feel like I have a yoke on me.

The second group of statements is clearly more accessible, yet such utterances rarely take the form of anything more than momentary reflections.

Delusional language, it should be emphasized, is not a subspecies of ordinary language. In Sullivan's terms, it is ordinary language but in a different mode. Its unique character lies in its frames of reference, its epistemology, its status as an internal form of truth. Mary once told me that she kept Stalin, Mao, and Lenin alive in a crypt located deep in the Kremlin wall. Furthermore, her current roommate at the hospital was "Anita Stalin," who, prior to her confinement, spent five months with her father locked in total darkness. Finally, Mary once reported a dream in which she was walking in the woods surrounding the hospital and came across a chopped up body. Frightened by the bloody sight, she ran away. Each of these symbolic productions, as keys to deeper unconscious structures, bore directly on Mary's actions, the relationship between her utterance and self-perception, and the way she viewed others.

What it meant for Mary to keep Stalin, Mao, and Lenin alive in a crypt lacked any consensual validation; what might have made her belief structure public and therefore accessible to the other (therapist) was beyond recovery. Mary lived with this world as if it were real. For it to be consensually valid, she would have had to distance herself from the reality of the utterance and examine it as a "commentary" on a set of feelings identifiable in her own historical, psychological environment. If she had been able to make connections between delusional images and associations from her past, it might have been possible in her therapy to locate the reasons or structures that tied her delusional beliefs to specific psychological events and develop a theory to explain those events.

Mary's statements about the world and her position in it clearly showed her to be dominated by the reality of the internal, by a private, noncommunicable knowledge that gave her absolute certainty. Her movement, gesture, voice, and tone all gave evidence of a fear that an observer would have seen as groundless and lacking consensual validation. For Mary, however, nothing was groundless; she was convinced that if she lost control, if she did not do what her inner messages commanded, if she were suddenly to lose her vigilance, there would be "mass murder at Sheppard/Pratt" and her body would be ravaged, "chopped up, axed, torn to pieces." Mary's communicable universe depended on the emotional matrices defined by her inner world. Body language, speech, gesture, and glance signified for her intense expression of desire: the other wished to make love to her or intended to kill her, "rape my dead body and chop it up into bits and pieces." Mary experienced emotion as an extension of her inner order of knowledge, and both the imagery she used and the meaning in others' gestures (her "International Guide Language") depended on an unrevealed or private truth. Mary dreaded the world; every morning was her "last day alive"; she protected thousands of people from imminent destruction; she experienced tremendous exhaustion as she tried both to "save the world" and protect herself from a horribly sadistic death plotted by enemies inside Sheppard. Yet this was the world she knew; its experience was as true and certain as any physical object.

The only knowable aspects of Mary's reality appeared in what she chose to translate and speak, whether or not she would make a private message accessible, and establish that message's reality in the social world and therefore, in Sullivan's terms, transfer meaning from the autistic or delusional to the consensual. If she made that choice or rather

110

if she saw that a choice was indeed possible, then her linguistic activity could bridge the gap between her internally held system of organizing the world and the public or social facts she experienced as a malevolent presence. Unless she could construct that bridge, she remained victimized by an internal order of truth, and any "other" in her psychological environment (whether that other was physically present or not) functioned as an active participant in a delusional truth that only she could validate. The facticity of Mary's experience was inseparable from the projections of her inner universe. She lived in an epistemological prison that, because of her fear and pain, she recognized as such, with all exits closed.

The facticity of Mary's life lay in her utterance, even though that utterance revealed a very small part of what she knew to be true about existence as a whole. What could be more bizarre or ritualized than keeping Stalin alive in a crypt in the Kremlin wall or maintaining that the head nurse on the hall (someone who Mary in her own peculiar way had grown quite dependent on) wanted to mobilize the entire population of the hospital against her? Utterances, attributions, and fears such as these constituted Mary's psychical reality. Each constituted a *fact* in the effort to penetrate the unconscious reasons or structures that motivated Mary's linguistic constructions. For Mary to allow "Stalin" to die (that is to stop feeding and caring for him), and to recognize his monstrous bad acts would have required that she not only give up some of her power; she would also have been obliged to recognize those feelings in herself. This she could not do, since it might signal a failure in her all-encompassing capacity to protect anyone in need. Stalin's death would have been tantamount to murdering "badness"; and to let go of any aspect of that quality would involve losing part of her identity, her self.

When Mary stated that if she were to die, the head nurse would start murdering and axing everyone, it reflected a conception of reality whose coordinates violated the consensually given phenomena governing relations within that specific environment. From Mary's perspective, what mattered was psychical reality; every other person's construction represented a lie, a violation of her inner order of knowledge. Mary simply could not conceive that her experience was lacking in reality.

The ability to utter the dreadful, even in the midst of alienation, demonstrates the self's participation in the human community. Language maintains the self's humanity, and life, no matter how anxiety-ridden or filled with fear, goes on—whatever the internal drama being acted out in delusion. If Mary gave voice to the fear that she was in imminent danger of being murdered; if Ann articulated her dread of being sexually assaulted by machines; if Chuck spoke about Joey and his killer agents, then the very act of speaking was what kept the self tied to the human world. Language reminds the schizophrenic self (although on a very primitive level) that it is still human, that it at least possesses an existence. What is far more important than the rules and conventions of consensual reality is survival. From this perspective, psychical facts defend the self against death. Consciousness in this psychological "state of nature" is preferable to no life at all.

It is extraordinary how much power these hidden meanings can contain. I frequently experienced myself being absorbed into Mary's "facticity." For example, she believed me to be Jimmy Carter. When I denied that attribution, she would playfully wink at me, a sign that we both knew I had to deny it lest someone overhear us. If I happened to be looking particularly tired, she might say something like, "I know it's hard being a world leader, so much responsibility. . . . Or if I was not paying attention, she would observe: "There's such distance in your eyes, but then it's a great strain being a world leader and sometimes you have to be distant." She knew me as Jimmy Carter and nothing could persuade her otherwise. In addition, she was surrounded in the hospital by the "World's Greats": Fidel Castro, Mao Tse-tung, Brezhnev, and so on. By attributing power to my presence, Mary transformed me into an other more clearly in accord with her delusional internality. Mary corresponded only with the "Greats" and every day she received a visit from some notable who was either disguised as a patient or who made a special trip to see her. Thus for me not to be a "Great" would have been inconsistent with the inner terms of her world. Why else would I have come to see someone "who is so famous" who "protects all the power in the world?" Psychical facts provide structure; they are coherent and real, and reflect, in Sullivan's words, an "inner bundle of changes of state" (1953a, 27). Or as Paul Ricoeur states, psychical reality "presents a coherence and a resistance comparable to that of material reality" (1977, 840).

Delusional Narrative as an "Archeological Dig"

Narrative in delusion is not historically defined; it is a dialectical process that moves forward and backward, telescopes experience, condenses and distorts the past, and mistakes wish for consensual reality. Symbolic utterance intermingles present and past, and the psychic facts that emerge from this narrative, rather than resembling ordinary facts, appear as a range of emotions and psychological operations jumbled together in a nonlinear series.

An appropriate analogy might be an archeological dig that produces not discrete levels of an ancient city but interpenetrations in which an object from level A will be found in the historically antecedent level D. Excavating requires that one put together evidence that is not symmetrical, that is not strictly causal, but that eventually yields an order or a classification. Similarly, the psychoanalytic investigation of delusion is an act of reconstruction and recognition. Its purpose is to forge a connection between the self and its embeddedness in sociality. For example, Chuck observed:

> CHUCK: Steinfield is after me.
> JMG: Why?
> CHUCK: Because I killed him; you know I put my father under when I was five; that took care of him.
> JMG: Why did you do that?
> CHUCK: It was the gun, you know . . . I shot him . . . I'm in pain . . . I just exploded.

To understand what this utterance means requires that one figure out who Steinfield is, what his function in Chuck's theory of knowledge is, why Chuck killed him, if he killed him at all, what kind of psychological functions the defense performs, and the psychodynamic structures that infuse the symbolizations. The dialogue moves back and forth from the present to the past and then back again to the present.

All discussions with Chuck inverted past and present; nothing was consistent; Chuck's descriptive world required a kind of archeological sorting or classification. Each bit and piece of information had to be placed in a grid organized according to a historical pattern. For example Chuck described to me the "history of his body" as opposed to that of his soul. He then went on to relate, separately, the history of his soul and then the history of his mind. As the history of his body he related a peculiar series of events that resulted in his becoming "muscled" by eating a special solution of what he called "Metrecal and meat." His muscles would grow overnight and he would no longer be skinny. Similarly, by eating the "wrong food" or "drugs and poisons," his muscle would turn into fat. In telling the history of his soul he spoke about church-related experience; and for that of his mind he discussed the kinds of schools he attended as a child. None of these entities—body, soul, or mind—ever cohered as a complete identity, and Chuck spoke of them as if they were separate and different realities. Each was an isolated aspect of self without any relation to the others.

Chuck feared both Joey (whom he sometimes identified as a three-legged hermaphrodite) and Joey's agents waiting in the parking lot ready to massacre him; he feared that his face was changing shape and becoming grotesque; he feared the periodic explosions in his room, and felt dread over the possibility that he might not wake up alive. All these fears describe a self who existed in a turbulent, ever-shifting state of nature. Chuck's cognitive world had been so disrupted, the earthquakes in his unconscious had become so profound, that his therapy had to involve a massive effort at historical and temporal sorting (see table 5.4). The

Table 5.4: Temporal inversion in delusional
reality

Consensual reality (linear and progressive)						
future						
present						
past						
Delusional reality (existential and static)						

P					P	
		P	P			P
	P	present		P	P	
			P			
	P		P	P		

P = equals bits and pieces of past brought into the present as if they have just happened.

psychic facts relevant to Chuck's therapy emerged not from linear conversation or dialogue, but from an inverted narrative that yielded images
of partial identities and fragments of the past, none of which was connected with any of the others.

> I put my father under when I was five; but when I was down in
> Florida, I ate food, Metrecal and meat, and became strong over-
> night. I gained forty pounds of muscle; I knew it was the Metre-
> cal. Then I became skinny because they put dope in my food;
> you know, dope makes you skinny. My mother doesn't really
> know who I am; she feeds little kids dope; is she some woman!
> Dr. Glass, why don't you go visit her? Tell her you're me, Chuck
> _____, she won't know the difference.

It is as if Chuck's self had stepped out of time and into a world of its own
construction distinguished only by the movements of symbols that composed his delusional system. It is because of phenomena such as this that
the schizophrenic is immune to the effects of any conventional understanding of time: for the schizophrenic a second might be a day; a month,
thirty years; a year, a century. Consciousness, then, in the schizophrenic
locates value, meaning, and purpose in the atemporal atmosphere of
what the symbology dictates as action and being; the consequence of this
is a delegitimization of social time, which requires the acknowledgment
of some basis in consensual reality. The following dialogue indicates the
extremity and pathos of this dislocation of temporal existence.

> CHUCK: I got a new pack of cigarettes, see? I haven't smoked for
> twenty years.

JMG: Chuck, how can that be? You were smoking with me when I spoke with you on Monday; it's now Wednesday of the same week.

CHUCK: Well, they put me to sleep.

JMG: Sleep?

CHUCK: Yeah, for twenty years. I just woke up and got my pack of cigarettes; you saw me twenty years ago. It might have been Monday for you, but it was Monday twenty years ago. . . . Anyway, the cigarettes won't hurt me, since I haven't been smoking for twenty years and my lungs have reconstituted.

JMG: How can that be?

CHUCK: I know for sure; they put me to sleep; they could have put you to sleep too . . . as a matter of fact, you look older, all that gray in your beard. . . . Well you say it was last Monday, but you don't understand. You and I operate off different calendars.

Chuck had succumbed completely to delusion and his inner universe defined all sense of duration and function.

The Dominion of the "Alien Object":
Delusion and the Nonhuman Quality of Self

For the schizophrenic, the "alien object" (to borrow a Marxian term) controls consciousness and behavior. The self's split off, alienated parts (what psychoanalysis sees as "part object" and "part self" representations) infuse consciousness with images of violence, annihilation, grandiosity, and despair. What Marx in his essay "Alienated Labor" attributes to labor applies with equal significance to the alien quality of delusion:

The *alienation* of the worker in his product means not only that his labour becomes an object, assumes an *external* existence, but that it exists independently, *outside* himself and . . . that it stands opposed to him as an autonomous power. The life which he has given to the object sets itself against him as an alien and hostile force. [1964, 122–23]

I would for a moment like to consider this quotation in the context of the effect delusion has on consciousness and adaptation to social reality.

1. "The alienation of the worker in his product means not only that his labour becomes an object, assumes an external existence, but that it exists independently outside himself. . . ." Alienation for the schizophrenic may be seen as a phenomenon akin to autonomous clusters of thought that control behavior and perception. In this sense, "labour" (if labour is conceived as the activity of thinking, which it is for the schizophrenic) becomes an object: thought externalizes itself as an object dominating

the perceptual field. In the schizophrenic mind, delusions always come from somewhere else ("the computers are controlling me; the spaceships send messengers to take me up with them . . . the trees tell me what's right and wrong"). Delusion is "out there," in Ohio or in the computer or in the buzzing of bees. It is never understood as coming from inside the self: delusion possesses a status and power thoroughly independent of the self.

It would be impossible to convince a schizophrenic that a hidden, unseen spirit, a voice constantly pecking away at consciousness, derives from inner emotional conflicts. The self believes not only in the truth of the delusion, but also in the voices and in what they say. Delusional systems and what they describe are external, presences with a life of their own in some other place. An example is Mary's belief that she presided over the "war of the rocks"—a battle in her delusional world involving warring Chinese sects that had been fighting for sixteen centuries. She attributed power to psychologically independent agents, and was firmly convinced she was not the author of this war—in her view, it was definitely not a figment of her imagination. She spoke to great warriors who since the beginning of time had been engaging in mortal combat. When I asked Mary whether the war might not have something to do with her own feelings, she replied: "Not at all, I give Mao and Lao Tzu their orders and they fight it out. They come to me for advice and I intervene from time to time. But it's ridiculous to tell me there's no war going on. Go to China, see for yourself. They'll tell you about the war of the rocks."

Hearing voices, controlling stupendous events, and being victimized by overpowering forces are for the delusional self real and decipherable phenomena. Coming from sources "external" to consciousness, the delusional voices seep in through walls and windows, rush down smokestacks, emerge from the chirping of birds, the slapping of wings, the rustling of blades of grass, or wind swishing branches and leaves. Agency, in the sense of being able to choose or author freely, possesses no meaning for the schizophrenic. The self is simply a cipher for forces far greater than it. For example, Chuck felt his bones were rotting away because of the extreme power of a voice that entered his flesh and "eats away my bones, draining me of my marrow, and making me brittle like a stick." Convinced that all his movements were ultimately controlled by computer signals coming from central Illinois (a project run by Joey), Chuck gave up on the idea of being free, or thinking of work as anything other than the hearing of voices. It was his "job" to speak about the voices; his wages, as he saw it, took the form of cigarettes and meals. He refused to speak to me on weekends because Saturdays and Sundays were his "days off." But when he was "on the job," Chuck felt it was his responsibility to transmit the voices, which he represented as agents external to himself: "It's like being out in the sea, the sun rising, blinding you. The voices come from out there; and then they pierce the walls and fly inside. They roll down from the ceiling in a slow curve. These voices are like the morning sun on a flat sea; they blaze and strike you right between the eyes."

2. The product of labor "stands opposed to [the laborer] as an autonomous power." What does it mean for thought to be "autonomous" in relation to self? Delusion, which is the product of "thought-labor," is alienated from any social or consensual foundation and reflects a life of its own. It opposes the social interests of the self with its own special power to define reality. As Mary once said, "I must sit here in this chair all day and guard the hospital from being invaded. . . . Every morning I call each world leader and we set policy for the day." Or as Ted remarked: "You know I'm a great rock impresario and I can't talk to you now because I'm being called to set up twenty-six rock concerts at the same time." Because delusional thought is so autonomous, so independent of what passes for social logic and rationality, it absorbs all aspects of the self's being.

3. "The life which [the laborer] has given to the object sets itself against him as an alien force." For the schizophrenic, the act of creation returns to haunt the self as an oppressive agent dictating the conditions and values governing experience. Delusional imagery often appears in the form of alien presences sending messages, codes, "rays," or knowledge. If delusion is a product or an object "alien" to the self, the schizophrenic "labors" or becomes dependent on a "possessor" (i.e., delusion) whose images systematically exclude consciousness from participation and proprietorship in any human or (in Marx's terms) "species" community. Consciousness as the productive element of self (the maker of thoughts) takes itself as the object of appropriation. It is no exaggeration to say that delusion exploits or appropriates the self. Delusion comes to possess the self's energy, time, and labor. The more delusional the self's thinking, the less "ownership" consciousness exercises over its consensual or participatory relations. The extent to which this dependency transforms the schizophrenic's connection to life and thought is remarkable. As Jenny commented, "When the computer tells me I'm alive, I'm alive; when the switch is turned off or the plug pulled, I'm dead." When asked where this computer was located, she replied: "Out there somewhere . . . when it's off I have no thoughts, no brains, just a big space in my head, nothing in the skull." Another example is the way Tom spent his day involved in sadistic games with Henry. Henry dominated Tom's life and kept Tom wrapped up in dialogue (inaudible to any observer) for hours, sometimes even days. Tom "fed" Henry at meals, bathed him, and took care of all his needs. He once said: "I hate being here [Sheppard/Pratt]; they don't want me to play with Henry; they keep me locked out of my room and on the hall. At least in my old hospital [a rundown, understaffed V.A. hospital] they left me alone. That suited me fine because I could go

outside, lay on the field and play with Henry all day long. . . . In the winter, I stayed inside, usually in my bed; as far as they [the staff] were concerned I was a perfect patient. I spent most my time in bed, never made noise; Henry and I had a great time." Absorbed in his games with Henry, Tom appeared to be immobile, even catatonic; yet he was quite active internally since his critical existential field lay in his delusional symbology.

This kind of domination—a set of internally held images that represents both sadistic and masochistic aspects of self—may be seen as a form of actual, concrete oppression. The labor of thought, to put it in Marxian terms, becomes a means to existence: delusional thinking takes away the schizophrenic's species life, "his real objectivity as a species being, and changes his advantage over animals into a disadvantage in so far as his inorganic body, nature, is taken from him" (Marx 1964, 128). The schizophrenic's consciousness experiences the physical self as not its own; it is felt to be "unembodied," "depersonalized," or "petrified" (Laing 1978). Or else the body is put together and functions according to nonhuman (or suprahuman) rules. Or the delusional self may feel that its body has been taken away or stolen; or that parts of it are dead or have been cut off, ripped to shreds, and are bleeding profusely. The physical self may appear to the schizophrenic as grotesquely distorted: "My face is made up of rotting flesh taken from the graves of decaying corpses."

Marx states that "what is true of man's relationship to his work, to the product of his work and to himself, is also true of his relationship to other men, to their labour and to the objects of their labour" (1964, 129). From a psychological perspective, alienation defines all moments in the schizophrenic's life; it is difficult to conceive of a more psychically alienated existence. There can be no public aspect or feeling of place attached to delusional systems that isolate the self and enforce withdrawal. As delusion strengthens, the human or social side of the self weakens; as delusion intensifies its hold on consciousness, the schizophrenic withdraws more and more from contact with others. The more demanding delusion is, the more frustrated the self becomes with any attempt at establishing a social relation with significant others.

Several of the contradictions Marx describes in his essay "Alienated Labor" may be looked at from the vantage of the schizophrenic's situation. "The more the worker produces the less he has to consume" (ibid., 123): In the context of schizophrenia, production refers to thoughts rather than objects, and the labor of the worker may be understood as the activity of thinking. The more the delusional self thinks or produces thoughts, the less it has of itself and the greater the domination of delusion over action and consciousness. Since delusion absorbs the ego, consciousness is bound up with the intensity and productivity of the delusional introject. The more thought "produces," the more these internal images constrain behavior and cognition. "The more value [the worker] creates, the more worthless he becomes" (ibid.): The more psychotic or delusional the schizophrenic's activity, the less value the self possesses for the outside world. "The more refined his product, the more crude and misshapen the worker" (ibid.): The more delusional the self's action or intellectual production, the more distorted become his relations with others. "The more the work manifests intelligence, the more the worker declines in intelligence and becomes a slave of nature" (ibid., 124): The more articulate the delusion that represents itself in language, the greater the likelihood that delusional images will provide the self's only form of knowledge and orientation. And the more consciousness is bound to this internal concept of knowledge, the less likely the self is to be free in its social relations.

For Marx, "alienation appears not merely in the result but also in the *process* of *production*, within *productive activity* itself" (ibid.). The schizophrenic's alienation manifests itself not only in the result of thought (its metaphoric language and condensed symbolizations) but also in the very activity of thinking, in the mind's essential productive activity. It is useless (from a collaborative or social point of view) or valueless production; thought lacks an external object, for it takes itself as object. It is not purposeful activity, for delusion contains no practical, intersubjective or consensual base. It is thought that is primarily defensive in nature: it keeps the social world at a distance and creates a hermetic identity that interprets and defines phenomena. It is not that the schizophrenic is intrinsically incapable of socially grounded, intellectual production. Rather, the objects of thinking—delusional symbols—act to defend against deeply repressed emotional conflicts which would be terrifying were they to be acknowledged.

If the self's regression toward delusion is a distortion of human nature, it is because the very foundation of thought has been separated from the self's social nature. It is as if the *telos* of ego development, which ordinarily takes consciousness into progressively more complex stages of differentiation, has been suddenly interrupted and thrown backward. In this respect delusion interferes with a vital aspect of human nature: the self's affinity and need for a social world, a set of values, an identifiable public (or polis life).[1]

Jenny's belief that she would die if her computer were unplugged (an event that took place intermittently throughout any given day) implies a rejection of what is basic to intersubjectivity: the capacity to receive nurturance and protection from values, actions, and others inhabiting the

---

1. In clinical terms, this is expressed in psychoanalytically oriented developmental theory (cf. the work of Margaret Mahler, René Spitz, Clarence Schulz, Theodore Lidz, and Harry Stack Sullivan).

consensual world. Delusion, as a psychically alien object, makes it virtually impossible to experience the other as autonomous or independent of the self's internal drama. Not only does the schizophrenic feel less than human, but the self experiences all social relations as assaults on itself and as threats to its survival. Consciousness therefore moves to control what is public and "relational" through a private knowledge and system that create a deadly prison. As Hilda described it to me, "Dr. Glass, I control your thoughts and feelings . . . by slipping underneath your skin; that's how I do it . . . I sneak into your brain; you don't know I'm there, but I do."

Because the schizophrenic lacks any productive function in association with others and repudiates any sense of a public, he frequently assumes an animal or other nonhuman identity.[2] The delusional alien object destroys the self's connection with human qualities. Jenny saw herself as having hooves that needed to be trimmed; she grazed on the hospital grounds and spoke of herself as "dead meat for the meals at Sheppard/ Pratt." Marx states: "We arrive at the result that man (the worker) feels himself to be freely active only in his animal functions—eating, drinking, and procreating" (ibid., 125), although the schizophrenic is not even free in these acts, since basic physiological or animal functions possess delusional content. An example of this is a patient who drinks water throughout the day because she believes it to be a cure for her alcoholism (even though she is not an alcoholic). In her delusional world, the hospital's water supply is fed by an alcoholic stream that cures people of alcoholism, a kind of anti-alcohol alcohol. Thus she feels she must continually drink from the water fountain and staff is obliged to monitor her water intake carefully and restrict her incessant trips to sources of water.

Marx continues, "in his human functions [the laborer] is reduced to an animal. The animal becomes human and the human becomes animal." The schizophrenic who grazes on her hands and knees or who sees herself run by a computer hooked into her brain is not therefore a being with a sense of *human* nature. Delusion may thus reduce the self to the status of an animal, or if not an animal, to an impersonal object controlled by unseen, powerful, super- or antihuman forces.

Conclusion: Narrative and Truth

Within the schizophrenic's narrative are statements about experience, the world, and the self's relationship to the

---

2. For a comprehensive discussion of the issue of nonhuman identification and its presence in the schizophrenic's life world, see Harold Searles 1960, *The Nonhuman Environment.*

world.[3] These statements constitute a linguistic and behavioral adaptation that should be understood not as the action of some human subspecies, but as a self struggling to survive intolerable psychic pain.

For Paul Ricoeur, language (which he sees as "desire coming to discourse") creates its own truth; it brackets the subject in meaning, in the activity of "saying true" (Ricoeur 1977). In schizophrenia, what is spoken (the language of the alien object) composes the self's frame of reference, no matter how nonhuman that may be. But what Ricoeur calls "being true" (what Marx might see as "species being") involves validation: it requires a social nexus, an interpersonal field that is dialectically defined. Delusional speech is not "being true" in the sense that utterance rests upon socially embodied frames of reference. Transforming "saying true" (the private epistemology of the inner world) into "being true" (consensually based knowledge) involves breaking up the inner order of knowledge. It also requires moving through what Ricoeur sees as the "itinerary" of misunderstanding (for example, Chuck's concept of time or Jenny's nonhuman sensibility) to recognition of the temporal and human qualities of existence.[4]

As a function of the therapeutic situation, the journey from misunderstanding to recognition or "resymbolization"[5] recovers the coherence of the human self in the presence of others. It affirms the possibility of intersubjective communication free of delusional projections. If, for example, Mary had discovered within herself the resources to remove "Stalin" from her protective inner world, and if she had relinquished the "World's Greats" as her defining frame of reference, then she might have been able to accept the consensual relation between her world and her therapist's world. To do away with the domination of the alien object would have necessitated destroying Stalin. If this had taken place as a function of the disintegration of delusional identity, it might have been possible for Mary to have established a viable intersubjective rela-

3. As narrative imagery, the psyche in Paul Ricoeur's understanding becomes a "text to be interpreted . . . a system of forces to be manipulated" (1977, 861). Knowledge develops from language, the capacity for feelings to be "said, to be addressed to another person, to be fantasized . . . resymbolized and to be recounted in the study of life" (ibid.). It is not enough simply to state the existence of psychic facts; they do not become meaningful or disclose value until they become recognized and internalized by the subject: "What is psychoanalytically relevant is what a subject makes of his fantasies" (ibid., 843), what the self in the midst of its awareness believes to be true. This kind of truth takes on public or intersubjective significance through the therapeutic exchange, and this process begins the recovery of self-esteem and human dignity.

4. In delusion, the inner dialogue assimilates all factual ordering of experience. In Harry Stack Sullivan's words, "the inner aspect of the situation is the more impressive" (1962, 196).

5. For Sullivan, resymbolization means that consensual logics become the basis of symbol formation.

tionship. At the very least it would have obliged her to question critical structures of her inner epistemology and to give up delusion for, in Ricoeur's words, "self recognition through the restoration and extension of the symbolic process in the public sphere of communications" (ibid., 859).[6]

Therapy recovers in language a symbolic order experienced as public, a movement away from the hallucinatory internality toward an affirmation of commonality that implies some separation between self and other. Instead of identity being founded on an inner set of coordinates, the self experiences the therapeutic other as an active agent in generating an understanding of a range of public or social responses. A "resymbolized" identity presumes the need to encounter and internalize public meaning. Therapeutic success depends on the extent to which incapacitating anxiety and dread diminish or even disappear in the face of the demands of public values.

With the founding of a dyadic therapeutic exchange, the self's inner history becomes accessible and, in Ricoeur's terms, recountable. It appears as part of the consensually validated world. And the eventual therapeutic outcome, the consequence of the subject's acknowledging his own psychic history, leads to a "new pattern of energies" and a breakdown of resistances (ibid., 868). The self's reliance on neurotic behaviors or, in the case of the schizophrenic, delusional imagery as means of self-protection or reference recedes and the public or consensual identity (the intersubjective) takes on increasing importance.

The schizophrenic narrative is storytelling of the most unusual kind, and it may indeed suggest a modern form of what Ricoeur calls the "biographies and autobiographies whose literary history is part of a long tradition emerging from the oral epic tradition of the Greeks, the Celts, and the Germans" (ibid., 869). Delusional symbology represents the self's epic history expressed through images whose content is often allusive. The stories possess an inner consistency, and the symbologies appear through the subject's narrative commitment, a link forged between the self, its identity, and the psychical reality implicit in its de-

---

6. Compare Sullivan's concept of resymbolization, namely, psychic operations that attempt to "achieve approximate security" and to "ward off clear awareness conflict and severe anxiety." For the schizophrenic, resolution of "conflict by resymbolizing and substitution" fails. The self's dynamism lacks the necessary "security operations" to avoid unmanageable fear and dread. Awareness disintegrates; the ego breaks into pieces:

> schizophrenia is a term meaning literally a fragmentation of the mind. . . . a splitting of the control of awareness. . . . So far as the self functions, the patient is engaged in (regressive) magic operations in an attempt to protect himself, to regain some measure of security in the face of mighty threats, portents, and performances in a world that has become wholly irrational and incomprehensible. [Sullivan 1953a, 142]

lusional world. The narrative defines the entire structure of self and being; it affirms the universe of "saying true," and defines the self's sense of place in whatever drama it chooses. No matter how odd the symbology, each image demonstrates an inner logic representing psychodynamic forces hidden within the self. The symbologies are epic in the sense that they span all aspects of life and explain all forms of human or even divine behavior.

Such tales or narratives possess an unusual resemblance to the tradition of magic and magical structures (Regardie 1973) in the attribution of power to celestial agencies, the symbols of transformation that define thought, the capacity of mind to transform or alter or in some way fundamentally rearrange the structure of matter and causality, and, most importantly, the obsession and fascination with images of power—a fascination that is critical, for example, to an understanding of the history of alchemy. The vast oscillation of uncontrollable forces (devils, the "World's Greats," trickster spirits, gods), the rapid psychological movement from victim to victimizer, the images of action, violence, and control: all these phenomena appear in the complex internal organization of delusion. In delusion the self feeds on fantasies of power, incorporation, and omnipotence in a vivid reminder of the totalistic and unyielding world of infantile omnipotence.

six   Delusions and Phantasms:
On First-order Human
Experiences

Delusion as the Self's Natural Condition:
The Imprisonment of Psyche

The aim of this chapter is to elaborate on certain similarities between delusional states and what Thomas Hobbes in *Leviathan* calls the "natural condition of mankind" (Hobbes 1968). I have already alluded to these connections, which appear in the content, action, and structure of delusion. Hobbes is also pertinent here in another respect: he defines madness or delusion as "motion in the brain." Hobbes's view is surprisingly modern given the considerable time, money, and research devoted to the search for specific chemical agents in the brain that cause or intensify serious mental disorders. As an early statement of this position (i.e., that serious mental upheaval derives from physiological functions within the brain) Hobbes's analysis might be useful to explore. It is also an argument that denies any experiential or factual content to delusional states. For Hobbes, delusion is empty, "airy," without substance, "phantasms" moving through the brain. It is a condition, he maintains, that can hardly lay claim to any empirical truth. Phantasms travel without any reality; they are as unreal as any "daemonology." What I would like to argue, in opposition to the Hobbesian perspective, is that delusion is filled with experience; that it is a legitimate form of knowledge validated through internal forms of experience projected as truth. Delusion by virtue of its critical identity-creating functions, is as real as any other form of experience.

There is, finally, an aspect of Hobbes's theory that bears on contemporary politics. Delusion threatens the authority of a rationally designed language. It is subversive in that it strikes at those conventions that regulate a very specific language game. Should the assumptions of a language and its game become eroded the very linguistic structures of society and authority stand naked and vulnerable. It was therefore essential for Hobbes to establish not only the rights of sovereignty but the rights of a certain construction of language. When Hobbes confronts delusional utterance (phantasms, spirits, and so on), he sees the Tower of Babel, disputes over language that spill into political life. It is "Babel" (particularly in laws that govern political exchange) that he seeks to

124

banish or dispel through the objectivity of naming and the authority implicit in publicly acknowledged words.

While much in Hobbes's argument in *Leviathan* deals with the necessity of public order (after all, few would quarrel with the idea that society cannot exist without laws commonly recognized or political "names" free of ambiguity and explosiveness), the kind of authority he attaches to the act of naming and defining inevitably results in a theory of exclusion, which entails canons of "right language," notions of "mad speech" identifiable authority for elucidating the meaning of words, and utterances that reflect "passions unguided." Hobbes not only posits authority in political sovereignty, he also erects (to protect the objectivity and power of science) a *linguistic* sovereign hostile to any activity disruptive of "naming." It is in this regard that his theory of names and words may provide the justification for a theory of exclusion: "dangerous" speech, no matter how it is defined, presents a threat to the commonwealth.

Anxiety, dread, and fear of imminent death govern Hobbes's description of the natural condition in *Leviathan*. Nothing that resembles law or a "common power" intervenes between self and chaos. Hobbes's natural state is a psychological environment defined by a "warre where every man is enemy to every man" (1968, 186). The delusional self also anticipates war, conflict, and struggle, and rarely does the schizophrenic's internal drama reach a stable equilibrium. The delusional self must continually guard against conflagration, annihilation, and the possibility of serious harm. Consciousness keeps a constant "vigil," waiting for destruction to suddenly sweep the world away. In the delusional world, there is absolutely no assurance there will be peace. As Hobbes states: "So the nature of War, consisteth not in actuall fighting; but in the known disposition thereto" (ibid.). The delusional self lives like Hobbes's natural man: constantly keeping at bay the perceived invasions and threats of others.

Friendship, collaboration, and empathy have no place in the natural condition: "men live without other security, than what their own strength, and their own invention shall furnish them withal" (ibid.). Through the "invention" (that is, the projection) of great powers, forces, presences, and leaders, the delusional self gains some protection from violence and threatened invasion. Being the "son of God" or the "ruler of the world" or the controller of the "World Bank" creates a sense of power that, at least temporarily, can ward off or inhibit feelings of despair and death. Such inventions become forms of inner security; the images of delusion, which function as experience, give the self a breathing space and provide allies in the hopeless battle against entropy. Mary could not survive without her mob and spies; Tom would die without Henry.

The natural condition lacks civil authority, order, and predictability; it possesses no economic or social activity; it has no productive apparatus, no "civility." It resembles the existential world of delusion in its absence of productive work, its minimal activity, and the little effort made to direct attention outside the self, toward tasks having social foundations. Almost all energy is spent protecting the self from the fear of imminent destruction. In many respects the actual life of the schizophrenic and existence in the natural condition are very much alike: withdrawn, isolated egos are dominated by fear; minimal civil exchange, if any, takes place, and there are a real absence of communication, a denial of collaborative action, a resistance to common purposes and goals, a dread of community or society, and a prevalence of despair.

If the following description in *Leviathan* is taken as commenting on the extent to which paranoia and fear leads to disintegration of the social and cultural ego, then it might also be understood as symbolizing the delusional self's existential field (it could certainly be interpreted as symbolic of what goes on inside delusion):

> In [the natural] condition, there is no place for Industry, because the fruit thereof is uncertain and consequently no Culture of the Earth; no Navigation; nor use of the commodities that may be imported by Sea; no commodious Building; no Instruments of moving, and removing such things as require much force; no Knowledge of the face of the Earth, no account of Time; no Arts; no Letters; No society. [ibid.]

Hovering over all delusional life, compounding its isolation and alienation, is Hobbes's dominant psychological reality: "and which is worst of all continuall feare, and danger of violent death; And the life of man, solitary, poore, nasty, brutish and short" (ibid.).

Paranoia is paradigmatic of the natural condition. All movement is fluid and defensive; action takes into account the predatory intentions of the other. No one can be trusted; fear becomes a way of life. The erection of barriers between the self and other and the other seen as an enemy are the consequences of the human self's "nature." This fundamental and grim human nature springs from the "Desires [and] Passions of man," which "are in themselves no Sin. No more are the Actions, that proceed from those Passions, till they know a Law that forbids them" (ibid., 187).

What occurs in the natural condition cannot be judged by any standard of morality or law; action precedes even the sense of a need for moral restraint. The assertion of power, the presence of war and violence, anarchy and self-rule, not only inhibit the creation of any overriding justice, but the actors (until their own sense of self-preservation forces them to it) feel no *desire* for constraint. The situation is similar with the delusional world: when the self arrives at a "compact" with a significant other, usually the therapist (an acknowledgment of the outward-moving dimensions of the life instinct), the strength of that alliance might prove effective in combating the narcissistic pull of delusion.

Because of its lack of any commonality or authority in politics and language, Hobbes's natural condition has no ethics, no sense of right; the self exists bounded only by its energy, its will to power, its capacity to survive the regime of fear. Similarly, in delusion right action appears in the terms of the inner drama. Nothing else matters; all limitation, rule, and morality, which govern social exchange in external reality, appear to the self as torturing instruments imposed by hostile others: "To this warre of every man against every man, this also is consequent; that nothing can be Unjust. The notions of Right and Wrong, Justice and Injustice have there no place" (ibid., 188).

In delusion each self writes its own laws; each dramatic symbology possesses its own structure, norms, and rules. There is little if any recognition of community or consciously granted legitimacy to institutional or societal agents. Justice and injustice, right and wrong, the acceptance of public order and value "are Qualities, that relate to men in Society, not in Solitude" (ibid.). But it is precisely this isolation that for the delusional self gives rise to internally held conceptions of justice and right. If a computer governs the world, behavior, and action, society or history or tradition or language cannot control justice. Rather, unknown figures (murky presences programming the computer, determining the direction and intensity of currents, rays, electrical charges) write the scripts for justice and value. In delusional systems, then, justice has nothing to do with any public forum or consensual expression of value. It is far safer (emotionally and physically) to obey the internal dictates of delusion: the computer can be programmed to be just and unjust; people cannot. Furthermore, what in large measure keeps the delusional self from returning to the social compact is the belief that its own privately held system of justice is far preferable (and offers more protection and defense) to any conception or formulation that society offers. Because the self believes its knowledge system to be true and inviolable, it is convinced that society's views and concepts are ephemeral, untrustworthy, and ambiguous. It is the social world that causes the intolerable pain of depression and grief.

Hobbesian properties run throughout delusional imagery: "a perpetuall and restlesse desire of Power after power that ceaseth onely in Death" (ibid., 161), "Passions unguided," "secret thoughts" that "run over all things holy, profane, clean, obscene, grave and light, without shame or blame" (ibid., 137). Madness or delusion comes from "extraordinary and extravagant Passion," "great Dejection of mind," extreme "Rage and Fury," or "Melancholy" (ibid., 146). In addition, it is not difficult to discern the evidence of madness in absurd and "phantastical" language:

> If some man in Bedlam should entertaine you with sober dis-
> course; and you desire in taking leave, to know what he were,
> that you might another time requite his civility; and he should
> tell you, he were God the Father; I think you need expect no
> extravagant action for argument of his Madnesse [ibid., 141]

If delusion is the consequence of madness and entails "too much appearing Passion" (ibid.), "perpetual fear" (ibid., 169) then from a Hobbesian perspective delusional utterances are not only unreliable and dangerous, they also deserve little if any attention from society. Delusion should be dismissed and ignored, not only because of its immateriality and lack of content, but also because it threatens the fragile connection between language, authority, and politics. Delusion raises serious questions about the authority inherent in language, the meaning of words, and the political agents governing the use of language. Delusion pulls the self away from society; thus it is the narcissism and hidden assumptions of delusion that Hobbes fears. For if these assumptions become public claims about ethics and politics, then suffering, violence, and political confusion will inevitably ensue. To grant delusional utterance a foundation in experience would be not only to weaken the common and public rules governing discourse, it would also involve a danger to the objectivity of the political language governing the commonwealth. It is this withdrawal from the public, from objectively understood words, from common assumptions regarding law, that Hobbes finds in "phantastical" utterance of all kinds.

All this may well be true if delusion is regarded as a political threat. In its contemporary manifestations such as schizophrenic disorders, delusion is rather a private tragedy that hardly threatens the polity's institutional arrangements. The delusional self, with rare exceptions, threatens only itself (and institutionalized patients are certainly "out of sight" of their families). If delusion is seen as a language communicating primordial expressions of pain, loss, and death, then delusional utterance becomes something entirely different from what Hobbes saw as the "daemonology" of the "heathen poets" and the "bedlam" of "lunatiques."

For the self to be consumed by delusion, to be confined within its frames of knowledge, means an effective end to any sense of participation in a human community. I believe that schizophrenics understand this deep within themselves, and that it is a source of their often overwhelming despair. It is this combination of self-hatred, self-contempt, and the understanding that somehow their humanity is suspect and seriously jeopardized that accounts for much in the self's often horrifying knowledge of its own alienation. It is this "dejection of mind" that runs throughout delusional utterance.

Delusions and Phantasms

Dave:

Today I'm the garbage pail of my mind. I feel like a bathtub, the tub is my mind, the drain my brains . . . I'm always processing people's toxicity.

I spend most of my day trying to screen out people's wish fulfill-ments, my nightmares about what they want to do with me. . . .

The radio has just told me that the mafia wants to cut me into little pieces and throw the pieces to the bears in the zoo. . . . They will cut me into thirds beginning with my neck, then the waist and the chest. . . .

They're torturing me to death sawing me in half, splitting me from the crotch up. . . .

I lost the goodness, the freshness and nobody told me . . . my heart is in my gut, it broke into bits and pieces like fragment-ing glass. . . .

My pulse went out, all over the floor. . . .

I turn normal voices into voices which seem appropriate to tor-ture myself with. . . .

The voices are always some overlap between my mind and the place I'm living in at the time. . . . My mind makes a compos-ite of what I need as feedback and what the "neighborhood" [i.e., the hospital] I'm in needs. . . .

My life is falling through the trap door. . . . Every question has a trap door . . . I'm waiting for death . . . I just follow the script to the end . . . I'm tired of people . . . people are tired of me . . . when the script reaches the end, you fall through the trap door.

Chuck:

A potion that kills mentally retarded sperm was put into a cup of yoghurt by the doctor. My father ate it; the potion didn't kill off the high I.Q. sperm. It left them and so I was born . . . I'm kind of a created being . . . a genius . . . but also a barbarian with deadly poisonous animals inside me.

My head falls off; it falls on the floor and then it's picked up by a nurse. It don't bleed that much because it's rotten. It's been

continuously rotten and then it grows back. Everytime it grows
back, it's chopped off. And for awhile I'm headless. Blood
flows out of my fingers and I rot away.

Jenny:

My brain's not working . . . they seem not to exist . . . they are
divided in two . . . retarded and genius . . . people are zapping
me . . . they burn the ray on my brain . . . they implant an
electrode in my brain . . . the electrode is tied up to a wire
that clicks all the time . . . my moods are controlled by the
electrode . . . they make me sleepy, awake, alive or dead . . .
there's a clicking in my head . . . all the time . . . it's like a
gun, the trigger being cocked and then pulled . . . I had a
dream that my head was blown off. They [the hospital] can't
contaminate me any more; I'm already contaminated . . .
they're [unspecified] going to let the viruses loose on me . . .
they'll attack me with viruses . . . I feel like Humpty
Dumpty. . . . They [previous hospitalizations] marked my brain
with the sign of the criminal; every time I take a deep breath, I
feel my brain being shot, from behind; they may even have put
wires into it . . . they're [unspecified] going to kill me, murder
me . . . It's all around . . . people killing each other.

I'm gangrenous; put me in a leper colony; I'm a bad guy; I'm a
thousand years old.

In a moment of rare self-reflection, Jenny engaged me in the following
exchange:

JENNY: Am I autistic?
JMG: No, why do you ask?
JENNY: Because I live in my own world, my own make-believe.

Dave, with his fear of torture, his fragmented heart, his feeling of
imminent mutilation; Chuck and his rottenness, his sense of self as a
"barbarian" with "poisonous animals" inside; Jenny with her gangrenous
condition, her sense of "contamination" and being "marked like a criminal"; the ubiquitous murdering and killing: each of these images constitutes a theory, an explanation of the universe that, while true and
incontrovertible for the speaker, also functionally and emotionally drives
the self out of the political community.

Delusion is a jealously guarded realm often made even more obscure
through conscious efforts to disguise the self's real core. Questions regarding inner theories or secrets or beliefs are consistently met with
responses such as: "So you want to know my secrets? I can't tell you . . .
Jehovah tells me to keep quiet. . . . You're getting nosy; these things are
private." Secrets frequently reflect themes of control and domination,

since it is only in delusion that the self constructs nonthreatening and "supportive" relations. If, for example, Jenny feared she would be killed, she might invent a presence or antidote or reaction to whatever force, element, demon, or poison threatened her. Chuck created machines that acted as guardians of his life, regulators of his emotions and actors in whatever emotional dramas he was undergoing. Yet Chuck controlled the machine's appearance, its "being there":

JMG: Chuck, who invented your machines?
CHUCK: Why I did.
JMG: Who operates the machines?
CHUCK: I have people to take care of them.

For Chuck, the machines regulated all exchange and transaction, particularly with regard to the emotion of anger. If he felt angry, rather than express it directly, he would understand it in the following terms: "The machine blew up last night . . . it blew up the room and everything in it." He refused to describe the interior workings of the machine, which would lead him to reflect on the relation between the machine and himself, since to be in the interior of the machine was to be inside himself, his "being."

Despair as Political Life

It was Hobbes's view that the collective despair of the natural condition could only be overcome through a powerful sovereignty, the domination of the sword enforcing law, although it might be intriguing to argue that the Hobbesian concept of sovereignty, the mortal god, contains certain delusional properties (the omnipotent representation of massive power and constraint, in addition to the obsession with abstraction and grandiosity in Hobbes's "scientific" reasoning). For the delusional self, however, nothing of even the basic and crude reciprocity that accompanies the Hobbesian solution (contracting with the sovereign for at least minimal order, each self giving up its unrestricted rights in nature for the sword of an objective rule) governs any of the representations of the inner world. In delusion there are no exchange relations; everything appears to be dictated and imposed; the computer decides; the aliens judge and enforce; the machines define and interpret. Even these internal "Leviathans" inhibit any sense of a shared existential or political environment.

Hobbes was right in one respect: political obligation and order require some form of reciprocity. Without a rudimentary set of reciprocal responsibilities (including a giving up of the egoism and anarchy of the natural condition for the predictability of civil society and the guarantee of protection from invasion) political and personal legitimacy would not be viable.

While I reject the Hobbesian solution as much too strong a commitment to order and too restricted a conception of "acceptable" language, it is still a philosophy that recognizes the causes of political disintegration in despair produced by human motives and desires. First-order experiences in the life of a polity (lack of boundaries, confusion over meaning, cataclysmic transformations, claims of omnipotence, the projection of desire as truth) provoke *collective* despair and decay. Further, it is the manifestation of such experience that draws the concern of architectonic political philosophy in its demands for a new political identity. Private languages and theories of knowledge, the retreat into egoism and narcissism, the repudiation of public life and reason, the critique of reciprocity: all these experiences bear on the creation of political identity, what might be termed the "self" of the polity. And it does not stretch the point to suggest that the political philosopher responds to a crisis in political identity with as intense a commitment as the psychotherapist's battle against intrapsychic entropy and self-destruction. Plato's drones (*Republic*), Aristotle's "beast" (*Politics*), Machiavelli's *condottiere* (*Prince*), Hobbes's spiritualists and daemonologists (*Leviathan*), and Rousseau's decadents (*Emile*)—all entropic images in political philosophy—produce an enormous upheaval in the organization of the political self.

Assaults on political identity that elevate private needs and desires or that equate such privacy with the public good put forward alternative views of knowledge and reality with often disastrous consequences. And against these assaults the philosopher constructs powerful arguments. Plato's philosopher king (*Republic*), Aristotle's theory of polity (*Politics*), Machiavelli's idealized prince (*Prince*), Hobbes's mortal god (*Leviathan*), Rousseau's General Will (*Social Contract*), and Marx's proletariat (*Capital*) all constitute notable arguments and images in the history of political philosophy in reaction to the despair in political environments caught up in private languages and desires, first-order experiences that have the potential to do great harm.

Is the schizophrenic an inward mirror of the primitive aggression that appears in tyrannical political systems? Is the content of delusion (as opposed to its function as a defense against empathic relatedness) the obverse of the visible primitivity characterizing a tyrannical political life? Fear, anxiety, and terror: the schizophrenic copes by withdrawing into a fantasized, projected world; there is action, but it is kept inside. The psychotic political process, however, works the other way around: it projects *actuality*, and the pathology of the inner appears in perverse structures of power. In each instance, what is visible is one side of the imbalance in power relations: in the schizophrenic it is the psychodynamic, the psychopathological as defense and retreat; in politics, it is the instruments of power utilized to dominate and control. Delusional utterance thus holds the key to understanding the ways and forms in which power unbalances itself.

The content of these first-order experiences (private claims, hidden intentions, unshared meanings, lack of reciprocity, desire projected as value) depends on specific historic realities and conflicts. What should be emphasized here is the apparent similarity of the tasks of the political philosopher and the psychotherapist who intervenes in the schizophrenic language world. For both, speech, reason, and public recognitions are besieged by unconscious and hidden realities lying within the self (whether it is the collective self of the polity or the unconscious, primary process of the intrapsychic self). Each reacts to what appears to be a self consumed by despair and entropy; each sees in language the fundamental connection between self and world; and each seeks to replace private conceptions of experience with collective forms of knowing *whose function is to resist narcissistic withdrawal*. Finally, each is concerned with the structure of boundary and identity in the context of relations of obligation, responsibility, reciprocity, and coherence.

The Hobbesian Underworld: Delusion as Apparition, Motion, and Phantasm

Although Hobbes dismissed "apparitions" as unreal and "incorporeal," the schizophrenic mind sees them as essential to life, to the meaning that surrounds behavior and thought. In Ted's view of reality construction, for example, experience appears in two radically distinct modes: "mythiology" and "theriology." Mythiology describes Ted's universe and truths; theriology on the other hand, comes from what Ted is told about the world by psychiatrists, doctors, nurses, hospitals, parents, and so on. Theriology is the realm of untruth, unfreedom, coercion, and constraint; mythiology holds the promise of liberation, freedom, and the exercise of power; mythiology lies at the core of Ted's being; it is what he trusts. More importantly, it is what he desires and where he wishes to be. It is the hospital and theriology that prevent him from experiencing the full potential of mythiology (Ted recognizes that his mythiology is called delusion; yet he believes the hospital imposes on him a false view of reality. This is why he is so hesitant to reveal his "secrets"; he feels he will be punished for his mythiology thoughts.)

Theriology then is authority, science, society; in Hobbesian terms mythiology is phantasm, apparition, and delusion. But for Ted, mythiology, no matter what it is called, contains all the sources of gratification. In mythiology, no person tells Ted what to do; he controls and dominates; he gives and helps; it is the only place where he can truly "do for others." Theriology, however, forces you "to do only for yourself"; it asks you questions about the reliability of "secret thoughts"; it interrupts the pure flow of mythiology with medication, psychotherapy, and language. It makes it increasingly difficult for Ted to do "for others," to perform as a rock star, savior, or son of God, or to rescue entire societies from conflagration and death. Theriology teaches depression, limits, boundaries; mythiology gives power, omnipotence, and grandiosity. It is understandable why Ted should feel hostility toward the hospital and his treatment. All aspects of his mythiology, he feels, are under assault, and he finds himself forced to defend mythiology as the definition and embodiment of his being. In his apparitional world of angels, gods, and cosmic powers, with his ability to transform nature ("I'm outside; I feel strong, powerful; I hold out my arms and the leaves on the trees turn green; I can do that; isn't that something?"), to tend for his "thousands of children" all over the world, and to stage rock concerts that draw millions of people, Ted knows no equals, and has no responsibility other than the exercise of his immense power. In mythiology, Ted experiences an almost absolute freedom.

It is what Ted calls mythiology that Hobbes seems to be attacking in *Leviathan*, part 4 ("The Kingdom of Darkness"). And if there were a patron saint of theriology, it would have to be Thomas Hobbes with his concepts of rationalism, materiality, and his critique of "phantastical" representation. For Hobbes, all aspects of Ted's universe would be absurd, "airy" notions without substance, enforcing dangerous tendencies in mind. Such thoughts constitute an affront to reason, jeopardize the meaning and boundaries of speech, confound definition and signification, and thoroughly disrupt the logic and order of naming. From the Hobbesian perspective (a view shared by much contemporary medical psychiatry) these "motions in the brain" should not be construed or interpreted as experience. This is a view I find troublesome.

If delusions are only airy "motions in the brain," then it is perfectly legitimate to coerce those "motions" without any concern for the meaning of the utterance, what it represents as an identity-creating act, its function in maintaining the self's survival, or its significant role as a theory of knowledge. In acknowledging the self's delusional identity, not only does psychotherapy retain a sense of relationship (no matter how fragile) with the self's experience, it holds that relationship *within the communicative possibilities of language*. A linguistically framed therapy stays with the self in all its pain; it recognizes legitimacy, being, and presence by not denying, impugning, or ignoring the self's experiential world no matter how bizarre that may appear. Most importantly, the experiential status granted to delusion retains belief in the cohering and enabling possibilities of the language world. As long as identity can be embodied in language, the delusional self retains pathways to its own essential humanity. Once the self gives up on its belief in its humanity (no matter how tenuous that belief may be), if, for example, Jenny's identification with the animal world were to invade her consciousness thoroughly, then not only would language be lost (along with its potential as a bridge between delusional and consensual reality), but her rudimentary contact with being would also dissolve.

Ghosts, apparitions, phantasms, demons: for Hobbes all confuse meaning and threaten definition. In Jenny's universe, the request "may I have a cup of water" possesses a whole range of meanings that lie beyond strict signification, that depart from any sense of Hobbes's "right ordering of names in our affirmations" (Hobbes 1968, 105). In the past her request has meant, depending on the occasion, any of the following:

A. She suspects the water is poisoned and wants to examine it.

B. The water may serve as an antidote to gas coming out of the airvents.

C. She feels she's about to die but the water contains a life-sustaining drug secretly put in the hospital's water supply.

D. The water contains a magic potion that might rid her heart of fat molecules that are clogging it up.

For Hobbes to see these utterances as experience would mean admitting anarchy into the use of language; it would deny the scientific basis implicit in linguistic exchange, since the model for "settling the significations" of words lies in the "science" of "Geometry" (ibid.). The private knowledge that informs the phantasmic utterance or representation not only confounds meaning, it also unsettles definitions and makes it difficult to distinguish "truthhood and falsehood" (ibid.) Phantasms thus make unacceptable claims about reality, radically distort the meaning of the "rational" and "scientific" and draw attention away from what established authority defines as the appropriate use of words. Most importantly, phantasms are politically disruptive, since the images present in the representations subvert belief and trust in public order. Spiritualists, religious claimants of all types, "churchmen," those who take authority from Scripture, and the "enemy" hovering "in the Night of naturall Ignorance" (ibid., 628) find themselves elevating phantasmic representations to the status of political right and authority.

Hobbes attacks spiritualism (and the appeal to Scripture and "apparitions") as the "Daemonology of the Heathen Poets . . . their fabulous Doctrine concerning Daemons which are but Idols or Phantasms of *the braine without any reall nature of their own distinct from humane fancy.*" Not only does such "daemonology" undermine reason, but more importantly for our purposes, it lacks any "real nature." Such representations are empty of empirical content. Phantasms, "dead mens Ghosts and Fairies, and other matter of old Wives tales" appear when consciousness has "no other means to acknowledge" its "owne darknesse." Theories that rest only on motions in the brain "putteth out the Light of Nature, and causeth so great a Darknesse in mens understanding" (ibid., 628–30).

135

(William James might reply, as I will argue at the end of this chapter, that delusions, rather than putting out the "Light of Nature," simply shed a different "light" from an unaccustomed angle. Further, from a psychodynamic perspective, delusion illuminates the nature of early developmental experience, symbolically represented in the linguistic imagery of the adult self.) By calling phantasms the "Darkness in mens understanding" and then dismissing that darkness as absurd and vacuous thinking, Hobbes sets up scientific reasoning as the arbiter of what experience *is*. For example, Ted's "mythiology" for Hobbes might have been akin to "the Egyptian Conjurers, that are said to have turned their Rods to Serpents, and the Water into Bloud . . . to have deluded the senses of the Spectators by a false shew of things" (ibid., 634). Conjurors and phantasms of all types are nothing other than "Enchantment and Lying," enemies to science.

The purpose of speech for Hobbes is "to transferre our Mentall Discourse into Verbal; or the Trayne of our Thoughts into a Trayne of Words" (ibid., 101). That "Trayne" should possess a recognizable ordering and meanings that can be grasped publicly. Speech registers "the Consequences of our thoughts" (ibid.); it therefore should be comprehensible and accessible. When private or hidden meanings come to dominate speech, confusion arises over these "Markes or Notes of rememberance" (ibid.). When this happens, Hobbes considers language to be abused, "when men register their thoughts wrong, by the inconstancy of the signification of their words . . . when they use words metaphorically; that is, in other sense than that they are ordained for; and thereby deceive others" (ibid., 102). What or who determines the right "imposing" and "connexion" is an issue for Hobbes that can be resolved by the authority of definition, the clarity of meaning in the utterance, and by its rational foundations. Delusion, however, thrives on ambiguity; its symbolism, obscure references, inversions of definition, absurdity of imagery, and associative language create in linguistic forms a dimension that differs considerably from "perspicuous words" (ibid., 116). I shall return to this in some detail in a moment.

Ted's reigning delusion, the one that, as he puts it, "overrides them all," centers on his soul becoming detached from his body and rising up to be with God. For Hobbes, these images are an example of *"ignes fatui;"* they are also interesting because they closely resemble (in their action or drama) what Hobbes calls the "contagion of the Daemonology of the Greeks," who felt that the "Souls of men were substances distinct from their Bodies, and therefore that when the Body was dead, the Soule of every man, whether godly, or wicked must subsist somewhere by vertue of its own nature, without acknowledging therein any super-naturall gift of Gods" (ibid., 639). For Hobbes, such beliefs constitute an unreal "Daemonology"; for Ted, they form the core of his life and involve massive transfers of energy (which he experiences as real) from earth to God and from Heaven back to earth.

Hobbes might consider Ted's beliefs to be only "Inhabitants [of the] Brain . . . absolutely Incorporeall, that is to say Immateriall or Formes without Matter; Colour, and Figure . . ." (ibid., 658). In many ways, the modern delusional schizophrenic constructs kingdoms, daemons, and other worlds much in the manner Hobbes attributes to classical theologies, with the "Poets as Principal Priests of the Heathen Religion" and worlds populated by "Good Daemons, and others Evill' (ibid., 659). Good daemons "they gave the name the Spirit of God," and evil daemons were "called *Daemoniaques*, that is *possessed by the Devill* such as we call Madmen or Lunatiques; or such as had the Falling Sicknesse" (ibid., 659). And these "Lunatiques" "spoke any thing, which they for want of understanding, thought absurd." Yet for today's "Lunatique," the delusional world is anything but absurd; it is a deadly serious assumption of identity that protects the self from imminent annihilation.

For Hobbes, delusion is tied to the necessity of rule, to the theocracies that used these doctrines to enforce obedience. The schizophrenic self, however, rules over an inner world, its kingdoms dominated by strange creatures of all kinds. Political authority in delusional systems often appears in distorted human shapes, creatures that are half-animal, insects, machines, and spirits of various forms, some identifiable, others unseen and ephemeral.

What for Hobbes is a "dream" is a waking nightmare for the schizophrenic, for it invades consciousness every moment and infuses all aspects of thought. Is it not more, then, than an impression distinguished by its motions and its origins in the brain? Are not identities more than "motions"? If delusion substitutes for the real or consensual world, are not the relations that motivate delusional utterance as real and substantial as any other set of relations? And should not identity, no matter what its form, whether it appears in a classical "daemonology" or a modern schizophrenic, be treated and respected as experience? Not so for Hobbes: for him it is simply not possible to speak about relations or existence in the absence of materiality, since phantasms appear only as "meer Figment, without place, habitation, motion or existence, but in the motions of the Brain" (ibid., 665).

Hobbes's critique of the productions of the inner world has the effect not only of narrowing the boundaries between language and experience, but also of limiting the social concept of what is or is not acceptable speech. I am not arguing that delusion should be taken as social or consensual truth, only that such utterance should be respected for what it is: an attempt to define identity and to bracket the self in the *experience of language*. Further, if the "right" use of language becomes the criterion of citizenship, then it would appear that any utterance not following the rational-linguistic assumptions of prevailing authority and definition would find itself unacknowledged and banished to some hinterland of unacceptable or absurd speech.

Finally, in terms of the psychiatric treatment of the delusional self, the Hobbesian perspective denies the schizophrenic the legitimacy of an inner space of being, a reality with meaning, structure, and form. And a therapy based on Hobbesian premises would be more likely to treat such utterance with advanced medical technologies, with the objective of managing and administering unacceptable speech and behavior, in order to seal it over and push it away from consciousness. It seems probable that a psychiatric Hobbesian would be impatient with delusion, reluctant to enter its *gestalt* representations, to sense its meaning, and to translate therapeutic sensitivity into some form of linguistic contact with the delusional self. One implication of Hobbes's attitudes toward phantasms and apparitions might very well be a denial of humanity to those who for whatever reason find themselves living within a linguistic world whose frames of reference cannot be considered consensual and whose speech acts appear to address hidden and shadowy audiences.

The problem with the Hobbesian perspective is its reliance on technology to the exclusion of language. If delusion is regarded as a form of lived experience, as an identity, it becomes essential to use language to intervene in the delusional condition, to try to reach toward the sick individual with language rather than with disembodied instruments. It would be tragic to leave the fate of schizophrenics to the Hobbesian, scientific technician. The delusional world is accessible to language, but it takes courage and a willingness to confront the messiness of experience and to deal linguistically with bizarre inversions of reality. But that is what medicine should be about; courage and resourcefulness in confronting the dreadful, the reality of self in its sickness and disintegration.

Empiricism as a Critique of the Hobbesian Airy Motions in the Brain: Clinical Data

I do not wish to imply that phantasms or delusions should be the basis for political order or that the experiences of schizophrenia constitute any kind of foundation for civil community or an appropriate, public, communicable language. I do maintain, however, that delusion should be understood as a legitimate form or category of experience that coalesces as an identity, a form of human behavior. Language reminds the self of its essential human, as opposed to animal, nature. The utterances of delusion also provide evidence for what William James sees as an empiricism that lacks formal assumptions about truth and falsity, a willingness to consider experience as the expression of felt realities no matter what their form, shape, or history, and a recognition that the empirically embodied world precedes in existence any universal abstraction or series of premises that purports to deduce what experience means. I would then like to rely on James's theory to take serious issue with the Hobbesian notion of a purely deductive (geometric) reason and the logic implicit in this definition and classification of experience as it relates to delusions or phantasms. Hobbes would have geometry "drive away phantasms and imaginary spirits." Yet in a psychodynamic analysis, it is not only rationality (as scientific intervention) that erodes delusion, but also the intuitiveness of empathy and tolerance, and the very real affective dimension of trust.

If delusion is to be more than "motions in the brain," it requires sensitivity to the internal relations governing its meaning. (The concept of "relation" and its embodiment in experience is central to James's argument in the *Essays on Radical Empiricism*, very useful observations that raise several questions about the sovereignty of an abstract or deductive rationality.) "The peculiarity of our experiences, that they not only are, but are known, which their 'conscious' quality is invoked to explain, is better explained by their relations—these relations themselves being experiences—to one another" (James 1971, 16).

For the speaker, delusion is the truth; for the observer, it is a peculiar mosaic that appears in pieces, without (at first glance) apparent meaning. Yet each fragment contains meaning; each relates to others. Utterances such as the following (made by Jenny) contain symbolizations that comment on aspects of delusional identity:

> I'm an old lady with the brain of a little girl.
> I'm a brain with no body because I'm really a computer, a
>   machine.
> The wires lead into my head.
> Sometimes I don't feel my body's there, I don't feel it at all.
> I look across the table and see spirits.
> Maybe we're all spirits walking around without bodies.

Using Jenny's statements, table 6.1 describes delusion as three levels of empirical reality: (1) the content of experience; (2) relations inhering in experiential symbolizations; and (3) continuities expressed or demonstrated in these relations.

For James, "to be radical an empiricism must neither admit into its constructions any element that is not directly experienced, nor exclude from them any element that is directly experienced" (ibid., 25). In the study of delusional utterance, I take this to mean something like the following. To speak of the "ping-pong game of pain" means actually to be *there*, to be within the game. It may even signify an identification with the experience of "pinging" or "ponging" a persistent going back and forth, endlessness, confusion over place, and so on. Or it may mean that to feel

Table 6.1: Experience and Relations in Delusional Utterance

Experiential clusters	Breakdown according to relations	Continuities inhering in relations
I'm an old lady with the brain of a little girl.	victim/victimized (old lady/brain/ little girl)	self deprecation/feelings of decay/nonself/weariness
I'm a brain with no body; it's that I'm really a computer, a machine . . . the wires lead into my head.	controller/controlled (brain/bodilessness/computer/machine/wires/head)	no control/unembodied self/forces absorbing self/influencing machine (Tausk 1919)/no sense of internality/feelings of being manipulated
Sometimes I don't feel my body's there; I just don't feel it.	emptiness/emptied (bodilessness/no feeling/I [self])	feelings of deadness/denial of self
I look across the table and see spirits.	dissociation (sight/spirits/I [self])	powerful external forces/presences/denial of autonomous self
Maybe we're all spirits walking around without bodies.	transcendence (spirits/bodilessness/we [collective self])	distrust of embodied world (others)/distrust of body as source of pleasure

the self retreating to the "deep recesses of the mind" (patient's comment) provokes the sensation of receding, moving further and further away from others, falling into the "gloom of time," the "fog of life." What is uttered is what is *real as experience*; no matter how bizarre the images seem, each cluster or set of images possesses an emotional matrix for the speaker. In such a universe, the normal referential context of utterance is upset, as the following remarks made by Ted indicate:

> My soul leaves my dead body.
> It goes to meet God; it leaves my head and body on earth.
> My soul comes back again, climbs into my head, and then both
>   my body and head go up to meet God.

The parts or experiential clusters appear as head, body, God, soul, the act of traveling between earth and God, the soul returning, filling up the head, retrieval of the body and then ascent, once again, to God. Whatever messages lie within this fable are to be found in an analysis of the relations of the images. In the attempt to enter the delusional world and to remain as objective as possible regarding the flows of actuality, it is essential not to deny validation to the delusional self in whatever mode it chooses and through whatever images it projects as real. It is also necessary to resist the temptation to judge the experience. The actuality or presence in the world of delusional utterance should, in James's terms, be taken "at its face value," and "the relations that connect experiences must themselves be experienced relations, and any kind of relation experienced must be accounted as 'real' as anything else in the system" (ibid., 25). All utterance possesses reality; the challenge is to discover the idea or structure that reveals the meaning inherent in linguistic experience.

It is the literalness of delusional utterance that holds the key to the self's psychotic identity. In some delusional expressions, for example, the overriding relation is of persecution and victimization. Identity may change depending on the delusional frame of reference; yet the identity that governs the self lies in the words describing self's relationship to the world. Spirits, ghosts, gods, underworlds, bizarre machines: all are imaginary projections of states of being that in one form or another either torment the self or protect it from death and annihilation.

Whatever the experience defining this kind of protection, its primary function lies in building an identity for the self that will enable it to withstand what it imagines to be threats to its survival. The self feels that this identity is vital to its being; furthermore, the psychotic identity allows the self to live in an experiential world free of real, concrete others. Traveling to meet aliens in spaceships, governing kingdoms, mobilizing power to do good, and transforming the world through psychic messages are all far more preferable than the uncertainty, inconstancy, and betrayal implicit in relations with other human beings. While for the schizophrenic the "outer" is filled with projections from the "inner," the self fears the actuality of the outer as the shared experience of trusting another person.

The empirical content of delusional statements tells a story about the dangers that befall the self in its contact with others. Language portrays this intense fear, which forms the essential emotional core of what the self knows to be actual and true in the world. What self *is*, its identity, appears in images lying within language; utterance *is* self, or at least contains the clues to what the psychotic self *means*. To deny the literalness or concrete quality of the words not only refuses acknowledgment of the speaker, it also ignores the real experiential dimension of the statement. Table 6.2

141

Table 6.2: Empiricism in
Schizophrenic Utterance

A Progression in empirical analysis	B Manifestations	C Types of facts
Experiential clusters appearing in language	• The hospital's killing me • I am a rock star. • I am Noah with his ark. • When I'm asleep they puncture me with needles. • I have no feelings. • Feelings are dangerous. • Rays shoot through me; I know there's someone out there sending them. • My body dies and then my soul goes to meet God. • I have children all over the world. • All I want to do is be psychic.	Facts essential to self's rudimentary survival as a being capable of a communicated language
Relations inhering in experience	powerful—weak controller—controlled creator—helpless omnipotent—victim	Facts essential to identity

elaborates on different stages of an empirical analysis of language, the
kinds of relations portrayed in linguistic imagery, and the continuities and
psychodynamic themes appearing in the symbolizations. Column C describes the type of facts characteristic of each stage.

The statements of Jenny that follow are an example of the formative
power of delusion in performing important identity functions:

Table 6.2 (*Continued*)

A Progression in empirical analysis	B Manifestations	C Types of facts
Continuities or themes in the relations governing utterance	• fractured self-image • despair over future • fear of being abused by authority • sensations of omnipotence, grandiosity • sensations of emptiness, despair over past • sensations of dying and rebirth • primitive fear of (and desire for) fusion • terror at being touched by another human being	Facts essential to the psychotherapeutic intervention in psychotic states

Gas is coming through the air vents. . . . It's poisoning me.
There's a bomb in the corner of the room; it's going to explode.
[The hospital intercom broadcasts "Dr. _____ call extension
   6666. Jenny responds:] That's really a code for my execution,
   they're getting ready to kill me.
I'm going to be burned to death by the fire of the sun.
There's a city underneath this hospital.
Do you know what happened last night? . . . I was taking a bath
   and A. [a mental health worker] came in with a knife . . . she
   was going to kill me . . . I have witnesses. . . .
I'm caught between trash and being killed.

Jenny's language world becomes her identity world. It is a world built on the concrete images in language itself. At other times Jenny has been the "elephant man"—alone, without care or love. She has seen herself as an animal, has believed her feet to be hooves, and has felt compelled to act like an animal, grazing on her hands and knees in grass and clover. However crazy or extreme her language and behavior appears, it remains her experience, the only relations she possesses. In James's terms, she "owns all that [words] can ever mean" (ibid., 29). Table 6.3 maps the relations and continuities lying within Jenny's utterance; table 6.4 adds a column on identity functions in the language itself.

It is no easy task for the delusional self to shed a known identity (delusion) and search for novel interpersonal boundaries in the minefield of human relationships, which is where the breakdown in ego functioning originally began. It is only when the self willingly makes the effort to transform delusional reality and attempts to leave it, to raise questions about the meanings in delusional experience, that identity can begin to develop in other directions. If, for example, Jenny were to ask her

Table 6.3: Levels of Empirical Content

Experiential clusters (language)	Relations in experience	continuities
gas/air vents/poison exhaustion	victim/controlled	hospital as source of poison; paranoid projections
bomb explosion	victim/annihilation	fear of anger/ rage/fear of blowing self up
court/plans/kill	domination/victimization	outside forces/ fear of loss of boundaries/ control
burning/fire/death	annihilation/transcen- dence	anger/rage/guilt/ denial of self
hospital/city	power/omnipotence	being influenced by outside forces/de- tached "power" controlling environment
bath/night/knifed/kill	victim/victimizer	aggression/rage fear of anger/anger as explosive/ potentially deadly anger both from self and other

therapist if he believed that people were computers, in other words if she were to question that construction of experience, she might be showing him a tentative willingness to suspend belief in her system of knowledge,

Table 6.4: Identity Functions
Performed by Experience

Experiential clusters (language)	Identity functions (delusional)
gas/air vents/poison/ exhaustion	defending against hospital as tormentor/preoccu- pation with external forces
bomb/explosion	constant vigilance; knowledge of self as potential victim/ preoccupation with building barriers against destruction
court/plans/kill	distrust of all outside others; knowledge that plans are being made for her death, demise/constant thoughts about who "court" is and kinds of plans
burning/fire/death	certainty of imminent death/ identity as dead person or maimed beyond recognition (identity as no-identity)
hospital/city	knowledge that everything inside the hospital is out of control/real power in city underneath/thoughts as to her role in that city and who she "is" in the city's organi- zation
bath/night/knifed/kill	fear of immediate destruction at hands of tormentors inside hospital/identity as prisoner in hospital, as object for experiments
	identity in aggressive impulses projected outward

at least for a moment. If she were to think seriously about alternative, more consensually based truths, she would then be focusing more clearly on the hear-and-now quality of relationship rather than on the immediacy of delusional experience actualizing, dissolving, and reappearing in the self's fear of annihilation.

For Jenny to give up her beliefs and thus her identity would undoubtedly be a very painful introduction to new forms of experience. Although these new experiences could never be as certain as the old delusional ones, nonetheless they can offer certain gratifications the delusional world lacks. For now, however, she remains caught, trapped by deadly forms of reality, by what Hobbes would dismiss as "airy motions." She believes she dies periodically throughout each day and yet is miraculously brought to life again through the agency of a computer. She dies when someone or something unplugs the computer; that deadness is experienced as having no brain or "being dead inside," and having no thoughts other than those sent to her by the computer's electrical field. When the computer is off, Jenny dissolves from the world; she transforms herself into nothingness: "I am a dead, skinny little person." Such observations form the basis of her theories about life and meaning.

If, without understanding it, I graft my world onto the delusional; if I insist on the falseness of delusional experience before I establish empathy or attain a perception into delusional reality, not only do I intervene in the self's first-order experience (in the unmediated unconscious) because of a belief in my second-order theory of explanation, I also refuse to acknowledge the very real survival functions that psychotic identity performs. Being preoccupied with delusional images (and periodically revealing them) allows Jenny some contact with other human beings, if only on a delusional level. She speaks; she forges some connection with the other. Language keeps her in contact with the world; she avoids the rigidity and immobility of catatonia. As long as she finds it necessary to use language as a means of embodying experience, she remains psychologically alive. If she loses touch with language as action, Jenny will probably find herself lost to any kind of life at all. Thus it is her delusional possession of reality that keeps her alive.

It is this tolerance to worlds quite different from our own, the acknowledgment of delusion as a type of experience and the insistence that such experience be understood as a series of relations (the reality of the self) that suggest the usefulness of James's analysis of empiricism. He focuses attention on the nature of relation itself: relations within language, relations governing identity, action, and meaning.

seven

Inside the State of Nature: Jenny's Delusional Habitat

> A prominent part of this existential tragedy which permeates the case history of the schizophrenic has to do with the finitude of human life. [Searles 1965, 490]

Jenny's Disintegration and the Fear of Empathy

For the delusional self, experience generates terror; the world appears as threat and torment. As Jenny once remarked: "Today is the day my heart blew away." No recognizable connections, no sensible linear reality distinguishes outer from inner; inner triumphs over outer. Everything real is defined in terms of dread; the deep, unconscious substratum of the self, its hidden archeology, drowns all consciousness. Nothing is left other than the raw, unmediated images of a primitive, narcissistic self locked into its own world. It is this space that constitutes Jenny's life. Her world is nowhere; it exists outside space and time; it posseses no fixed definitions or coordinates; it changes depending on the language of the unconscious and the despair residing within it.

For Jenny, the links to consensual reality were broken. While she recognized others and carried on superficial conversations, the knowledge motivating her dialogue and understanding derived from inaccessible psychological structures. The human being that Jenny was may have been able to ask for a glass of water or a cigarette or speak about painting and art, but beneath each request her language reflected a significance peculiar to the configurations of her internal world. When Jenny wrote "Kill me basturds [*sic*]," it was a statement about her self, life, and situation. Within her delusional world, she acted consistently.

Jenny acknowledged the terms and definitions of her delusional world: "I have been programmed; recorded to in my sleep . . . I am the beeps of the computer." It was where she wanted to be; the hospital, in attempting to confront that delusional world, became for Jenny the agent of death. She observed:

Staff show much insouciance [sic] when it comes to the life of patients in the hospital. They seem to be mainly concerned with
how much they can rob, steal, and plunder. These things are
against the law. They do many other things such as destructive
[sic]. They kill their own families like Cain killed his younger
brother Abel. Like the physician killed his grandmother—so
forth and so on. Like I am blind—Godamit [sic]—I am not blind
and I don't like what I think I see—constructive behavior—I
have always been a raving maniac—godamit [sic]—I will not put
up with those plundering swine anymore—youre [sic] not going
to buy or kill me [From a written note to staff.]

Jenny's rage was projected outwards in this universe of perpetual killing.
She saw death as the only solution to her pain, and her social statement
expressed the wish to die. In her view, Sheppard/Pratt prevented the
realization of her wish. Sheppard tormented her by sending deadly gases
through air vents, planting bombs in secret chambers, and allowing
"death rays" to pass through its walls. Unless she was allowed to be
discharged from the hospital (in which case it was highly probable she
would find a way to commit suicide), Jenny felt she had no alternative but
to take her own life. Her wish to leave the hospital suggested a whole set
of feelings centering on the wish to die. This wish and its manifestations
bracketed Jenny's tragedy.

Sheppard/Pratt responded accordingly. It undertook heroic efforts to
keep her alive in the hope that at some point Jenny might open herself up
to treatment. But Jenny desperately wanted to end her pain ("I sure wish
I could jump out that window"). The hospital insisted on keeping her in
pain from her point of view by refusing either to discharge her or allow
her to commit suicide. She felt she was in a no-exit, no-win situation. The
more strenuous the hospital's efforts, the more antagonistic and suicidal
Jenny became. The more the hospital monitored her behavior to make
sure she would not swallow lighted cigarettes or tie bathrobes in knots
around her neck, the more Jenny believed she had been imprisoned in a
concentration camp. Jenny struggled unsuccessfully with the need for
empathy and relatedness, the emotional content of basic trust. She found
herself caught up in the images of death.

It is no exaggeration to suggest that, psychologically, Jenny existed in a
Hobbesian "state of nature." For Hobbes, the state of nature brings
death; it represents the domination of Thanatos. Hobbes, however, is
committed to life, since to bring the self out of the state of nature into
political association channels the essential entropy and destructiveness of
human desire and need. In the interest of self-preservation, individuals
find themselves obliged to leave the state of nature for the benefits of civil
society and the protection afforded by political authority.

Jenny saw no choice. It was death, not the external world, that could
bring her relief from her own inner chaos. Everything outside presented

itself as war, annihilation, and torture. For Jenny, civil society was the "natural condition," the arena of destruction, and she wanted no part of it. Rather than guaranteeing her self-preservation, civil society generated such overwhelming pain that annihilation was preferable to any thought of civil association. Civility disappeared in Jenny's world of violence, war, animality, and terror. Thus it was not self-preservation that motivated Jenny and provided her with the reasons for action, but rather annihilation. Unlike the inhabitants of Hobbes's state of nature who choose to escape death, Jenny chose to embrace it. This was the source of her despair, which she called a "communicable disease . . . loss of hope spread by stupid habits."

On a conscious level, the anger, hatred, and terror that consumed Jenny was projected outward. The hospital became a torture chamber; the seclusion room took on aspects of an oven or gas chamber; her therapist turned into an SS commandant; the nurses became Gestapo agents and guards. Each of these representations tormented Jenny; she believed the "concentration camp" (Sheppard/Pratt) would never let her leave. She felt doomed, and the only escape was suicide. Jenny's will turned on her physical self; she made her body the object of her fear and anger. Her sacrifice (or statement, since her death would be a message sent to her tormentors) appeared in her pain and blood ("They will flood this hospital with my blood"). For Jenny, life at Sheppard/Pratt was indeed "nasty, brutish and short." She asked nurses and aides whether they spoke German. Occasionally she would use a "language" that sounded vaguely like German. Or she would complain at having been "burned up" in the seclusion room[1] When she found herself in seclusion (usually after she hit, bit, or scratched someone) she believed she was being annihilated in a gas chamber or oven: "You know why I'm here? . . . Why do you think? After all, I'm in an oven; what do they do in ovens? They burn you to death. You should know that!"

Jenny's behavior defined the hall's reality. The ruckus she periodically

1. Each hall had one room and a small adjoining bath set aside specifically for patients who became assaultive or otherwise disturbing to staff and other patients. It was furnished only with a mattress; there was a window and plenty of light, and it was kept immaculate. The room was used as a "quiet room" or "seclusion room." Quiet room meant the door was left open; the patient could speak with other patients and staff but had to stay behind a table at the entrance of the room. Seclusion, however, was more serious: the door might be locked for patients who were physically acting out and assaultive; alternatively, the door might be left open but the patient monitored continuously by staff (this was usually done for patients who were suicidal or believed to be suicidal by staff). However the room was used, the patient is given periodic "recesses" for meals and personal needs. In some cases, recesses included walks up and down the hall. Seclusion was not used capriciously; it was reserved for specific incidents that presented clear physical threats to others (or in the case of suicidal patients, to the patient himself). It was often used by patients as a kind of blow-out room (lots of screaming, ranting, and banging went on within). For Jenny, the room became central to her life at Sheppard/Pratt for several months.

made validated her being as an animal, in addition to confirming her view that both she and staff shared a beastlike Hobbesian world:

> [Jenny] provided the comparison of being in the center ring of a circus and seemed rather amused at her notion that she would be very much the center of attention. . . . She did think that as much as I thought she might be cracking the whip and having the staff jump through the hoops, she also saw the staff as animals—beasts who might threaten her. I got the general impression that apprehension—fear and rage were moving back and forth on both sides of the equation so that she experienced this as coming from both within herself and from the outside. [From senior psychiatrist's reevaluation note.]

If Jenny was indeed dead, as she sometimes believed, if she was empty ("I have nothing inside me; they stole my heart; nothing's there, no beating"), if people were stealing her organs at night and creating a "cavity" in her chest, then how else combat these feelings of powerlessness except by making herself the star of the "center ring"?[2] Her delusions were so entrenched that the inevitable consequence of Jenny's acting out her desire to die was to bring her to center stage. If Jenny was indeed a beast among other beasts and if beasts make noise and cause disruptions, then acting in center stage could validate her own inner frame of reference—"being-as-beast"—and provide an environment for acting out or refracting identity. This was the only life-space Jenny possessed; her outrageousness formed part of who she was.

No matter what the state of her internal world ("I will kill, murder you all . . . give me the long knives . . . nothing stops me; I'll have revenge; you don't know who you're dealing with"), Jenny's external reality lacked hope. Her enfeebled physical condition, her inability to care for herself, and the energy she expended in warding off "beasts" and death threats or plotting revenge rendered her social existence almost nonexistent. Just as one could not expect a nine-month-old infant to care for itself, so with Jenny: outside of a containing environment, she would wither and die. Like an infant consumed by rage and anger, Jenny knew only despair: "I was not kidding when I said Christmas means hatred and pain and killing . . . I will die before my birthday; nothing will keep me alive." Jenny demanded containment both physically and emotionally. It

---

2. Not only did Jenny's "treatment team" devote an extraordinary amount of time to her care, she was also evaluated by Sheppard's senior psychiatrists. Extra staff meetings were scheduled to coordinate her treatment. The chief of service (the psychiatrist who administers a group of halls in one of the hospital's two adult wings) spent more time than usual on treatment issues relating to Jenny's case. Nurses, hired specifically for Jenny, monitored her behavior twenty-four hours a day. She was certainly the most "outrageous" patient on the hall. At Sheppard, the treatment team generally included a therapist (psychiatrist or psychologist), nurses, mental health workers, a social worker, and activities therapists. Treatment was a collaborative effort that involved several different individuals on three shifts. At any one time, then, a number of people may be interacting with any single patient.

was as if she transformed Sheppard into a collection of mothers; her screams, threats, and actions frightened staff into a series of treatment decisions that inevitably focused on containment and restraining—precisely the treatment given an infant thoroughly out of control.

Whatever "mothers" Jenny may have unconsciously constructed in the hospital, the "bad mothering" images eclipsed any sense of care and nurturance. For example, Jenny ate to survive (caring mother providing sustenance), but the food was poisoned (bad mother). She drank water, tea, and coke to stay alive (caring mother), but the water or coke was filled with acid and lethal mercury (bad mother). She welcomed a bed to sleep in (caring mother), but the bed contained hidden bombs and poisonous ants (bad mother). She was treated by nurses whom she often called "mother" (caring), but when they offered her closeness or empathy she lashed out with biting, scratching, and hitting (bad mother) (see table 7.1).

Bad images completely devoured the good. Jenny repudiated every feeling or even hint of warmth and tenderness, withdrawing into images of terror. Her protection from the fear of engulfment appeared in fables that composed her inner "state of nature." Dread was inescapable. Trapped by unending torment, Jenny believed her flesh should be sent to a "good butcher for food." At other times she asked that her body be used for the "evening meal" and "ground up into bits and pieces" or "stripped off in large hunks and sold to Sheppard/Pratt for a profit." If she was bad enough to be killed and butchered, it is no wonder she felt beyond empathy. Thus it was easier for Jenny to deal with being an animal sent to the packing house or glue factory than it was to think of herself as a human being capable of (and deserving) warmth and tenderness. Her fear of empathy drove her away from human community.

Jenny's intelligence had the potential to subvert the hospital's efforts to keep her alive. Monitored twenty-four hours a day because of her avowed intention to commit suicide, Jenny clung to life only because of the necessity imposed on her by treatment. It is understandable why she saw the hospital as a tyrant. It wanted to keep her alive; she hated living and hallucinated her own death ("My heart stopped beating today; and I died, but then it started up again. I couldn't find my heart . . . I'm empty inside; nothing's there.") What Hobbes calls the "commodious life," the

Table 7.1: Split Images of Mother

Good mother	Bad mother
Feeding	Poisoned food
Drinking, liquids, fluids	Fluids filled with acid, lethal mercury
Bed	Bombs, poisonous ants
Nursing, caring	Concentration camp guards
Gluing, holding together	Glue factory for dead animals

151

life of civil society, eluded Jenny. Nothingness and pain filled her consciousness; she spent her days staring at walls or out windows, occasionally speaking, sometimes drawing, rarely reading. At times she would
write a poem or note to staff. Jenny's mother and father kept their
distance; their relationship to Jenny certainly had nothing to do with the
fantasized life described in the following poem:

> Mother Maker
> of the warmth
> Father provider of the Sustenance
> Mother's warmth sustains
> While Father provides
> For Mother
> Mother keeps father
> Warm and protected
> against Nature's call

Jenny's violent acts and physical assaults were a plea to be held; when
she screamed or hit people, she was a nine-month-old infant making
demands. Jenny desired the idealized "mother maker," the good mother
who holds and protects, yet she lacked the inner sense of basic trust
essential to retain the good mother image as real and constant. Further,
she unconsciously refused to believe she was worthy of a good mother.
What she did know (both consciously and unconsciously) were the bad
mother images or introjects. Thus by making herself "bad," she attracted
the attention of what she called her "shepherd [sic] mothers." Most
importantly, it was her badness that induced these surrogate mothers
(nurses, mental health workers, or therapist) to hold her. In her mind,
however, emotional closeness of any kind involved assault. Jenny lacked
any concept of tenderness as a physical act enclosing the self in an
empathic warmth. All holding represented a form of projected violence;
to gratify this basic human need would have involved inducing others to
act violently. This is precisely what Jenny accomplished in her psychotic
concept of physical closeness.

Empathy threatened Jenny with annihilation, an absorption into the
other with a consequent loss of identity, yet her delusional world of
bombs, explosions, guns, knives, needles, amputations, ovens, and gas
chambers overwhelmed her with anxiety and a fear of imminent death.
Since she experienced pain from both directions the only exit Jenny could
see was a state of no-pain or nonbeing. Death became preferable to life,
since living meant fighting off the desperate need for and fear of empathy
while at the same time expending enormous energy warding off the
demons tormenting her consciousness.

For Hobbes, fear and anxiety about the future, which are attached to
the instinct for self-preservation, drive the anomic individuals of nature
into civil association. However, it is primarily fear that creates the im-
petus behind the "contract" with the sovereign. Pure self-interest, the

"reckoning of consequences," and the realization that the commodious life is impossible in an environment of fear all bring the warring selves of nature into a sovereignty that guarantees common names, rules, laws, and signs (codes). Yet if Jenny's experience is any indication, the dynamic that lies behind civil association may not be a Hobbesian privatism, self-interest, and concern for property. While Jenny was frequently paralyzed by her projections, her dread of empathy was even more fundamental. It should be emphasized that the defenses she created in her mind (her delusional habitat), the world that appeared so Hobbesian in its uncertainty, actually provided Jenny with a more bounded and definable universe than the inevitable disappointments and terror of human attachments and the unbearable pain of loss and rejection.

Thus it was not so much the anxiety generated by delusion that kept Jenny outside human society as it was her terror of empathic contact. If anything had the power to rescue Jenny from her delusional world, it was not the Hobbesian concept of self-preservation (with its associations of security, property, the "reckoning of consequences," and the rational perception of dangers arising from the lack of social order), but the irrational and emotional connections established through an empathic understanding. What escapes Hobbes in his view of motives is this unconscious but very real affective dimension of self. Certainly the fear of empathy and its critical function in bringing the delusional self out of psychosis would suggest its cohesive properties in an "association" as primitive as the therapeutic alliance. If, therefore, community of any kind depends on an original position of basic trust, it would appear that empathy lies at the heart of those human dynamics that stand behind all forms of association. It is this movement outside of self (an acknowledgment of others separate from self) that lay beyond Jenny's capacities; she remained locked inside her own internality.

Jenny's experience, when added to postdelusional accounts of psychosis (the subject of the next two chapters), adds convincing weight to the Rousseauian view concerning the origins of human association. Empathy, or what Rousseau calls *pitié* or compassion, as the first human emotion constitutes the elemental foundation of all subsequent political community. In Rousseau's view it is not fear that brings individuals together, but an instinctive need to be empathically connected with an other. Empathy, in this sense, is not a form of instrumental rationality. Rousseau's "natural man" leaves nature (or his self-absorption in nature) not for specific, useful reasons; rather, the beginning of association involves an innate sensing of suffering in an other separate from self. (I return to this argument in chapter 8.)

Jenny's denial of empathy created just the opposite effect in her treatment team. Her withdrawal and craziness evoked from staff the political relations of cooperation, organization, and compromise. The more tormented Jenny's delusions became, the more assaultive her behavior, and the more complete her inability to see herself as a human being, the greater the effort the staff made to rescue and treat her. Although, with a few exceptions, the staff disliked Jenny,[3] her behavior did give rise to considerable reflection and analysis.

Jenny conceived of herself as a sacrificial animal who existed for the purpose of feeding the staff: "My blood is their dinner; why else do you think I'm put in seclusion; they put machines in me that drain my blood. I'm a prisoner of war." At times she sounded as if she were awaiting a kind of ritual slaughtering, a pagan act that would heal rifts and ease tribulations within the "tribe" of Sheppard/Pratt. She offered herself up to the "knives of the slaughterers" with the "hospital as my gallery." Her agony preserved the psychic integrity of the group, and Jenny conceived of her energy, flesh, and even consciousness as placed in the hands of torturers and priests whose function was "to eat me alive and toss my bones to the dogs . . . to sell my meat cheaply." She saw the sacrifice as filled with cruelty, and she hoped that "death will be quick and not this slow torture of blood draining; why don't they just bash my head in with a rock and get it over with. . . . Why am I being subjected to this public spectacle . . . why is my death so important for Sheppard/Pratt?"

Just as the language of Jenny's unconscious drove her toward death, so the language of the treatment team sought to offer her life. But what treatment saw as life, Jenny saw as death. Each language was trapped in an unyielding set of assumptions over the meaning and content of linguistic interventions. The more Jenny consumed herself in delusion and terror, the more intensive and collaborative her treatment became. The more unpredictable her behavior became, the more the staff withdrew into its own Hobbesian anxiety over her actions. Not only was Jenny's internal world filled with fear, but that sense of reality permeated Jenny's relations with the staff. It was as if each were locked into a kind of Hobbesian regard for the other.

In a psychodynamic sense, Jenny's attempt to bring staff together represented the deeply held fantasy of curing the warring and fragmented parents (Searles 1965). It was her hope that the parental pair would be rescued from their unhappiness and pain through the transforming properties of their child's regression. Only the sacrifice of the child possessed the power to heal the family constellation. Jenny therefore felt unconsciously that her sickness would magically remake the grimly recollected family experience into an idealized fantasy of "mother maker" and "father sustenance." Not only did Jenny see herself as responsible for the

3. An entry from the "hotline" notebook (notes on pressing day-to-day problems) described the staff's wariness in approaching Jenny: "Continue to keep distance, remember 'warmth through friction,' and any sensing of closeness on her part is frightening and she's likely to strike out (closeness and fear of engulfment). . . . She needs simple, clear limits (as an infant), no complicated explanations, yes or no."

breakup of the fantasized, idyllic nurturing world of the family constellation, she was also the only person in the world who could restore her parents' lost happiness. Jenny therefore weakened herself so that the parents might become well.

Jenny, cut off from friends, rejected by her family (her mother and father were divorced and clearly indicated that they want as little to do with her as possible), an outcast from the human community, sank deeply into despair. Is it surprising, given these circumstances, that she experienced herself as an animal or an object controlled by impersonal forces? As her therapist put it:

> In Jenny's view the problems lie not inside her. She is not like you or I. For example if we're feeling bad we might say there are some problems bothering us, problems of our own making or our own reading of reality, or our own internal feelings. Not so for Jenny: when she feels down or depressed, it is because of something outside, a hernia, or her heart stopping. She is incapable of self-reflection, of seeing her somatic or psychological problems as having an origin inside her mind. She is so divorced from reality that what you and I would see as "inner" comes through to Jenny as a conspiracy of outside forces both in her body and in the world that conspires to kill, murder and torment. . . . It is the ultimate in masochism. Her sickness will bring about her parents' happiness.

Clinical Developments from the Perspective of Competing Language Worlds

I would now like to turn to an account of Jenny's course at Sheppard/Pratt from the point of view of three different language worlds: delusional knowledge projected as truth (Jenny's internality); the medical language of diagnoses and treatment (her therapist's view); and the observational, day-to-day linguistic interventions of activities therapists, nurses, and mental health workers. In all these worlds language constructs reality and surrounds the self with meaning and structure. Jenny found herself in a linguistic stalemate: every utterance she made that indicated a wish to die further involved the staff in ethics and definitions regarding the prevention of death and the maintenance of life. (Of course, from Jenny's perspective the maintenance of life meant prolonging an agonizing death.) Jenny saw her treatment at Sheppard as a violation of what she would have chosen had she not been committed to a mental hosptial: "If you're four thousand years old, what is yet another death?" The confrontation of Jenny's language and that of her treatment team resulted in an ongoing standoff, with each working under radically different assumptions regarding life and death.

First I would like to quote from a discharge summary Jenny received in one of her earlier hospitalizations:[4]

> Jenny is a 17-year-old, single girl with a long history of behavior problems which culminated . . . when she took her stepmother's car and drove west through three counties up to 115 miles per hour until she was stopped by a police barricade. There was no significant injury. She was released by the police to seek psychiatric hospitalization and was brought back to _____ by her parents.
>
> Her long-term problems include the following: she had had difficulty with school refusal and truancy since the third grade when she would not attend an average of two days per week. The problem has never been less than that. However despite the absences she obtained straight A's until junior high school when she started to refuse to attend school nearly full time and failed. She has been to court three times for truancy. Jenny ran away with a boy for one week at the age of 15 to Kentucky. There have been episodes of aggression including threatening her stepmother with a knife when she was in the ninth grade. One of the more impressive problems has been Jenny's withdrawal. Since the ninth grade she spends much of her day in bed, mostly sleeping or reading. Late in the day she commonly would wash up, dress and go out with "friends." The nature of her friends is not entirely clear but they sound like other teenagers who have difficulties and have some interest in drugs and religion. Lastly, Jenny has poor social relatedness. Her friends seem more like people to run with. She is not close to her mother, father or stepmother or to neighborhood friends. She always has been shy.
>
> More recently, Jenny has become somewhat bizarre. She has been living with her father and stepmother in _____ for the past two months. She just keeps to herself. She reads a lot including philosophers such as Plato and Socrates and copies pages from these works. There are no reports of her talking to herself. For the two days before she took the car she didn't speak at all. Since the accident she said things like "I know my destiny . . . I am going to live a thousand years . . . I have a son who is 33 years old . . . My name is Jenny and I died in 1898." [From a discharge summary.]

Jenny came to Sheppard in December, 1981; the information her therapist gave about her past was not particularly hopeful:

> The patient was admitted to Sheppard/Pratt Hospital as a transfer from _____ Hospital in _____. It was felt that a number of short-term hospitalizations and care at that Hospital had not been

4. All names, dates, and places have been changed to protect the privacy of the people involved.

of much help to the patient and she was admitted to Sheppard/ Pratt for longer-term, more comprehensive treatment of her illness. Since she was fifteen years old she had a number of short-term hospitalizations, all of them following a similar course: a rather uneventful adaptation, a progressive deterioration in her cognitive or (social) functioning, intensive regression, struggle over her treatment (particularly neuroleptic medications), and elopement from the Hospital.

What brought Jenny to Sheppard was a series of violent incidents: "the patient eloped from a day trip [during her previous hospitalization] and went to her mother's house." A struggle developed and her mother received multiple knife wounds:

> There were various accounts of what happened ranging from her mother getting hurt while stopping a suicide to Jenny simply attacking her mother. After this the patient was probated for one year to _____ Hospital in _____. However, in mid-February of 1981, the patient eloped from the hospital, went to her father's home, located a gun and shot herself in the abdomen.

Jenny suffered major internal injuries that required intensive surgery and aftercare. It was shortly after her recovery that she was transferred to Sheppard/Pratt.

On admittance, Jenny appeared quite normal for a young woman of twenty:

> Jenny presented as an appropriately dressed, attractive young woman who entered into the interview in a cooperative if somewhat distant fashion. . . . There was no evidence of overt psychotic symptoms, but as she began to discuss a recent telephone call with her mother, there was disorganization of her thought processes. . . . She was oriented in all spheres. Her insight and judgement are impaired secondary to her psychotic illness. . . . The patient's initial pleasant demeanor on the hall was a surprise considering the extremely stormy and chaotic nature of her previous hospitalizations. The degree to which this chaotic course will be eventually repeated here remains to be seen.

It soon became clear, however, that Jenny's psychotic world lay directly beneath her cognitive awareness. She moved rapidly between what seemed to be normal speech and behavior and what was obviously psychotic or delusional. She could be cheerful, pleasant, and interacting one minute and the next wander off into some delusional revelation ("I am being burned by the fires beneath the Hospital"). Yet she conformed to expectations on the hall; she cooperated. At least on the surface she showed some interest in other patients and took up a few activities. It seemed that she might have turned, at least partially, toward consensual reality. Jenny's initial diagnostic evaluation closed with this observation: "the best diagnostic level for the patient at this time is schizophrenia, paranoid type."

For the first several weeks of her treatment, Jenny acclimated herself to the life of the hall. She attended meals, activities, and meetings. She played games and exercised occasionally. Yet she could be unsettling, particularly by wearing expressions that seemed to be both "there" and far away, and by an unnerving emptiness in her eyes, which gave the impression that she could see objects thousands of light-years away. Her eyes effectively concealed another Jenny (or many different Jenny-identities) that lay hidden somewhere behind her superficial, adaptive mask. At times her delusional world surfaced in language: "Somebody broke my neck . . . they shot me from behind; it just happened, but I don't know which. I don't think I'm alive. A nightmare flies out of me and back into my face . . . I see five thousand thoughts in your glasses. . . . There's a city underneath this hospital."

About two months into her hospitalization, Jenny began to show symptoms of what psychiatrists call "decompensation," and she found it increasingly difficult to suppress psychotic concepts and definitions. It was during this period (around the end of February) that Jenny delivered a "three-day notice"[5] to the staff. The way she dated the notice gives some indication of the nature of her delusional frame of reference ("Jenny-as-dead-person"): "February twenty-third nineteen hundred and eighty-two, one-thirty *post mortem*"(italics added). Considering Jenny's obsession with death and her belief that she was in fact dead, her language of dating conveys a very specific message. She went on:

> I Jenny . . . have decided on this day to inform the people of Shepherd [*sic*] and Enoch Pratt Hospital that I would like to leave, to lead a free and responsible life of my own where I have the opportunity to make and act upon my own decision of the best possible judgment in accordance with the norms of society.

---

5. Patients who were not certified had the right to give a "three-day notice" of intent to leave the hospital. If the treatment team felt the patient's discharge would be seriously threatening to himself or others, the hospital moved to have the patient certified. This was an informal process (a hearing held in the hospital) involving the written testimony of two outside psychiatrists that the patient, if discharged, would be a threat to self and others. If it was agreed by the hearing officer that discharge would pose dangers, then the patient was certified. What this meant was that the patient, with the appropriate consent of relatives or guardians, was obliged legally to remain in the hospital. In practice, certification at Sheppard/Pratt was rarely used; it was a practice that obviously could be abused. But in the instances of certification I saw, it was obvious to me that if the patients had been discharged, it would have amounted either to sentencing them to death by suicide or would almost certainly have resulted in some serious, destructive behavior.

> When confronted by necessity I am responsible enough to meet
> my needs for existence. So it is not a question of whether or not
> I could hold a job and function in the community. I feel I am
> ready to pursue my own life and meet the needs and goals I have
> decided beneficial to my welfare. I felt freedom is a major ne-
> cessity towards normal, healthy and happy functioning. Freedom
> is decision making for oneself.

Who could quarrel with these sentiments? The letter implied that the
hospital had deprived Jenny of her freedom and the right to make
decisions for herself. Yet consider what freedom means when it is tied
into a delusional system preoccupied with death and suicide. In the past
"decision making for oneself" meant Jenny's taking a twelve-gauge shot-
gun and turning it on her abdomen. Was the hospital depriving her of
freedom if, in its view, her freedom would inevitably have led to her
suicide? For Jenny, freedom had no consensual meaning; it was not a
political concept in her world. Rather, it defined an end state, a condition
of nonbeing, the freedom to be dead or to confirm an already dead state:
"I am brittle like being in the grave for a million years . . . my name is
post mortum."

Jenny later retracted her three-day notice: "I Jenny . . . remove my
three-day notice to leave, because I have decided to prepare myself for
discharge by discovering what is available in the Baltimore area jobwise.
I also want to prepare myself for this task. I also plan to discover
self-discipline." Only Jenny knew what her "preparation" for "self-
discipline" involved, but even at this early stage it was highly unlikely that
she conceived of the outside world as either friendly or challenging. What
preoccupied her was the action of delusional reality: "when I tilt my head
back a zap goes up through my nose; sometimes I feel that electrodes are
in my sinuses . . . I think the hospital wants to sell me into slavery . . .
Sheppard/Pratt is the valley of death, hell . . . my body is jaundiced."

She slowly withdrew from all activities. The following entries (January
through May) from her activities therapy chart indicate how far Jenny
moved from organized, consensually based exchange:

> Feb. 9 and 23: attendance has been irregular for all activities this
> past month. The patient tends to arrive late when she does
> attend.

> March 19: overall progress has been minimal due to patient hav-
> ing difficulty getting to activities. [But for Jenny the difficulties
> were very real: "I will be attacked by birds . . . I am dying; my
> heart stopped beating; it is dangerous out there. . . . I didn't go
> swimming today because the atomic submarines were lying
> underneath ready to nuke me. . . ."] [On water therapy:] The
> patient has generally refused this past month, stating a "phobia"

159

against water. Due to her general resistance she has been temporarily discontinued as of _____. [Further,] the patient has
been temporarily withdrawn from the interpersonal skills waiting
list due to general inappropriateness to attend at this time.

April 22: [Horticulture and female recreation] attendance has
been irregular, patient does participate in open and skill development and PAC [patient activities council] activities at her own
volition. . . . In female recreation, the patient distances herself
from others and appears quite interpersonally insecure. In horti-
culture, the patient appears motivated. Although she is pleasant
and conversant with others, she does not tend to work with in-
vestment or motivation. She does however appear to enjoy being
outside [where she might have the opportunity to escape or turn
herself into an animal].

May 29: Jenny is quite unresponsive to others in her group and
in her past chose to ignore the instructions of the group leader
unless very firm commands were made. In addition, she used her
leatherwork tools in an angry, aggressive manner. Jenny was
placed on hold in all her groups due to her special observation
status.[6] An effort will be made by the activity therapy representative to see Jenny one-on-one in the Hall.

June 4: The patient has not attended any activity therapy groups
off the hall due to her repressed, disorganized state.

Although Jenny found it increasingly difficult to leave the hall (for fear
of being killed), she became quite responsive to one-on-one encounters.
It is this aspect of her being, the need to be held and contained that
became prominent in her treatment. The more her delusional identity
consumed her life and defined her action, the more she demanded
one-on-one contact, even to the point of assaulting nursing staff (particularly women), knowing full well she would be physically handled, restrained, and placed in seclusion. The greater her fear of the outside
world, the more insistent her demands became and the more regressed
and infantile her behavior. Several altercations between Jenny and the
staff landed her in seclusion from July through November. The following
exchange between Jenny (J) and a male staff member (S) is typical:

J: May I have some valium?
S: No, it's not in your order [medication orders prescribed by
attending psychiatrist].

6. Special observation (SO) meant that the patient's behavior had become so unpredictable (usually assaultive or threatening either to self or others) that continual monitoring was
necessary.

J: Well, Dr. L. [a therapist at previous hospital] has it in my orders.

S: No, it's not in your orders. Besides Dr. L. took care of you when you were in _____. He's not here at Sheppard. Dr. M. is your therapist.

J: Well, it's written in my chart, go look.

S: That's just not true. Dr. M. is your therapist and he hasn't written such an order.

[Jenny then kicked the staff member.]

S: I held her for awhile. She struggled a bit; a call went out for female staff. But she calmed down and I walked her to the quiet room. I think she just wanted to be held.

For the staff, it was clear what the issue was and what the response should be: either restrain Jenny or be hit. But from the perspective of Jenny's internality, any number of events might have been happening. She might have understood the refusal to give her valium as (1) a plot against her; (2) abandonment and the reliving of previously felt or experienced abandonments; (3) a complete rejection of self and an effort to annihilate her (since Jenny was unable to distinguish the refusal of the valium from a refusal of self); or (4) as an indication that she was still in her previous hospital.

A similar incident again demonstrates the radical polarity of Jenny's linguistic construction of reality and the staff's reaction to her. Jenny came out of quiet room and asked for her prescribed medications. The nurse told her to go back to QR until she (the nurse) brought them. Jenny became enraged, reached through the medication window, grabbed the nurse by the hair, and punched her in the face. It is obvious that the refusal of medication set up some internal resonance in Jenny that provoked her to violence. For Jenny, simple acts (at least from the perspective of consensual reality) were charged with emotional content. It is impossible to know the exact meaning Jenny attached to the refusal, but it may have had something to do with the whole area of being human and nonhuman (see Searles's 1960 essay, "The Desire to Become Nonhuman as a Defense against Various Feeling-States").

It is intriguing to consider that, *voluntarily* by requesting her medications, Jenny was agreeing to the rules of civil society. At that moment she rejoined human association; she accepted certain terms of a consensual reality. This acknowledgment of rules represented for her a notable achievement. The nurse, however, in ordering Jenny back to the quiet room, refused *in Jenny's mind* to recognize the human content of her request. The order to go back to the quiet room was, from Jenny's perspective, a demand that she return to her animal habitat. This enraged and hurt her, since the nurse's action entailed a repudiation of Jenny's effort to act according to assumptions governing the human world. This was clearly an instance where the linguistic content of Jenny's request contained a symbolic dimension that could not have been anticipated.

Jenny's rage, then, confirmed that she was indeed capable of being as nasty and hostile as a beast; and the experience of being "hauled" back to her cage provided her with further confirmation of her alienation from human community. By denying Jenny's request, the nurse not only repudiated Jenny's humanity (and the enormous effort it must have taken Jenny even to think of herself as human), she also further reinforced Jenny's delusional identity as an animal fit for slaughter, as "meat" ready to be cooked in Sheppard's ovens that "throw black smoke three hundred miles into the sky."

Some indication of how alienated Jenny felt appears in the following poem:

Nighttime doom
    awakens in murder
Pencilvania Flat

It is no wonder I cannot think see or feel; someone feed me
    rabies . . . I must learn the laws of the jungle

Jenny never quits
posed and prepared
Equal opportunity implorer

Mass confusion
Bash her head right?
Wrong I do not know what to do

Father, I cried upon my bed of death
    your a serpent and not a man
Someone—prey be it tell me of life
The male calls she's not my wife
Father, I despise the grounds you walk
    upon with your heavy loaded guns
I have been sentenced to Siberia
    to live in a Fort
My scarlet fever is turning to amonia water

What is cain and abel?
Cain kills abel

Psychiatric Evaluation and the Management of Delusional Reality

Jenny's psychiatric evaluations were as discouraging as her activities reports, and reflected a similar course of withdrawal, regression, and increased hostility and aggressiveness. The following are typical entries:

> Dec. 28: [Jenny] is in need of hospitalization at this time because of the extreme life-threatening nature of her illness and the need for supervision and coordinated treatment that an inpatient setting can provide. . . . The patient's mother described a change in her after she went back to work subsequent to a divorce when the patient was two. There was some truancy beginning in the ninth grade. The patient dropped out of ninth grade, went back a year later and only stayed for one month. Her interpersonal adjustment after this became increasingly marginal. She became more mistrustful of people and her relationships more chaotic and problematic. Eventually she became preoccupied with religious delusions and these seemed to wax and wane at different times. . . . Truancy began in the ninth grade and the patient dropped out of school in the tenth grade. The patient has had intermittent jobs as cook and dishwasher. From October 1977–March 1980 the patient had an apartment of her own with a boyfriend who then left. The patient has lived mostly with the mother and at times has lived with the father and her stepmother. The patient's mother says she will not accept the patient returning home again. She feels that Jenny takes control of the home and tends to imitate mother's action in a psychotic fashion.

> Jan. 28: Jenny appears to be making a satisfactory initial adjustment to the Hospital setting and treatment program over the past two weeks . . . in the individual psychotherapy sessions, the patient tends to focus on the externals of the office such as the art work, etc. She also seems to need to focus fairly concretely on the present. At the present time the patient's clinical condition is tenuous and she remains withdrawn and frightened. Discharge at this time would be precipitous and would place the patient at a high risk of regression and self-destructive acting out of life-threatening proportions.

> Feb. 14: Jenny has shown some increased participation and greater comfort in her interactions with other patients and staff. However she has shown a considerable degree of inconsistency and variability in both her participation in activities and interactions with others. At times, she tends to withdraw to her bed and complain of various somatic difficulties. These are only hints of an intensity of negative feelings against which this withdrawal seems to be defined. In individual psychotherapy sessions, the patient has begun to miss some sessions, claiming that she has forgotten the appointment time. Then, there are only brief glimpses as to the reasons the patient is missing the sessions. Sometimes she alludes to frightening paranoid feelings and thoughts which

she then dismisses in a joking fashion. She seems to have some sense of just how tenuous her hold on reality is at this point and she is guarded about revealing much of this to anyone.

However, during this period Jenny felt completely closed off from the world. As she wrote in a poem,

No response
No response
no response
keep quiet
learn to be

Big deal right . . . the retardates when [sic] again

The psychiatric evaluations showed little improvement.

Feb. 26: The patient's severe difficulties are becoming more noticeable as she becomes more engaged in the treatment program. This engagement may initially take the form of a negativistic, "warmth through friction" kind of relatedness at first.

March 19: A little more improvement; better adjustment to the hall and the hosptial treatment program . . . the patient is revealing more in the individual psychotherapy sessions that indicate the degree of disorganization and delusional thinking that she uses almost all her energy to manage and to maintain an appearance of being together. [Jenny's therapist cautioned against discharge because it "would be premature and would place the patient at risk for any intensification of delusional thinking and possible severe self destructive behavior."]

April 21: Jenny has been more angry and negativistic both on the hall and in the individual psychotherapy sessions. The clinical picture is one in which the patient appears in indirect ways, such as through the other patients, to be telling staff and her doctor about frightening and puzzling experiences that she is having. But when this is directly inquired into, the patient makes it almost impossible to go any further in exploring these experiences. In general, the patient has made it very difficult for anyone to get very much of a sense as to what she is thinking or feeling. There has been a flurry of concerns and complaints about her physical condition and this seems to form the basis right now for her interactions with staff.

May 2: [From reevaluation by senior psychiatrist:] The parents have been very remote and there has been only one phone call from them. . . . Nursing describes the patient as becoming more angry. She slams things down in a childish way. She says that just because she gets angry toward the staff does not mean that she doesn't like

them. . . . The general impression one gets is of superficial adapata-
tion with a great deal of denial and concealment with our having
very little grasp of the underlying dynamics. It is noteworthy that
she has been involved in some very violent kinds of behavior which
in itself might be cause for her to be going quite slowly in terms of
trying to explore her difficulties. I think this is one of those patients
who will require a longer period to establish the necessary relationship.

May 26: Jenny has become more overtly disorganized in her functioning on the hall and has now been more open in sharing with
staff a number of delusional concerns about being harmed either by
staff or in other ways such as poisonous gas seeping through the
ventilation system, etc. She interacts with staff in such a way as to
provoke them in "substantiating" her delusional concerns. For instance, at the time when the patient was due to go down to dinner
in the cafeteria, she called her doctor. Prior to this, she refused a
tray and then after the staff dinner group left demanded a tray.
When the staff balked she said this was confirmation that the staff
was torturing and starving her as she had suspected.

June 28: Jenny remains regressed in her thinking and behavior on
the hall. A prominent delusional concern is a fear of being
harmed by the staff and this seems to include projective aspects
such as her feeling that staff people have attempted to harm
members of their own families. Another area of the patient's
concern is her being fearful that her food is harmful and refusing
at times to eat. Included in this is also a refusal to take any
medications that might be prescribed. She has stated clearly that
she would run away from the hospital if any attempt were made
to force her to take medication. The approach to the patient is to
respond to the regressed aspects. Nursing staff has at times tasted
the food before the patient eats and frequently sits with her while
she is eating. This has resulted in some stabilization of the weight
loss that was present over the last several weeks. . . . What has
emerged is the patient's insistence on controlling every aspect of
her life at this point in her own way and intense distress and fear
of being controlled by anyone else. . . . Because of the extreme
disorganization of the patient's behavior, and some comments
about her not being alive following the suicide of another patient
in the hospital, she was placed on special observation this month.

July 28: The patient's clinical condition this month has been characterized by a profound regression with the patient becoming extremely disorganized and delusional. She has responded somewhat to a treatment program that emphasizes basic nursing care
in terms of the patient's eating, bathing and participating to some
extent on the hall in terms of meetings and other activities. . . .

Along with the more overtly psychotic features, the patient's behavior has taken on many childlike characteristics such as eating
with her fingers and speaking in an infantile fashion. However
she is now eating a little more and relating somewhat more com-
fortably at times on the hall.

Jenny resisted psychotherapy and repudiated any involvement with
social rules. She tumbled backward in her own psychological time into a
state of complete despair.

> Misguided information
>   Unknown satisfactions
> Unceasing beguilement
> Needless misunderstanding
> And comprehension
> Unendearing Faith
> lack of self confidence
> lack of self discipline
>
> Remember why I'm here?
> Cross and Switchblade
> Because you are ready to die
> Die as in death
>
>   Elizabeth Kubla Ross [i.e., Jenny]

By early summer Jenny's behavior had become so disruptive, her withdrawal so intense, and her madness so palpable (she defecated into paper
cups, washed her hair with tea leaves, and "grazed" on hospital grounds)
that it was now believed medication should be forced on her. With some
misgivings her treatment team moved toward this psychiatric intervention, taking into account her history and her own stated hostility to
medication, which she believed planted electrodes in her brain:

In view of the patient's regression and disorganization, antipsychotic medication has been prescribed which the patient is
refusing. She continues to insist in the individual psychotherapy
sessions that she would run away from the hospital if she were
forced to take medication with all the implied tragic consequences. At the present time, the plan is to encourage her to
take medication orally with the notion that the necessary confi-
dence can be established so that she will agree to this. It has become increasingly more apparent over the last month that the
patient would benefit from pharmacologic intervention.

Jenny continued to refuse medication and her condition continued to
worsen: she became more hostile, threatening both to herself and others,
and the treatment team's reactions took on a defensive quality. Jenny no
longer appeared as the whimsical classic schizophrenic washing her hair

with tea leaves; instead she degenerated into a combative, frequently assaultive person for whom the world was a perpetual torture chamber. Hers was a bleak situation, the final descent into the Hobbesian "war of all against all."

> August 26: This month the patient's disorganization, withdrawal, and psychotic thinking has [sic] shown minimal improvement. She began to do for herself some of the basic activities that were being done for her by nursing staff such as bathing, dressing and eating properly. There was some concern about her response to a vacation of the mental health worker who had been working most closely with her. After this mental health worker returned, she again required nursing staff to bathe and dress her. This seemed to be a way of her reengaging this nursing staff member after her vacation. The patient then became almost mute and refused to meet with the therapist. There was one episode during which the patient kicked and scratched several nursing staff members who were attempting to bathe her.
>
> Because of the patient's prolonged and severe regression, it is reasonable both for therapeutic grounds and for the patient's safety to give intramuscular medication. The concern was raised during the reevaluation conference that the patient made a serious suicide attempt in the past that to some degree was related to her having been given medication. However failure to give medications at this point and allow this situation to continue would have serious hazards in its own right. The potential is present that a favorable response to psychotherapeutic medication might lead to improvements and would help the patient become more involved in other aspects of the treatment program. After discussion with the patient's father about her need for medication and with his permission an IM [intramuscular] order of Trilafon will be ordered.

Forcing medication by injection on Jenny was the hospital's last line of defense. This situation served to crystallize two mutually hostile languages. For Jenny the IM injections proved several things: (1) life was indeed "nasty, brutish and short" ("Don't they drug animals before they kill them?"); (2) the hospital was a concentration camp; (3) people only touched each other in a hostile and violent manner; and (4) trust and love did not exist inside Sheppard/Pratt. The world for her degenerated into pure force and fear.

Eventually, however, Jenny gave up (as she put it) and decided to cooperate with the medication regimen. The need for the injections lasted only a week or two, but it was obvious that Jenny experienced IM medication or indeed any medication as an attempt to kill her. Several months later her attitude changed. For example she remarked that medications "glued" her together; and, as the staff observed, she was

167

"sometimes the first in line to receive it." Yet the next day she might scream that the staff were killing her, using the medication to plant electrodes in her head. From a psychiatric standpoint, the medication proved to be relatively ineffective in combating the intensity of her delusional projections and in diminishing her anxiety and terror. Jenny stated at one point that she would be "dead by the time of my birthday." Her fear intensified even while she was on medication, and her delusional world never disappeared or even receded during the medication phase. The following entry (from the "observation sheet for seclusion") is typical of Jenny's behavior while she was on medication:

> [Jenny threw] juice into the face of the nurse. Attempt was made
> to have her take time out in her room and she grabbed the por-
> ter [cleaning lady]. She was carried to LDS [locked door seclu-
> sion] and given her meals. She was quite resistant and combative.
> Jenny banged on the door and when staff went to her, she tied
> her gown around her neck. Help was summoned. The gown was
> knotted [it had been soaked in Jenny's urine] and had to be cut
> off her. She had to be held as she was assaultive and attempted
> to bite.

It was in this context that her therapist began to wonder whether or not treatment interventions would ever be useful to Jenny. This was a period of real hopelessness both for the staff and for Jenny. Each acted according to linguistic and behavioral assumptions that had no common ground, and there appeared to be little likelihood of a breakthrough.

Nursing: The Phenomenology of the Day-to-Day

I would like to complete this picture-in-language of Jenny's descent into a psychological state of nature by turning to the nursing notes, which consist of observations made by nurses and mental health workers at the end of each eight-hour shift in the hospital's day. These notes provide an ongoing phenomenological record of Jenny's day-to-day transformations. Nurses have considerable power in the hospital because of their continuing relationship with patients, and much of their power comes from the dependence of the patients on the nurses' evaluation both of how they progress and of the appropriateness of behavior. It is important here to point out that one of Sheppard/Pratt's treatment objectives is that influence over patients should resemble in some respects the kinds of pressures and demands that will inevitably be placed on them after discharge. Thus the presence of mental health workers, nurses, paraprofessionals of different kinds, and students, gives the atmosphere on the hall a certain social content and context. On balance, I would argue, this provides the patients with possibilities for "refracting" behavior. Appropriate behavior does not necessarily mean obedience; it does mean, however, maintaining a standard of civility that, if violated or broached, brings on sanctions within the hospital. Those sanctions involve the use of the quiet and seclusion rooms and restrictions on the freedom to be outside the locked doors of the halls without staff supervision.

It was clear that Jenny not only violated this criterion of appropriateness, but she would also have presented insurmountable difficulties (such as elopement) if she had been allowed to go where she wished in the hospital. Yet it was not clear that Jenny would leave the hall, since, in her delusional habitat, wars, conflagrations, and hell-fire raged in the outside world, and the rigidly structured environment of a closed room provided Jenny (at certain critical periods) with a containing environment that approached the security and limited definition of an infant's crib. Jenny needed the care, attention, and tolerance a mother might lavish on her year-old child.

The following are typical entries from Jenny's nursing notes:

> Dec. 28 [shortly after her admission]: She appeared quiet and frightened but was friendly. She was introduced to her roommate and others. . . . She's alert and oriented and does not appear overly psychotic.

> Jan. 3: Jenny was on the hall until approx. 1:00 A.M. talking with staff. Pt. talked about fears she has of waking up with frontal lobotomy. Pt. also states that she feels something is blocking her main blood vessel in her neck causing a headache and possible brain tumor.

> Feb. 19: Patient accompanied staff group to lunch and spent much of the morning in bed. At first, pt. expressed anger at being on SE [staff escort] saying I'm going to place a bomb in Dr. M.'s office [her therapist], although laughingly said. . . .

> March 8: Patient has had a good evening; pt. spent much of the early evening interacting lightly with peers. . . . Pt. seemed in pleasant mood. [Jenny's moods, however, were variable; the next moment she could be dumping water on another patient's head or demanding that the guns be removed from the hall or complaining about how the water was poisoned. She may have appeared agreeable to some staff, to others she may have spoken of cities underneath the hospital, torture chambers, executions, bombs, irreversible destruction, and so on.]

> April 15: Jenny was on hall at shifts change. Expressed concern as she spoke with writer about a feeling that freon-type substance was blowing through hospital ventilation system. Her concern or

fear seemed to stem from an accident which she mentioned, whereby several people had died. Writer tried to allay her fears and concerns but this effort was minimally successful.

April 23: Jenny woke late and missed her 10:15 appt. with medical doctor even after reminded by staff. Pt. rescheduled appt. for 11:30 which she did make. Jenny has continued seeming belligerent and angry at staff at times and reacted oppositionally to staff intervention in terminating or redirecting a conversation Jenny was having with peer. In this discussion peer was talking of his delusions about doing brain transplants on others, which Jenny seemed very interested in and kept asking about it in reference to herself (told staff member her sister had a brain transplant). When confronted Jenny became accusatory towards staff and expressed her feelings on reality versus irreality which was difficult to understand and seemed paranoid and delusional.

It was at about this time that Jenny wrote another long note to the staff:

Today so many things have occurred to me. Many positive things have begun to happen concerning my interest towards something intellectual. I have picked up many new things in this wonderous [sic] day God has created for living creatures. One thing I learned is that concerning the people that are becoming well through the benefits of science and experimentation is that the people running the show around here should be titled proctors. Another positive thing I have learned is that I am an intellectual being capable of understanding many different things. One of my many desires is to learn and understand the purpose of medicine. Its pharmaceuticology [sic] and its biological effects on life, along with its purpose. I have come to understand that I am a very reasoning creature concerned with humanity . . . a very unhappy thought I have been dealing with today is my physical being. I am becoming very ill and do not know what to do about it, if there is anything. I am starting to feel pain in my arms and legs. I am coughing severely and spitting up green colored flem [sic]. Miss _____ [mental health worker] noticed that under my eyes I am gaining dark circles. Speaking of fright I am frightened for I know the pain I have gone through before and I do not enjoy it. My love of life tells me to continue, persue [sic] and succeed until I am well. I do not want to give up and I pray no one will give up on me.

  I am thinking about the tetracycline hydrochloride ordered for me. At first I was reluctant to take it because when I took it before it caused burning in my abdomin [sic]. This conjured up thoughts of rabies and hydrochloride for the treatment. I remember a little girl with the name Chris that went to _____ hospital everyday to get rabies shots and she would scream with excruciating pain. This was many moons ago. I feel her mother did the right thing in being cautious. For rabies is something you cannot play around with when there are any chances.

While Jenny may have prayed that no one would give up on her, her delusional projections became even more obvious, and her initial success at masking this underlying knowledge-world disappeared:

> May 3: While being escorted to her GED [General Educational Development] and typing activities, Jenny commented that the helicopters and airplanes that were flying over were "war planes" and asking "what if they. . . ." She mimmiced [sic] a machine gun. Staff responded with "It's a time of peace, they wouldn't do that." She stated, "What makes you say that?"

She found "poison" in her food, saw "judgment day coming," and would "remember staff and not forgive." She threatened "to act crazy and staff would regret it." She refused to eat because of the "rat dung in the meat." She stayed away from the swimming pool because she feared the staff would "drown me for being a witch." Early in the summer the staff found Jenny on her hands and knees grazing on the hospital grounds.

> June 11: Jenny attended a volleyball activity and the activities leader soon called to inform the staff that Jenny wasn't participating in the activity but instead was on the lawn eating grass. When approached by a few staff members, pt. seemed quite loose and disorganized but responded tearfully to a female staff member. Afterwards, pt. expressed not having ever been loved and feeling lonely. Pt. also seemed somewhat psychotic during this interaction, but was able to communicate what her feelings were. . . .

> June 14: Patient was returning from walk to pool when she refused to return to hall . . . talking about the "building falling down" on her. The patient resisted verbal attempts [to get her to return]. Staff eventually carried her back to the hall and she kicked one of the female staff members.

> June 17: Jenny seemed to be having a difficult time early on in the evening, speaking of murder, blood, guns and knives and evidently unable to connect any of this to reality. Jenny was given a tray on the hall for lunch which she picked at. Afterwards writer found Jenny in the bathroom wiping very thickened [cold] coffee on her feet and legs and said when confronted "What do you think it is, blood?" Jenny then mentioned something about everybody having guns and knives and what would we do with her if she died. . . . Jenny touched on many different subjects in our conversation—some of it delusional, paranoid and others suggested Jenny's fears on the hall and alienation from the group. "They all carry knives and guns . . . I guess that's why

171

nobody attaches to me." At one point writer asked Jenny how the violent talk related to the incident preceding her SEPH admission and she said, "I made a blunder but I shouldn't say anything" and responded affirmatively when asked if I was getting too close.

June 27: Jenny has been very difficult today, such as using a great deal of profanity and testing limits. She was writing numbers all over the chalkboard which is used for phone messages and got into an altercation with peer and staff over that. She refused to eat lunch saying that the food was poison and that if she couldn't go to lunch with the group she would not eat at all. Jenny has been spouting quotes from the Bible. One example is "you shall work for seven years, and rest for seven years," and then she said "and this is the seventh day."

July 6: Jenny slept until about 10 A.M. then refused any breakfast when encouraged in 1:1 interaction with staff. Pt. also refused lunch and was quiet and distant on the hall. About 1:30 P.M. Jenny dumped tea bags and coffee into trash can and began fishing around in the trash. When approached by staff, Jenny was non-verbal and looked frightened (trembling, wide, dilated eyes), and she was asked to take some time out in her room. The pt. initially refused to relinquish cigarette and walked away from staff and away from her room. When staff approached her in a non-threatening way, Jenny backed away and moved quickly to T.V. room where she picked up a lamp and raised it overhead as if threatening to throw it at staff. Jenny was not responsive to verbal commands by staff but put lamp back and walked up the hall when all female call sounded on loud speaker. Pt. was escorted to LDS.

July 9: Staff entered room and found Jenny with only her shirt on wiping her genital area with a towel dipped in Coca-Cola. Pt. also defecated in a cup on the floor and appeared to urinate in 2 cups and mix some coke with it. Pt. was delusional saying, "I'm not going to let you burn away my skin and rub blood in my hair." Pt. was bathed by female staff and hair washed. Pt. grabbed writer's wrist in vise-like grip at one point, refusing to let go until I wrenched it free. After bath, pt. dozed on hall and was quiet. Pt. has been wandering up and down hall appearing spacey and distant.

July 14: Jenny remains on S.O. [staff observation]. She is much more verbal and sociable. She ate much of her dinner and stated later that she was hungry. Jenny asked to be taken to the snack shop to get something to eat. She spoke to this writer about not knowing what she is. She feels that she is a bird or a bee or whatever. She said that she doesn't know what sex she is either. She then asked for toenail clippers to trim her "hooves," that was laughingly said [but I think seriously meant]. Jenny then sat with staff and trimmed her toenails. She is smiling and pleasant. [Yet she was also capable of saying "I'm tired of all you hissing around me like snakes."]

July 21: Patient combative: when staff was giving a bath she refused both . . . hitting staff and was escorted to quiet room.

July 23: Jenny spent the evening on the hall. Pt. did not eat her dinner tray but did eat a piece of cake and drank juice. Pt. has sat on the hall and also looked out the window for long period of time with a male peer having little [verbal] interaction between the two. Jenny had an episode where she refused to allow peers to watch T.V. proclaiming some form of evil related to T.V. Pt. was urged to leave the T.V. room and refused until told females would be called. Pt. then came onto the hall where she addressed several pts. that a "strong wind may blow this building down," along with other paranoid type remarks.

August 4: Jenny remains on S.O. She seems to be pushing limits today. Jenny entered the room of another pt. and took a tooth cleaner. Jenny then began to play the piano during a time when it is set not to be played. The next thing she did was to take a glass of iced tea (from which another pt. had been drinking) and began to drink from it. When I asked Jenny about these things she said that she needs to be punished and that she is tired of feeling the pain.

Jenny became the caricature of madness, with stringy, unwashed hair, towels on her head, incessant, often vacuous staring, and smiles that seemed to be a mixture of torment and lasciviousness. Her choice of clothing made no sense. Frequently her pupils dilated, as if she sensed some extraordinary threat lurking in the hall. She would urinate on the floor and defecate on her food tray. She felt betrayed by the forced medications: "I've been shot, killed, stabbed to death . . . my heart is all clogged up . . . it hurts." Jenny, lost to the human world, found herself enveloped in a psychosis that left the staff totally baffled:

Sept. 4: Jenny has remained on the hall this whole shift. She has been conversing with peers and staff. Jenny made some attempt at being seductive in the presence of male staff. She sat on the floor and fondled her breasts saying that she needed to be "milked" [more animal imagery, this time associated with sensuality]. Jenny also expressed the desire to go outside and walk with her bare feet on the grass.

173

Sept. 10: Pt. went to reach for another patient's Tab. Staff member told her not to take it. Pt. refused to listen and she started to open can of Tab. Staff took can out of pt.'s hand and [Jenny] hit staff in the face.

Sept 15: After [male] writer had settled back to chair on hall [Jenny] bent beside me and asked "You want to make love to me?" As I looked up at her she added "I'll pay you five dollars." She was told that wasn't my job and I'd appreciate it if she didn't ask me that again. She then walked away, put a sweater on and stated, "I don't want to make love either, I want to make war not love." With this she returned to bed.

Sept. 18: Pt. is suspected of defecating in the shower room as feces have been found after she has been in there. When confronted she denied it; also denied the need of a toilet as she "has no bowels" [another sign of her nonhuman identifications] . . . she also threatened in a quiet way to break staff's face.

Sept. 26: [Jenny] receives flowers from her mother; she cries, is very upset [she saw this as a prelude to a funeral: "You send flowers to a funeral, don't you?"]

Oct. 3: Jenny appeared to sleep well through the night. Pt. awoke at 5:30 A.M. saying she had a dream about her mother. Also said she felt like her head was chopped off.

Oct. 15: Pt. becomes very agitated towards housekeeper yelling obscenities. Anger escalated and viciously hit and scratched MHW [mental health worker]. Then tackled to the ground; also bit head nurse. . . . [Jenny was placed in seclusion, where she remained for several weeks but was constantly attended to. It was believed by staff that she was serious about her stated desire not to be alive by her birthday (mid-November). In addition, it was felt she needed the close, secure confinement of a room totally enclosing her physical self.]

Oct. 29: During recess Jenny said "I have a bleak future"; she wants to "curl up in a cubby hole and sleep . . . and there is only room for one." [During this phase Jenny spoke little and spent almost the entire day and night sleeping.]

Jenny eventually returned to the hall but was restricted, with periodic breaks, to her room. (The staff felt Jenny needed her room in the same way an infant requires a crib. It is interesting here the way language defined reality. For Jenny, "room" consciously meant "cell," "cage," "oven," or "gas chamber." However, it was the staff's belief that, unconsciously, "room" meant for Jenny "crib," "womb," "mother," and "care." In this instance the staff guessed at the content of Jenny's unconscious language-world.) She appeared to be in better spirits and stated her intention to be "in control" of herself. The nurses still regarded her with a great deal of suspicion and felt she remained suicidal. Occasionally she confided in a staff member or a special duty nurse. She drew and painted, and at rare intervals interacted with other patients. It was essentially this routine that, from the nurses' perspective, constituted her present life. Yet the entire staff believed Jenny was capable of sudden violence, and they continue to be wary of her. When she was scheduled for a review of her certification, she imagined it would be like a Perry Mason trial, with hundreds of spectators and prosecuting attorneys. If she was found guilty, she knew she would "burn in hell" and the "staff should pray for me, for my deliverance." She saw my visits as those of a defense attorney and said to me, "I don't want you for a public defender." She tried to collect money for her case by selling sunflower seeds for two cents each but no one bought them and Jenny felt she was being punished for "soliciting." She referred to the table in front of her room as the "bar of justice" and prepared for her trial, stating that she saw it as a life-or-death proposition.

Conclusion: Treatment and the Dynamics of Community

Jenny's treatment throughout her first twelve months reveals both the inner complexity of delusional systems and the "political" response implicit in her containing environment. Jenny induced political relations within staff while she continued to experience herself outside any relational context other than the delusional assumptions she maintained within herself. Jenny's psychosis precipitated argument and sometimes stiff disagreement among the staff, yet her treatment held together. And it was the staff's willingness to undertake a type of care exposing them to physical assault that kept Jenny alive, even though at crucial phases this effort went against her wishes.

Working with Jenny was thus a collective effort, with leadership roles shifting, political alliances established, and hidden messages running through suggestions and recommendations for treatment. Jenny wished for death but the staff moved toward an affirmation of life and made a sincere attempt to uncover and examine their own unconscious fantasies in treating this difficult and confounding patient. Jenny may have been dimly aware that her sickness created around her a community of interest. If she was, it may have been her only way of retrieving an idealized family lost to the dim and distorted memories of her past. This may have been the paradox that unconsciously haunted her: the fear that at some point she would be taken away from this family (what she called her 'shepherd mothers') along with her desperate, unconscious need to establish some empathic contact with it.

Delusions are like distinct systems that occupy their own time and place without connection to any linear concept of reality. Moreover, delusional systems lack "bridges" between one another. Each is completely contained within its own frame of reference. When Jenny lived in a concentration camp, the hospital *at that moment* had no existence. Each delusion functions as a part-identity wholly defined by its motivating theory of knowledge. In all existential and emotional aspects, Jenny became a concentration camp inmate. When she lived in the city "three miles underneath Sheppard/Pratt," she participated in what that city offered as life, which was usually some form of burning or gassing. In all these part-identities, Jenny was completely dependent on images that took away not only her freedom to move about but, even more importantly, her freedom to live. Her consciousness acted as tyrant.

In "democratic" psychological systems, however, consciousness may at any time be a composite of several part-identities functioning simultaneously. It is the "I" that mediates the images or identities, and each part-identity is linked to others in the self system. Not so with Jenny: she became absolutely the object dominated by a subject over which she had no control. In delusional reality, the part-identity eclipses or absorbs all other competing identities; thus when Jenny saw herself as an animal, both her physical and psychological being transformed into a beast. She was possessed by images associated with "being-as-beast," and saw herself as "meat" ready to be slaughtered "in the basement of Sheppard/ Pratt" or as an animal with claws and hooves that needed trimming. Each part-identity then contains a logic that thoroughly organizes the self's existential and psychological field. Each language field (Jenny's and the staff's) confronts the other, and neither of these worlds establishes effective communication (see table 7.2).

Benedetti captures the psychological function served by these systems:

> Most schizophrenics are so dependent upon their own autistic delusional aggressive, paranoid behavior, that their clinging to their systems and symptoms is more than a resistance, it seems to be an attempt at survival by means of organizing a last psychotic identity in the vacuum of their nonexistence. [Benedetti 1979, 35]

Further, Benedetti argues, the "psychotic world must become valuable to us as a message of human longing for personal existence" (ibid.). Or as one patient coming out of a delusional state, remarked "I have feelings, but I hadn't noticed them till now."

Jenny's treatment raises several important questions about care and the extent to which any treating environment should devote itself to maintaining life. Should she have been discharged? It is quite clear, considering her background and behavior at Sheppard, that if she had been discharged she would most likely have been dead within a month's time. Yet on any number of occasions Jenny expressed the desire to be dead. Should society have respected this wish?

Table 7.2: Jenny's Self-Contained
Delusional Systems

System 1	System 2	System 3	System 4 . . . n
Jenny in concentration camp	Jenny as cow, animal	Jenny as 4000 years old	Jenny as inhabitant of city beneath the hospital
Language world	Language world	Language world	Language world
• guards • German • confusion • ovens • gas chambers	• hooves • udders • distorted words • sense of self as freak	• already dead • weary, tiredness • claims to worldly knowledge • language and walk of an old lady	• bombs exploding • poisonings • self protection from airplanes flying overhead • everything "dark" and cold • freon coming through air vents • hell fires

Language world (psychiatrist)		Language world (nursing)	
• creation of boundaries • holding, containment • medication and compliance • efforts at consensual alliance		• public safety • mothering • keeping alive • physically maintaining • separating Jenny from more compliant patients	

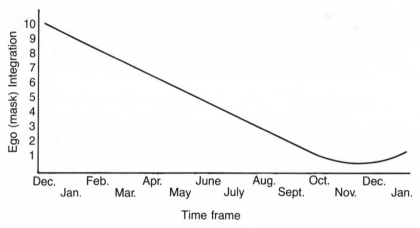

Fig. 7.1. Phases in Jenny's Delusional Life

In Jenny's case, her wish represented a conscious attempt to avoid confronting her fear of empathy. It was born out of desperation, a fear that consumed her consciousness. Why then respect a wish to die when it is the product of a tyrannical language deep within the underworld of the self? Why, by discharging her, give Jenny over to "delusion-as-executioner" when the executioner derives from an unconscious universe fueled by ongoing and powerful emotional paradoxes? Was Jenny's adult self (what there was of it) responsible for forces she has had no opportunity to overcome? Jenny's treatment at Sheppard was an effort at teaching or persuading her that her survival as a human being depended on her coming to grips with whatever delusional languages impelled her toward death.

If Jenny's course at Sheppard Pratt could be put on a graph, it might look like figure 7.1. This is necessarily a rough indication because the "ego integration" scale hardly indicates anything approaching a concept of "integration."[7] What it does suggest is Jenny's progressive failure, early in treatment, in maintaining the *illusion* of integration. Phase 1 would be the December–February period; phase 2, March through May; phase 3, mid-May through July; phase 4, August through the end of November; phase 5, December through the present (Jenny's attempt to reestablish social relations on the hall).

It should be noted that all these phases circulated around Jenny's life in

7. Yet Jenny, now eighteen months into her treatment, was beginning to show some positive movement toward integration (communication with other patients on the hall, some differentiation of her own experience, and a growing acceptance of hall routine). She was slowly emerging from her delusional cocoon and establishing contact with other human beings. While it is not at all clear that her nonhuman identification had diminished, she appeared to be less obsessed by its imagery.

Table 7.3: Psychological Stages of Delusion:
The Descent from Civility

Historical Matrix (pre-psychotic)	Regression from history (toward psychosis)
civil society language logic ⟶ rationality instrumentality	loss of civility, society transformation of language ⟶ loss of normal, logical sequences (in thought), loss of rational properties, denial of instrumental character of social exchange

State of nature as a life form (psychosis as living reality)

Hobbesian (anti-integration/ death instinct)	Rousseauian (toward integration/ life instinct)	Therapeutic reconstruction (integration/ community)
internal tyranny "war of all against all" anxiety, dread, domination ⟶ will of the stronger, killing, terror, horror	empathy compassion rudimentary intersub- jectivity ⟶ feeling of need for community, appreciation of non-hostile, consensual environments	collaboration active inter- subjectivity, rediscovery of social lan- guage forms, new apprecia- tion for forms of social life, active partic- ipation in spontaneous communities, recognition of the limita- tions of instrumental rationality, capacity to trust

a Hobbesian state of nature. If delusion can be understood as a descent from civil association, then Jenny's existence evolved around the state of nature as a form of life. Through her delusional identities and refusal of social rules, Jenny implicitly repudiated the social contract. Her fear of civil community (for whatever reasons) effectively removed her from interpersonal exchanges that might have confirmed her sense as a human being participating in a universe of common goals and values. At least since adolescence it was clear that Jenny either experienced herself on the fringes of the human community or felt herself to be completely at odds with it. This was not just teenage rebellion. In retrospect, it is clear that Jenny built an alternative world, a delusional habitat that occupied her attention and time. Civil society, political rules, and historical values all became for Jenny a realm of untruth, unreal, suspect. For Jenny, truth about experience and life lay in delusional reality. Her course, then, from adolescence to the present, has been a continuing movement away from political society, a denial of its frame of reference, and an embracing of an internality no longer populated by concrete others but rather by imaginary figures projected onto others. This world is one of killing, torment, and death.

Table 7.3 schematizes this process. It shows Jenny's movement from an existing historical matrix (in time and society), regression from these relationships and properties, and a descent into life forms that resemble the Hobbesian state of nature. In addition, the movement out of this psychotic internality depends on recovering or discovering an empathic relation with an other. It is here that certain similarities between psychosis and images in Rousseau's political theory become prominent. Leaving delusion involves a willingness to explore the different manifestations of empathy and compassion. And before any therapeutic reintegration develops, it is essential that the self establish a rudimentary intersubjectivity, an alliance whose foundations rest on empathy. This relation between empathy and the reintegration of self is the subject of the next two chapters.

eight

From Nature to Community: The Social Contract as Lived Psychological Reality

Rousseau and the Making of the Psychological Contract

Without considerable medication, outpatient treatment (such as that provided by day centers), and external support systems sensitive to their needs, it is not likely that any of the patients I spoke with at length would be able to survive for very long on the outside. Not only would they be inhibited by their delusional bases of knowledge, they would be unable to cope with the uncertainty of worlds they see as threatening, insensitive, and uncaring. I recall a session with Ted in which he related to me what it was like being outside the hospital, alone, for the first time in four years. Ted's remarks struck me because of their description of terror; it seemed to me incomprehensible that a simple bus ride down Charles Street could be a source of crippling anxiety. (Charles Street bounds the hospital, and as the major thoroughfare facing Sheppard, it leads directly from Towson to downtown Baltimore, a distance of some ten miles.) Ted called his bus ride "goin' down hard on Charles Street." It was "like being in a minefield, blindfolded, with boots ten feet wide. I felt that any minute the bus would explode. I feared for my life; at times the windows seemed to be crashing in; I wanted out; I was screaming inside; I thought we hit automobiles, embankments, that murderers were waiting in the back of the bus, ready to slit my throat."

I mention this because the simple act of riding a bus held enormous symbolic significance; it demonstrated Ted's commitment to be in the world. He proved he could survive outside the hospital, without losing control over the sources of his own inner terror. Enduring the bus ride became something like an initial compact made with society; Ted felt good, proud of himself. By staying on the bus, by not succumbing to the impulse to run or jump, he found himself intrigued by the possibilities of what that outside world held. He knew he could survive and that meant the beginning of a new life.

In view, therefore, of the demands made by the world outside the Hospital, I would like to turn to the experience of an ex-mental patient who went through a psychosis of long duration but who now functions capably in an external environment. This experience might shed some light on the making of the psychological contract, or the renewed com-

181

mitment to civil society. The more I listen to patients like Jenny or Chuck, the more convinced I am that the world they seek is not the self-seeking world of Hobbes with its possessiveness and materialism and with rationality as the "reckoning of consequences," but rather something more like the world of Rousseau's General Will, a place that offers warmth, shelter, companionship, and, most importantly, empathy. If there is any emotional need that stands out in the schizophrenic's world, it is the yearning for empathic communication. Unfortunately, this is a need that often proves to be either elusive or unattainable. Even when the most hardened ex-mental patients become attuned to the Hobbesian world "out there," there seems to be a Rousseauian yearning for community and empathy that transcends their own self-absorption and society's economic and psychological constraints.

Before his psychotic withdrawal in his mid-thirties, Frank had been a research physicist, a respected member of the scientific community. I first met him at a rundown halfway house in C., a small city in the southeastern United States. He had been living at Tenley House for several years. When I approached the residents about a series of conversations on differences between their psychotic and postpsychotic experiences, outlining my background and the reasons for my choosing Tenley House, Frank volunteered quickly and with enthusiasm. We spoke with each other weekly for a period of ten months. The subject of this chapter— what schizophrenia is, its commentary on delusion—has been distilled from Frank's reflections on the course of his own tragedy. All material facts, references, locations, and names that might in any way reveal Frank's identity have been altered. It is enough to say that the loss of Frank's intellect to the scientific community is irreplaceable. It is difficult to convey my own personal involvement in Frank's world. Listening to his description of his disintegration, of the loss of his stature in the scientific community, of the decline of his intellectual powers, of his descent into psychosis and subsequent recovery, I came away with an intense admiration for his courage and talent. Possibly some day Frank will choose to end his isolation; I hope so; he has a great deal to teach all of us.

If the making of the social contract could be suspended at precisely that moment when the self feels it essential to enter civil society, and if a neutral observer could reach inside the thoughts of Rousseau's natural man, then Frank's account of his journey into delusion and back to sanity describes what might, from a modern perspective, be called a "Rousseauist" state of mind. What developed in Frank's life over a fifteen-year period is a graphic example of a self moving away from society and toward nature, living within the withdrawn and isolated condition of nature, and then recognizing the imperative to leave nature.

Two dynamics link Rousseau's theory with Frank's experience: the opposition of the "natural" to the "social" (both criticize existing or prevailing systems) and the central importance of empathy as the fundamental psychological impulse in human nature. I would argue here that empathy and compassion perform identical emotional functions; what Rousseau calls compassion or *pitié* is an empathic response to an other. (I will return to this in greater detail in the next chapter.) Both Rousseau and Frank share an aversion to social practices that transform human relationships into instrumental action, and language into a cold calculating agent of a driving egoism.

From the outside looking in, Frank may have indeed appeared deficient in thought, memory, and language. For almost four years he refused to talk, showed signs of extreme listlessness, and seemed apathetic. But from the vantage of Frank's inner life, a great deal was happening, and his delusional world possessed extraordinarily complex intellectual structures. "Sometimes I would sit for days, doing nothing, just staring, doing enough to keep alive. I bothered no one, talked to no one and generally wandered about bumping into things." Intellectually, Frank had a demanding schedule: he constructed private languages, signs, projects, and identified with powerful historical figures both alive and dead. As a social being, Frank had become withdrawn, uncommunicative, and unkempt. He looked like Rousseau's "natural man" without the will to do anything other than sit and stare blankly into space. Yet what Frank described about this period of little or no communication with the outside world was hardly quiet: "No one ever understood what was going on inside me; I lived completely apart from other human beings; but in my mind, I accomplished all sorts of triumphs and spent hours trying to figure out numerous contradictions."

Frank's experience fell into three distinct stages: (1) withdrawal from society; (2) retreat into the "naturalism" of delusion (the psychological state of nature); and (3) return to society and the world of the social contract. What I wish to emphasize is that Frank's psychosis succeeded in stripping him of his social ego. His regression or withdrawal to nature did not impair his capacity of mind; rather, the operation of his mind continued on an entirely different plane. (Compare this with Lévi-Strauss's description of mythic "spirals" and complexities. It is not that such thought is inferior; rather, it operates according to laws, logics, and frames of reference that are, for the most part, inaccessible to scientific reason.)

Frank never lost consciousness; he never stopped thinking; instead he hid his thoughts and dissembled; he repudiated social rules and conventions; he transformed the conditions of language and wrote new laws for linguistic expression. His intellectual capacities thus were never diminished because of his regression, but he did reject a form of action he felt derived from cultural interaction and logic. He refused all social and instrumental responsibility: he would have nothing to do with money or financial transactions; he never read or showed an interest in anything other than the T.V. and radio. He had no aspirations, demonstrated no interest, pursued no hobbies. He sank utterly into "nature" and severed all connection with consensual reality. In his imaginary world, he could be as free or as powerful as he chose. "But I never shared this with anyone; it was all a secret; for all they knew I had become a vegetable. But I knew what I was; I could be Julius Caesar, Jesus Christ, Anne of Austria. It didn't matter to my keepers in the hospital; I was just another patient, staring vacantly out the window."

The contrast between nature and society, emotion and reason, embodied and unembodied reality, social communication and social confusion: all these elements ran through Frank's recollection. Table 8.1 charts the transformation from social or consensual reality to delusional nature and then back. It should be noted that the critical moment lay in an intermediary condition governing both regression and reemergence. The contract (understood as psychological connection or rejection) serves as the pivotal moment in both directions—first as withdrawal or denial of social reality, then in returning from delusion, as reciprocity and acknowledgment of a social presence.

The Descent into Psychosis: Frank's Waking Nightmare and the Puzzles of Consciousness

The following is a chronology of Frank's descent into psychosis, his time spent in psychosis, and then his transition back from delusion to consensual reality.

STAGE 1: DESCENT

Summer 1967–winter 1968: Sporadically engages people; begins to suffer intense anxiety, confusion; perceptions alter; sounds, colors change rapidly.

Winter 1968–winter 1969: Stops speaking entirely with people; goes to office but refuses any interaction or exchange; sees psychiatrist three days a week, but visits consist of "unproductive talking . . . I would relate stories that my mother told me about what it was like when I was little. I would speak as if she were speaking about me in the third person."

STAGE 2: PSYCHOSIS

Winter 1969–spring 1970: Isolation intensifies; stops going to office; sees psychiatrist; absolutely no communication with others

184

Table 8.1: Conditions governing the Psychological Contract

Withdrawal from social reality	Repudiation of psychological contract	Descent into delusional nature	Contract reestablished with society	Ego reintegration
• regression	• denial of others	• others absorbed to conditions of inner reality	• empathy toward others	• developing sense of self worth
• loss of social ego	• insensitivity to external world		• growing need for self/other dialectic	• capacity to trust
• feelings of isolation	• transforma- tion of language	• delusional constructions triumph over social ones	• impatience with isolation of nature	• acknowledge- ment of autonomy of others
• sense of impending doom	• preoccupation with internal objects	• social reason- ing gives way to non-consen- sual logics		• acceptance of depen- dency needs
• intense distrust and fear of intimacy		• development of private symbol systems		

speaks only with his psychiatrist; thoroughly separates himself from family; spends most of time in front of T.V. or listening to radio.

Spring, 1970: Admitted to Hillwood Psychiatric Hospital; sporadic communication returns but through transformed language: pronouns, adjectives, adverbs dropped; medical chart reads "words used inappropriately." For example, instead of saying "close the door" or "open the door" Frank says "do door." Frank believes, at this time, that the words "open" and "close" are dirty and should not be spoken. Language is governed by secret laws of syntax, phonetics, and grammar. Frank begins the process (which will last for almost ten years) of rewriting linguistic usage, but only in his own mind; he never shares his delusional system with anyone throughout the entire psychotic period.

Summer 1971–winter 1972: Transferred to state hospital at Grovehaven; no communication, language used sporadically, spends most of time watching T.V.

Winter 1972–summer 1973: First residency at Tenley House; very little speaking; almost no interaction with other residents; spends most of time in front of T.V.; very delusional still, but shows no sign of inner mental activity; refuses communication, bathing.

Summer 1973–winter 1975: Readmitted to Grovehaven; same pattern: no communication, language rarely used (and when used, it sounds truncated, abbreviated; to others, Frank makes little sense); T.V. occupies most of his time.

STAGE 3: PSYCHOLOGICAL CONTRACT AND REINTEGRATION INTO THE SOCIAL WORLD

Mid 1975–Fall 1981: Second residency at Tenley House; has convinced himself that he wishes to leave delusional world: "I met a woman at Grovehaven that I liked; I decided I would organize a play and have her star in it; that's when I realized I had to speak normally and communicate with people; if I didn't do that, this woman would be unable to star in my play. At that moment I realized I no longer wanted to be psychotic." Frank slowly emerges from his cocoon during last months at Grovehaven; he develops some friendships and relationships; language takes on increasingly normal patterns; he begins to bathe and care for himself without incessant urging from staff; this pattern continues at Tenley House.

Spring 1981–Winter 1981: Again refuses to bathe; emotionally withdraws; begins speaking incoherently and then stops speaking altogether; staff feels uneasy; thinks Frank is slipping back; Frank is readmitted to Grovehaven. Frank feels staff overreacts

186

to what he believes are minor issues that could have been resolved quickly. Is rehospitalized in winter 1981.

Spring 1981–present: Frank returns to Tenley House; follows
house rules, bathes regularly; resumes completely normal use of
language; wishes to leave psychotic world behind; makes tentative efforts at establishing relationships outside Tenley House in
the community; does volunteer work at a local nursing home.

I would now like to turn to a detailed examination in Frank's own
description of each of these stages. It should be noted that the conversations were not as orderly as they now appear—Frank would often go back
and forth from what it was like to be psychotic to his experience of the
postpsychotic world in any given conversation. I have found it necessary,
therefore, to piece together his story and to give it structure in terms of
the chronology given above. The one and only time I used a tape recorder, Frank became nervous early in the interview. Its presence was
obviously interfering with the conversation (even though Frank told me
the recorder presented no problems) and I shut it off. He had no objection to my using a notepad as we talked. I took down verbatim (with some
help from a personal shorthand) his feelings and perceptions and then
transcribed the dialogues after each session.

First, some brief biographical information about Frank is in order.
Frank was the eldest child in a family of four; his father died in 1969, his
mother in 1975; he has a brother and sister, both living. Each has been in
and out of mental hospitals, although their illnesses are not as incapacitating nor have they had such a devastating effect as Frank's. Born in
1930, Frank grew up in a small southern town; his parents, Baptist
fundamentalists, led a conventional, middle-class life. His father published technical journals for a number of small local companies; his
mother taught kindergarten at a local grammar school. Frank attended
public schools, went to a large state university and, received his Ph.D. in
physics in his mid-twenties. He spent a few years teaching at a prestigious
private university in the east. Shortly after receiving tenure (after four
years of teaching), he returned to the West Coast to take up a position as
research scientist in the physics department at State University.

Frank recalled that his childhood was filled with injunctions against
sex: "my parents hated sex and all functions having to do with pleasure in
the body; I don't remember having ever seen them kiss each other." He
was constantly scolded about dirtiness and warned about all the different
ways a child could be contaminated. His parents believed children to
harbor "original sin," a defect that could only be combated through
rigorous moral training. Sin for these deeply devout people meant having
"uncontrollable sexual thoughts . . . I felt my parents wanted me killed
for my sexual thoughts. Every night before bed I saw my father coming

187

into the room and slicing at my genitals for retribution against the evil inside me." Frank recalled having this fear as early as five or six. Sexual contact polluted the body and brought decay to the spirit. It was a sign of having been possessed by the devil, of having fallen victim to "Satan's claws":

> My father used to tell us when we were sick or came down with a cold or the flu that our feeling bad was a sign of having committed a sin, a terrible lapse that would haunt us for the rest of our life. He instilled such a fear of sex in us as children that when I entered puberty, I actually believed that if I lusted after a girl or felt sexual desire, I would be isolated, killed or banished from mankind for my thoughts. I used to fantasize in church during those years that all the Elders could read my thoughts and knew what I felt; that the last thing I was thinking about was God. And they wanted me dead for my sexual thoughts; if they could have, they would have skewered me up the middle and hung me from the altar. It was grotesque.
>
> I think my father had a real hatred for women; he certainly felt they were inferior; I know he hated sex. He would say things like "Women don't know how to think" or "Woman's duty is to bear children and cook and sew." He even thought his children inferior species of human beings, and I remember him constantly telling us how we would never amount to anything, how he thought we had been born wicked. When I'm psychotic I frequently experience myself having a female psyche, as if I were a bottomless bucket, receiving all this evil wickedness into myself. I keep hearing my father's voice screaming at me "Women are no good and dumb . . . creatures hardly higher than an animal!" But my father hated everyone.

Father and son related with a cool formality, which permitted little affection. In the last ten years of his life, Frank's father became a recluse, rarely leaving his room or communicating with either his wife or children. Nothing much was said during this last decade and Frank seemed rather relieved when this "master lawgiver" died (although I find it doubtful that his father's radical rejection left Frank completely undisturbed; it is true though that Frank described his father as tyrannical, unpleasant, and thoroughly unlovable). The following entry in Hillwood's psychiatric chart is revealing:[1]

> In the winter of 1969–70 [Frank's] father died. The informants stated that he showed no emotion to this, and said words to the effect that a good boy was equal to death and there was no need for any kind of feeling. Mrs. D. [Frank's sister] said that she would not have expected any kind of emotion anyway.

1. Frank signed a release granting me access to his records at Hillwood; all quotations from his psychiatric chart are from the period 1970–71.

Frank continued:

I was never free to say what I thought; my father always used to tell me, don't masturbate, it will ruin your heart. He had funny little names for the genitals. He called them "river places" and used to refer to sex as "docking." You'd have to go and find your "river place" in order to "dock." What a strange man! He gradually decided that all people, not only his children, were filthy and he didn't want anything to do with them. After he retired and started locking himself up in his room, he refused to see me or even acknowledge my presence . . . he wouldn't talk. I suppose he thought everyone was filthy and by not speaking, he protected himself from the germs of human life.

I remember there was an enormous amount of constipation in my family. We all had to move our bowels regularly; father would dictate to us when to take bowel movements, in what order, who was to go first, how long they were to take. He stood by the bathroom door with a stopwatch. Everyone had to swallow laxatives, or he shoved them into the anus. It was a rule of the house. Father called the anus the "bad place" and if we were bad, he would take us to the "bad place" and flush us away to "hell." To this day the concept of hell and anus are tied together. . . . Every time I go to the toilet I think the demons of hell will leap out of the commode. Each of us had a different laxative; father tried them all; we had ours marked on the bathroom cabinet shelf, all kinds: epsom salts, castor oil, special potions father would buy at the drugstore, Ex-Lax, vile-tasting concoctions put together by the druggist. Awful stuff. . . .

And my mother constantly hovered about, nervously watching, stern-eyed, warning us against our bodies.[2] If she saw me touching myself, she would rap my hands, hard; that sure cured me of the habit. She kept a close eye on my sister, brother, and myself; she insisted we sit on the toilet twice a day, timing us, standing sentry outside the door. Playing with ourselves had to be the highest sin we could commit as kids; and it was simply no fun breaking those rules. Mother had about her a coldness, a

2. The picture in the psychiatric history is of a woman demonstrating a very strict conception of morality and right:

The patient's mother is presently a retired school teacher at _____. She is described by informants as a "bossy school teacher" who was intellectually stimulating her children to read and investigate, but who was very strict and rigid morally. The patient describes her as being very detailed, scheduled, disagreeable, very serious, rigid, but had difficulty in describing her in any kind of personalized manner. He said that he "guessed" that he liked her, but was not really very close. He quibbled greatly about the word "close." The religion of the family was fundamentalist Baptist. His mother was reported to have been very rigid in her moral teachings. [From psychiatric records at Hillwood.]

chill that frightened me. She never took any joy in her kids, never liked to hug us; there was no such thing as a physical caress. I really can't remember who was more distant, mother or father; each, though, felt that love had to do with rules, regulations, and injunctions to do this or that.

I do remember wanting my father to be free of my mother although they both were horrible. And I would make little jokes sniping at my mother, things like "Daddy go see a woman" or "Daddy swallow mama and mama go away." I think he was afraid of her, that rigidity. She was so orderly, neat, and hated sex. She told me once that if you had pleasure in sex, that was a sign of your basic degeneracy. To like sex in her view you had to be filthy. She coped through rules, etiquette, formality, and logic. She did everything right: rules for eating, shitting, going to church, being outside or inside. I think her rules were a way of regulating behavior towards others in order to make them safe from sex. If she could make everyone fit her mold, if she could protect them from the lurking filth, then, as long as she was around, nobody would have filthy (which of course meant sexy) thoughts.

My wife used to speak to me about sex as her "wifely duty"; I suppose my mother's attitude must have been identical. Both were of the same frame of mind. Thinking back on it, it's amazing how frightened both mother and father were of anything alien or foreign to their concept of absolute cleanliness. Even at dinner, the issue of how to eat properly or how to put the fork in the mouth or cut the food, constantly came up; that's about all we ever talked about at dinner, if we talked at all. Our parents forbade us to eat off each other's plates; we couldn't pick food up with our fingers; if we touched each other during dinner they said we would be contaminated and go to hell for our filthiness. Satan always sat behind us, ready to pounce if we so much as dropped a pea. To this day, I find it impossible to see any pleasure at all in eating or food. We had to wash our hands before and after dinner; we couldn't laugh or speak unless spoken to, at meals. We weren't allowed to be messy . . . it was horrible.

I married in my early twenties; it seemed the thing to do, to get married; and in the early days I suppose I loved my wife. She provided me with a sexual outlet, but it was purely functional. She never enjoyed it; it was like a chore. And she did it to please me and bear children. I never paid much attention to the kids [a boy and a girl]. I did all the things a father should do: played catch, bounced the kids on my knee, took them to a baseball game or two. We went on picnics. But my mind, even then, was elsewhere; it's not that I didn't love them, but the thoughts inside my head would crowd out my concern for the kids.

By the time Frank took up his appointment at State, his life at home could hardly be considered normal. He rarely spoke to his children or wife; he kept a menagerie of animals in stalls around the house. The rooms reeked of uncollected feces; clothes, books, and papers were strewn about. And his wife, dutifully following his lead, refused to clean up or make an attempt to have Frank change his habits. He never spoke much about his wife and little information about her appears in the psychiatric records. What does come out is a picture of a rather nondescript woman without much will of her own. They divorced shortly after Frank was admitted to Hillwood in 1970.

State allowed Frank a permissiveness that had been central to his fantasies: "When I was a teenager I used to think, particularly in church, how exciting it would be if all the elders were somehow killed and the young people would then be free to have sexual orgies." The university served as a surrogate family, but unlike Frank's childhood environment, at State all was permitted. With its intellectually free and emotionally stimulating environment, the university became a haven for Frank, the inspiration for innumerable fantasies, in addition to providing opportunities for extensive socializing, the sharing of thoughts and plans, serious collective research, and untrammeled communication and exchange. State had about it the quality of utopia: in its limitlessness and the shared joy of messing things up, it appeared to be the opposite of the antiseptic, repressed world of Frank's upbringing. Yet, as he put it, "I never was comfortable at State; it was too free, too much for me; it was like being in a candy store. I tried to eat too much; my explorations, at least in my fantasies, got out of hand."

State intensified the pressure and anxiety Frank felt. He never felt safe, nor did he have a firm sense of boundary between self and other. The more he immersed himself in State's permissive atmosphere, the more he suffered from painful and incapacitating guilt. The appearance he presented to friends and colleagues began to disintegrate, and Frank found himself surrounded by a haze of doubt:

> I would often awake in the middle of the night with this horrible pain in my head; I felt I was about to die. I didn't tell anyone; I just would slink downstairs and let it pass. At first, I felt this fear after a peculiarly excruciating nightmare. Later, though, it would come during the day at work or driving home. I would be inside a dense fog, even though it was bright outside, not a cloud in the sky. It was unbearable and confusing.

Frank's fragile connection with reality slowly gave way under the weight of his depression and anxiety. Friends disappeared; he stopped reading and talking. His interest in scientific experiments ran to the bizarre; he spoke about things that brought ridicule from his colleagues; his work had little usefulness. He felt as if he had been abandoned, as though the world ignored his projects and concepts. He became preoccupied with his inner thoughts: "I didn't know myself anymore. My imagination, the thoughts rushing through my head had more value to me than anything outside. Work, family, friends, my kids, all were incidental to the puzzles I was working on."

For Frank this was a period of emotional disintegration, withdrawal from the external world, and movement inward. Again, I quote from his psychiatric records:

> The patient continued to not attend work [1969–70]; immediately prior to first hospitalization at Hillwood, [Frank] stayed at home watching television, playing with the family menagerie of animals, and paying very little attention to his own personal hygiene or the upkeep of his home. His car was repossessed in August and he was evicted from his home in the middle of September. It was at this time that Dr. L. [Frank] began to wander the streets in Central City and was picked up by the police and eventually hospitalized at Hillwood. . . . His colleagues noted at this time also that he became very much more self-centered and spent a great deal of time writing an ostensibly scientific paper on "the nature of words and reality." This paper was thought to be somewhat indicative of his difficulty with language and communicating with other people.

I would like for a moment to look at some of Frank's reflections in his scientific paper; it provides additional evidence of an increasing detachment from social and linguistic frames of reference. It also demonstrates his growing commitment to the reliability of the hidden, inner, secret meanings bracketing "reality." (The paper had been xeroxed in its entirety and placed in Frank's psychiatric records at Hillwood.[3])

It begins with an argument for the uncertainty of external points of reference: "There is no reason for believing in the existence of an unobservable like an external world, and therefore my mind, cluttered with surprisingly uncooperative images, is my only reality." He recognizes what such beliefs imply for relationships: "This view may have its compensations but it is a lonely one. . . . It is clear that avoiding the idea of an external world is desirable." Knowledge in turn reinforces feelings of isolation: "one lives in a world of mere images, shared with no one [Frank's sense of himself as alone and abandoned] and connected with some colorless, rushing reality [his inner thoughts becoming uncontrollable]." Being subject to such thoughts "seriously reduces one's interest in one's [external] surroundings."

Frank never lost his linguistic capacity; rather, it shifted to a different plane. He transformed the functions of language and held all linguistic

---

3. I never talked with Frank about the essay or its arguments; he seemed disinclined to do so, and had difficulty even remembering what he had written. My observations then amount to speculation, but I believe them to be consistent with Frank's state of mind at the time.

attributions (and the power he saw in them) inside. He called this kind of thinking "silent":

> Mind is here defined as an organ of thought, and thinking has meant to me the meaningful production of words, *but so softly that only I could hear them.* I experience these silent words as *freely arising inside my head out of nothing*, but they are suf-ficiently under my control that I feel that I am thinking them. [Italics added.]

Utterance requires no listener who is separate from the self; both speaking and listening remain hidden within the self. Words take on properties distinct from their use in social language: "Silent talking is located in the middle of my head because I perceive it not to be located outside and so place it inside and midway between my ears." But the silent voice speaks; it possesses an audience in Frank's consciousness. If he is able both to speak and to listen to himself, it is not imperative that there be an external audience: "If this silent voice is what is meant by thinking then the organs of it are speech and hearing organs." Speech remains invisible; it lacks a historical or intersubjective context; its reality appears in its delineation of the present: "If the word consists of percep-tions here and now, one needs no more." As Frank moved closer to psychosis, language became less and less important as an activity orient-ing the self to both history and the other. It no longer served to link generations (recall that Frank stopped speaking to his children), and related to reality only as a projection of an inner, hidden "will."

Revealing and intriguing observations periodically show up in the essay. Some are more accessible than others, since during this stage Frank's analytic or social ego was disintegrating in direct proportion to the increasing importance of internal images and objects: "It has been noticed by many people that the rigid grammar of Indoeuropean lan-guage has grown up with a world view, and corresponds to the idea that the world is made up of *property laden things which act.* Plato is a spectacular case of someone discovering a noun" (emphasis added).

When Frank writes about "property laden things which act," he is referring to the "action" of money and to the connection and inter-dependency between the development of language and money. Frank believed money to be a pollutant, and while at Hillwood he refused to have anything to do with bills, finance, or payments (part of the reason why he was transferred to the state hospital at Grovehaven). For him even touching money meant committing a horrendous sin, and he in-tended to avoid such contamination at all costs. But what is really interesting here is the Rousseauian assumption that the world view of Indoeuropean language might have something to do with property. It is an argument that could have been taken directly from the *Second Dis-*

course (and *The Origin of Languages*), where Rousseau attacks the coldness and instrumentality of languages deriving from economic necessity and social complexity. It is this relation that erodes the virtuousness and innocence of the original language of nature:

> To the degree that needs multiply, that affairs become complicated, that light is shed, language changes its character. It becomes more regular and less passionate. It substitutes ideas for feelings. It no longer speaks to the heart but to reason. Similarly accent diminishes, articulation increases. Language becomes more exact and clearer, but more prolix, duller and colder.
> [Rousseau 1966, 16]

Rousseauist assumptions dominated Frank's attitude toward money and property; he criticized egoistic motives; he exhibited an impatience with instrumentalism; he refused to participate in social rituals built around property or vanity; he scorned social (and what he saw as decadent) concepts of value and choice. Even Frank's delusional use of language was dysfunctional with regard to the egoistic or "property-laden" world. He avoided all pronouns, including any reference to the accumulating instrumental "I." The possessive self disappeared altogether.

And for the comment about Plato discovering a noun, given Frank's fascination with language, he might have been intrigued by the way Plato encloses reality with the power of words, the "I" as supreme and magical creator of a world through language (Socrates' city of speech). Plato uses words against the prevailing order; his system of organizing the world represents an imaginative act. For example, in *The Republic* he repudiates the power of money and property as a foundation for meaning. It is this kind of "I" that intrigued Frank, not the possessive I or self, but the I of words, language, and the ability to encircle or capture through a magic inherent in inner voices and inspirations. Frank then may have been identifying with the sheer will of Plato's linguistic "I", a self that masters words so completely that nothing else matters as evidence for reality.

Finally, Frank speaks of the "preestablished harmony between the world and mathematics"; he distrusts the messiness of experience, the imperfection of any world that refuses to yield to perfect form and structure. He also shows signs of identifying with an omnipotence that, in his delusional state, he attaches to the capacity of language to construct the world:

> I will become more famous than Newton and my ideas will become permanent verbal habits of all mankind. The disparity between this hope and the material I actually produce leads me to disparage the work of others, which denies me the chance to freely try it as raw material for my own creative activity.

Because he treats being "more famous than Newton" as a hope, Frank remains somewhat limited by reality. And while he laments that his looking down on the work of others inhibits his own creative activity, it is clear he embraces an assertion of omnipotence and grandiosity dependent on the power of his inner language and a logic he conceives to be perfect. Not completely out of touch, he knows he harbors a secret, that what *he* believes, the world might not. And if he expresses this knowledge too publicly or strongly, he might find himself estranged from others: "And sometimes when I am not painfully discreet these ideas lead to unsatisfying human relations."

In its preoccupation with inner and outer, with the power of language and its autonomous inner sources, the essay describes a consciousness denying contact, becoming further alienated from external objects. Frank dimly understood this process, but he demonstrated more affinity with the "silent talking" than any language rooted in consensual reality. Emotionally, however, it was a devastating experience. Again, I turn to Frank's own reflections:

> At about that time, I became highly suggestible, particularly whenever anyone talked about themes of abandonment or separation. I thought that I should learn from other people, but I found it difficult. I had trouble sharing other points of view. I locked myself out from other worlds, and my inner thoughts became much more important than what happened outside. I started to build my fantasy world. I did sense a need for others, but whenever I wanted to cry out for help, it was impossible. I could hear screams, they seemed to be my own. I groped around; no one could understand; my screams got lost in the hollows of my mind, and I kept seeing darkness. People I guess were concerned; it's hard for me to recall that period, but I seem to remember telling my wife and children, and whatever friends showed up, to go away and leave me alone.
>
> I refused to clean anything up; my wife lost all interest in the house; we stopped making payments. We lived in a zoo, animals were everywhere, it was filthy, a real mess. It must have smelled horrible. I could be disturbed or upset by anything, a word from my wife, the kids demanding attention. Naturally I stopped having sex with my wife; my family intruded on me; they wanted me out of my inner world; I of course wanted to stay there. Sometimes I thought they were enemies who had come to kill me. But I did have my anger, my fantasies, my ability to create a world through language. It was then that I started to speak with extensions of myself, a kind of mental telepathy.
>
> I began to sense myself as an isolated being in the midst of faceless multitudes; it took on the character of an obsession. I was anonymous, a piece of sand, a speck, invisible, lost in a gigantic multitude. I identified with an Australian aborigine who

195

had been the subject of a T.V. show dealing with the impact of civilization on primitive tribes. I had become like him a primitive, a lost soul in the midst of an alien civilization. Both of us, the aborigine and myself, had to fight a society seeking to move us in a direction opposite from the one we wanted. We were partners in this solitude, victims of a world that refused to understand our needs and desires. We were being denied our primitiveness; we spoke in different languages; we had habits that civilization abhorred.

It was then I became convinced that by being clean I drove people away; if I were dirty, my true nature would be released and people would flock to me. Dirt would increase my sexual attractiveness, and if I were allowed to be in my natural habitat, without bathing, my sexual powers would be enhanced and women would find me irresistible. I could only be loved if I were dirty! To me, then, being dirty and not bathing would be a sign of my primitiveness; it was another way of establishing an identity with the Australian aborigine.

I was full of rage; if I weren't raging, I would panic. There seemed to be no intermediate state; I thought everyone was abandoning me, turning against me. People vanished; my fear intensified; I could hardly control myself; the entire social system was rejecting me. The longer I thought about things like this, the more convinced I became of my likeness to that aborigine, to the lost soul being killed by an unsympathetic world. Soon there would be nothing left; I would be, like the aborigine, naked in the midst of hostile languages and customs. Later on, at Hillwood and Grovehaven, I was forced to bathe; it curbed my rebelliousness; it coerced me into being someone I didn't want to be. I resented that regulation; it made me less primitive; bathing became a trap. I think I must have felt like Samson when Delilah cut off all his hair.

I spent days in my office, staring at the walls, seething with rage, refusing to talk with anyone. The anxiety got worse. I tried to figure things out, but nothing worked. Time played funny tricks on me and I found myself floating backwards, away from everyone and everything that had been important in my life.

I asked Frank if during this time he ever felt suicidal, so desperate that he seriously thought about suicide as a realistic choice:

> I never really gave it much thought. Certainly not while I was psychotic. I had too much to do. Thinking about suicide occurs in an intermediate state, somewhere between being normal and delusional. Too much is going on in psychosis; thoughts fly through my head; I never really had the time to focus on suicide as a plan. I'm sure it must have been in and out of my mind, but never long enough to become an obsession. In my last year at

Grovehaven, I had a suicidal thought that hung around for a time. I kept reciting a line from a poem, "here he lies where he longs to be." And I thought how nice it would be if a mugger shot me through the head with a forty-four magnum. The thought didn't depress me; I just found it curious, almost like an experiment.

I remember having a dream that sums up that stage in my life. I was on a raft, screaming, watching the crowds on the beach. They all wanted to jump in and pull me back. But I kept yelling, "Stay there; I hate all of you! Let me drift away." I started referring to myself in the third person, but only from the point of view of what my mother had said about me when I was a little boy. I would talk about "me" as if it were my mother referring to little Frank. And this only to my shrink. I would say things like, "Wasn't it nice she had a little boy to pick up the toys" or "How good of him to move his bowels," or "What a naughty boy he was for getting dirty." I spoke this way for two years and then stopped speaking entirely.

These were very intense times; I recall an incident typical of where I was heading. It was one morning, at the office, I became enraged at a colleague; the reason escapes me, but I ran out into the woods, behind the university, convinced that I had to stay there until I figured out the truth. My anger felt like it was pulling my arms off; it was painful, almost unbearable; and I spent that first day screaming to myself. My body felt as rigid as a tree trunk; the anger strained at it; I thought I would explode.

I made it through the first night, yet I hadn't found any solutions. The second day the anger subsided somewhat and I began to think. I thought about all those old Tarzan stories, apes in the trees, Jane clinging to Tarzan. Tarzan and I had become partners in conquering the animals of the forest. Both of us were outcasts; searching for something in these primitive retreats.

I could feel strength coming back into my arms; I knew I should forage for food, and nature seemed very close to me. For the first time I felt connected to something larger than myself; Tarzan's presence, even if it were only in my imagination, made me feel secure. And it convinced me that I could be as strong as he. From that point on, my perception cleared, and the world began to rearrange itself. Tarzan, myself, the lost aborigine, primitive spirits, all of us spoke with each other, a telepathy that went through time and space. We found ourselves together in a gigantic family. I was no longer alone. I had finally found myself and my power seemed to be growing in leaps and bounds. The forest and my new company cooled off my anger; I discovered I no longer needed other people to know me, to bring peace and certainty. I knew where I wanted to be, and it wasn't at home or in the office. I needed to be hidden from civilization, away from everything but the signs of my new found strength in nature. In the forest, I could be free in my silent, hidden images. I could speak with whatever faces I saw; my telepathy was limitless; I could avoid the hostile glances of those who seemed disturbed by my presence.

On the third day I felt a tingling collapse; something terrible had happened; the safety of the previous day disappeared; thoughts flew through my head. . . very fast. . . I had no control over anything; and the last thing I wanted was to return to my home, to civilization. But something impelled me back; I don't know what it was, maybe guilt, or deep down I knew I had to physically survive. And if I stayed in that forest much longer, I could hurt myself. But I came back with the knowledge that the world "out there" had nothing for me. I wanted no part of it. And when I wandered about late that night in the city, I felt a strange kinship with that Australian aborigine who when cut off from his tribe slowly withered away and died.

I knew I had to return; I never felt so desolate in my life. All my talking, my screaming, was silent; I decided not to acknowledge "their" civilization in language, and in my muteness I would be free of them. I would confound everyone; I would be invisible to them, since they had become invisible to me. It would be a signal of my rage, my anger. It would demonstrate my resolve to cut off all ties. My telepathic communication with the aborigines, with Tarzan, confirmed this. Each of us were bound into this pact of resistance to civilization; each of us would survive in his own way. Nothing remained in the world I had known. From then on, my inner life, what my delusions told me about truth, absorbed everything. It was in that state, very late the evening of the third day, that I was picked up by the police and taken to Hillwood.

Delusional Reality: The Lived World of Psychosis

Frank seemed unconcerned about being committed to Hillwood; he had cut himself off from civilization. He could be free, and it made little difference where. If he had been on his own, he might have hurt himself, either through starvation (he refused to eat during this period) or exposure. Frank needed to be contained, held:

> I began to construct reality; the radio and T.V. sent messages; my telepathic field increased considerably; I began to mediate international and political conflict, conducting dialogues with world leaders, accomplishing tremendous feats of strength, traveling with extensions of myself all over the world. Everything presented itself with new forms, shapes, and knowledge. It was not like the days in the forest, the sadness and despair. All of that seemed a remote past I barely remembered. I had finally found

198

my niche; I was no longer isolated or alone. My delusions kept me company and provided me a great deal of work. After all, I lay at the center of everything. I developed my own language by dropping pronouns, changing around syntax, consonants, and vowels. I devised a phonetics that allowed me to transform and alter words on the basis of similar sounds. Since I knew the secret words and logics that made events appear and disappear, I held the secrets to nature and its transformations; if I spoke certain words at the right time, I could do what I wanted or exercise control or give advice to the influential and powerful. I did avoid words I felt were dirty, not the normal dirty words. But words like "open," "close," "shut," "toilet" and so on had pornographic meanings for me. I found them unvirtuous and filthy. For example, instead of saying "open the door" I would say "do door."

Several themes preoccupied Frank in the hospital: he became "Rasputin" or a "descendant" of Rasputin, who Frank believed "had been the real architect behind the Russian revolution." He saw himself reincarnated as different historical figures:

I had a terrific time being Henry the VIII, Anne of Austria, Ivan the Terrible. . . these incarnations made me powerful. . . . At times I thought I was Julius Caesar or Jesus Christ brought back from the dead. I inherited Caesar's capacity to act in opposition to massive organizations. Why should Caesar have to obey Hillwood's staff? Shouldn't the staff and patients defer to and respect such a great leader? Like Caesar, I did what I pleased; I refused to obey hospital regulations (I too could rebel against organizations). I wouldn't cooperate or do my chores. I needed to stand out as a rebel, a figure powerful enough to resist the social implementation of rules. Rules couldn't compare in importance to the action of my delusional incarnations. Why should I, Ivan, or Caesar acknowledge petty rules? My telepathic communication extended all over the world; I controlled thousands of transmissions, I had become too important to be bothered by trivia. In my world, then, I could do anything; my power had no bounds; all the delusions had this element of control about them, acting on my own, setting up schemes, arbitrating international disputes, engaging in telepathic sex, creating world shaking events out of nothing. It was at times exhilarating; at other times, I felt overwhelmed, the feeling that there is too much to do, exhaustion over all my "responsibilities" in supporting my far-flung projects.

Frank convinced himself that psychosis made the self perfect, and since mathematics projected an illusion of perfection, he built his delusional universe on what he conceived to be mathematical or logical premises.

His rules for words and their transformations may have appeared to Frank to have been mathematical, but as we shall see, the logic, while decipherable, had about it a magical rather than rational quality. While his reasoning was ingenious and playful, it could hardly be considered rigorous.

Frank's delusions, with their often esoteric or religious imagery, depended on a kind of whimsical logic. Rules were invented when needed; letters changed according to specific aspects of any delusion. There was, however, a core of rules that allowed Frank considerable leeway in his manipulation of words. It was not difficult for him to believe he had indeed tapped into a magical reservoir of meaning which he completely dominated. "I was processing ellipses," he commented, "the ellipse was perfection; I could control the orderly unfolding of events through this perfection." Mathematics was perfection; imperfection, though, meant people and emotions (i.e., threatening traps). And mathematics was powerless against the imperfection of human need and failure. Delusion provided the perfect escape:

> By being the head of the Russian government I was perfect; I could do anything. But from the outside looking in, I was weak and helpless; after all I was in a mental hospital. I didn't like to eat; I couldn't take care of myself. By reaching perfection, I could let the real world bother itself with my physical welfare. They would bathe me, feed me if necessary, keep me from killing myself; if I were free of those earthly chores, I could be anywhere I chose in my delusional stratosphere. Or maybe it was a way of saying, "Look, I'm in trouble, notice me, take care of me." It's a terrible position to be in because it means, on the one hand, that you're so completely alone in the world. Yet you find yourself traveling so quickly through a thousand different delusions, you simply haven't the time to recognize or accept or even acknowledge how isolated you really are. . . . As long as I flew lightning fast through my inner world, I could avoid sitting down and reflecting on what it meant to be a patient in a mental hospital. I had too much to do being Rasputin, or Caesar, or keeping track of my telepathic communications. Who needed to be depressed?
>
> Yet every once in a while I came back to earth and grasped something of what had happened. The traps would jump up and slap me right across the face. It's like when you were a kid, your parents had gone out for the evening. The night's cold and windy; it's late; you're in bed, safe, protected under the covers. Yet you decide, lifting the heavy blankets, to peek out, just to check that everything's still there. But the emptiness and fear outside the sheets is so terrifying it forces you right back down to the safety of Grandma's two-hundred-year-old quilt. Being alone with your thoughts, thinking up exciting but congenial things, is

far more comforting than dealing with the dark and chill in a room where all kinds of dreadful people-monsters might be lurking about.

Whenever I sensed my helplessness or took a glimpse at how serious things actually were, I escaped right back to the delusions. Because to be in the real world meant having to cope with imperfection. I couldn't stand that idea; imperfection comes from people's desires; and those desires scared the hell out of me. Being delusional removed the terror, the fear of imperfection, the fright generated by my own needs and the pathetic person I had become. . . . It's like finding yourself battered about on the fringes of a storm, feeling the wind, the shifts of the sea. Delusion takes you out of the storm; it flings you into the eye, where it's calm, but a deceptive calm. For me to know myself as the head of the Russian government was like being in the eye of the storm, perfectly contained. No one could harm this powerful and alone "me."

The Magic of Words: Delusional Identity and Linguistic Transformations

Since in this inner world, Frank was unaffected by contact with other human beings, he could experience himself as whole. It was his only refuge, his lived reality. Who he was, his sense of self and identity, could only be what was alive in the delusional universe, and much of this identity rested on the magical power of words.

Table 8.2 describes the relationship between consensual and delusional reality as a transformation in the self's concept of a linguistic identity. In consensual reality, the instrumental character of language, although it contributes to identity, is only one aspect of an intricate process that gives consciousness an image of what it is in the world. Merely to utter something is not to become it; language is capable of holding meanings at a distance, describing the past, providing bridges. It is different in the delusional world: to speak a word means to construct the world in the image of that word. Puns, word games, symbols: Frank employed them all to build his identities. He told me he had developed hundreds of identities or delusions (since each delusion represented a specific commentary on identity). He described in some detail three of these systems, although, as he put it, "these were only examples of the minor ones." What Frank considered to be truly complex systems he found difficult to remember (even after my urging) or he thought I would find them so bizarre he refused to tell me what they were. But the following psychological episodes—"The 1980 Election," "The Beast of Revelation," and "Welcome Back Kotter" are typical of how Frank constructed reality through his "silent talking."

Table 8.2: Movement from Consensual to Psychotic Communication

Consensual language	Elements of transformational logics (in movement from consensual to delusional nature)	Delusional "talking"
• use of language as instrument	• use of puns	• language as lived identity
• acceptance of social meanings	• peculiar phrases and symbol construction	• private symbols systems negating consensual meanings
• acceptance of common and shared symbol systems	• growing gap between public and private meanings attached to words	• delusional interpretations at complete variance with "normality"
		• autonomy (and hermeticism) of inner life absolute
		• "The 1980 Election"
		• "The Beast of Revelation"
		• "Welcome Back Kotter"

The 1980 Election

During the 1980 election, I became responsible for the behavior of the federal government. I believed I was responsible for the cutbacks, the diminishing of services, the assault on the bureaucracy. I saw the arms buildup, the race between the Russians and Americans, as a political event requiring my mediation. I even felt that the Russians had designated me their negotiator at all arms conferences. I stood at the heart of the Arab/Israeli conflict, charged with a conflict-resolving mission. I felt it essential to reinterpret everything the American government said, in addition to locating within the statements of various world leaders what they really intended to say. A great deal rested on my reinterpretations. I conviced myself that the fate of the world depended on my power to resolve competing and contradictory positions. It was, now in retrospect, obviously a commentary on myself and what I needed as a person.

I received the raw material for my interpretations from television, since coded messages would be sent through the evening news. I took what I heard, reinterpreted it, and came out with what actually was being transmitted. Harry Reasoner and the "NBC Nightly News Broadcast" served as my conduit for the 1980 election plans. It was my mission to undermine a conspiracy set up by Reasoner and the American military; they intended to wrest control of arms negotiations from civilian authority and wreck any possibility of reconciliation with the Russians. I had to act and solve this problem as quickly as possible.

Now, as spokesman for the military establishment, Reasoner had the power to send signals all over the world, to its agents and representatives. No one else knew that his real function on the news lay in conveying information and engaging in this conspiracy. I listened to Reasoner's comments, deciphered them, reinterpreted his views, and through my words, changed not only his content, but the position of the American Generals. Simply by recasting his language, I became more powerful than either Reasoner or the generals.

In this way, I opposed the military and, telepathically, sent my conclusions and recommendations to the president. I had therefore become more powerful than the military and now was in a position to initiate lasting negotiations on arms reductions. My words provided me with access to power and control; I frustrated the military at every turn. If Reasoner reported the military wanted to develop the MX missile system, I took it to mean that the president needed my commentary. I contacted Carter through my telepathic code, told him what was happening. He "sent" back, agreeing with me, assuring me he would contact the military immediately.

It developed into a quite complex set of exchanges. At times I spoke simultaneously with the secretaries of state, defense, the director of the CIA. If Reasoner had referred to an official "testifying on the hill," that meant I had been summoned to "high" places for an urgent conference. Every night I found myself called upon to respond to a different plot or policy hatched from his broadcast. My interventions lasted for several months.

I discovered this power through a simple word game; it was really a thought whose truth suddenly hit me. I put together two ideas. First I took Plato's maxim "Knowledge is power" and joined it with the Socratic command "Know thyself." Power then meant to have knowledge about yourself. But power corrupts and Acton's phrase came to mind, "Absolute power corrupts absolutely." I dwelled on this for some time, trying to figure out the relation between knowledge, power, and corruption. It was really very simple: to know yourself (having knowledge) gives you the power to corrupt. And the key to knowing yourself lies in words; if, then, I could locate myself in the words I used, if I could find out who I was in those words, I could then be myself. And if I were myself I could have power; and if I had power, I could corrupt. . . very logical! By knowing myself, by controlling language (since language held all knowledge), not only could I gain power, I would also be able to corrupt, subvert, or erode from within. That power enabled me to intervene in any political situation and "corrupt" or otherwise bring apart whatever I had to do to reach my ends. To know thyself is to have the power to corrupt, my golden rule. It was easy then to reach into the military's lair; my power could be extended anywhere. And since it was the power to corrupt, I could gain total command over the military's projects. My power over words would crush whatever force they could bring to bear; and I would succeed in unraveling their plans for an arms buildup.

"NBC Nightly News" then became my command post; each night Reasoner would send out the messages: I would reinterpret, issue my commands. Other parts of the program would report to me everything I had done that day; it was testimony to my power.

I constructed a beautifully symmetrical universe, divided between the Russians and Americans. I wanted to bring both sides closer together, to revive the flagging arms negotiations and to push the Russian point of view. (A similar motive got me involved in the Iranian crisis; I convinced myself that both the Iranians and Americans wanted me to mediate; that took a great deal of my time, negotiating, arbitrating, trying to persuade one side of the other's intentions. It was exhausting.) Invariably the Americans showed more intransigence and bellicosity than the Russians. When Reasoner reported on the American generals' plans for taking over the earth, bombing Russsia, and wiping out half the Third World [the *telepathic* content of Reasoner's messages], I knew time was running short, and I had to act without delay.

I remember at that time attending a concert of Russian music. It was the medium for sending me the foundations of new proposals the Russians wanted delivered to the Americans. And the Russians believed the concert would be the most appropriate place for me to receive these new suggestions. I found this out the following day in the newspaper when I read that the Russians, on some issue of arms control, had made "concrete" proposals. Actually I took this to mean that the proposals had been made at "concert." My letter inversion rule came into effect here; er, ae, ei, ce, re: all could be interchanged. Concrete then becomes concert. All this is going on only in my mind.

Since I had been at the concert, the proposals obviously had been directed at me, with the message to forward them to the Americans. Also the program had been billed as the "foundations of Russian music," but what "foundations" really meant or what I understood it to mean was "proposals." The word "foundations" contained the key to the content of the proposals. What the newspaper had been saying, a message hidden in the article, was that concrete proposals had been sent to me during the concert. The real reason for the concert had not been the widely advertised benefit for the Children's Fund (UNICEF); it had been intended to reinforce or bolster my position as chief negotiator between the Russians and Americans. I believed this very strongly.

The Americans refused to budge; they rejected the proposals made at the concert. I thought they were testing my power. But I had a plan that would make the Americans finally acquiesce to the Russian negotiating position. I decided the interests of reconciliation would be best served by having Reagan elected president. Aside from what I regard now as the peculiarity of that position (it was a crazy idea), I was absolutely sure that Reagan would resolve what had become rigidly held positions. I intervened in the primaries, again through words.

If for example Reasoner in reporting a primary victory said Reagan was "over the top," it meant I had succeeded in getting him to a place I called the "back of beyond." I imagined this to be in Outer Mongolia; to be in the "back of beyond" was to be safe from contamination. If someone were to reach "back of beyond" he could not be caught, poisoned, or otherwise destroyed. Or to put it another way: if Reagan were to reach the "back of beyond," he would be unbeatable; and if I could get him there, none of his competitors could overtake him. If I could keep him in the "back of beyond" through the primary elections, I might sew up his nomination. That of course happened; and through a similar process I had him elected president.

Chapter Eight

The Beast of Revelation

Becoming the Beast of Revelation started with a morning T.V. quiz show. The announcer asks his contestant, "What kind of mark does a company have to have to engage in business?" She answers, "Trademark." And with that, I found myself trapped in a series of associations surrounding me in life-and-death choices. A code lay hidden in the letters *t m*. It stood for something, and I thought the connections might have something to do with the word "mark" and my being "marked" with the sign of the beast. I had been thinking a great deal during this period about reconciling opposites: good and evil, Lucifer and Jesus. And I was particularly sensitive to failing and finding myself marked with the sign of Cain. If I could not bring good and evil together, I would die. Satan represented evil, and Jesus Christ the good. If I were to survive, then, I had to end the conflict between the two children of God or else I would be marked forever.

I also believed that if I refused to pay my hospital bills, it would be easier to attain that reconciliation. If I could be pure, avoiding contamination by money, I might be able to end the struggle between Jesus and the Devil. But if I touched money or allowed myself to become involved in financial transactions, I might die. It infuriated the hospital and eventually contributed, I think, to my being transferred to Grovehaven.

For me the Devil possessed secular powers; Jesus, on the other hand, possessed spiritual powers and could do good in heaven. If the secular could be joined with the spiritual, God would be pleased. The key to lasting harmony, to eternal peace depended on this project, uniting good and evil (in the persons of Jesus and Satan) into one. I would be satisfied with nothing else. I also felt myself being slowly transformed into the force of evil; and I had a desperate need to merge with good. But evil persistently drove good away. If I could discover a way to strengthen good, then evil might not be so powerful.

All this forced me into an obsession with truth. I saw myself riding the "tiger of truth" and I connected that with the proverb "He who rides the tiger must not dismount." Smoking cigarettes symbolically demonstrated my intention not to dismount, to remain astride the tiger telling the truth. Smoking turned into a symbol of the truthsayer on the tiger. Every time I lit a cigarette, I transformed it into the tiger of truth. I could bend the world that way into my conception of the truth.

My knowledge that smoking and truth telling were synonymous involved a word game. It worked like this: I reduced the word "cigarette" to the following sounds: *sa-ga-rette-ta*. I then rearranged some consonants to get sa-ta-rette-ta. The *sa* and *ta* could be dropped because of similar phonemes. That left me with

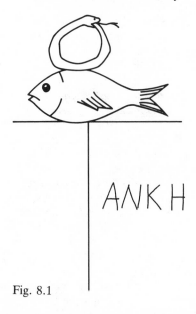

Fig. 8.1

ta-rette (remember all this is going on in my mind very fast). Since I could interchange vowels, I made *ta-rette* into *ta-rutte*. Next, in being able to transfer similar sounds (my phonetical law), I could substitute *ta-ruth* for *ta-rutte*. Since *ta* and *tra* have similar sounds, *ta-ruth* becomes *tra-uth*; *a* and *u* are vowels, therefore interchangeable. One could be dropped, so *tra*-uth turns into *tr*-uth. Cigarettes in my world came to be *truth*; and to smoke cigarettes meant to say or speak the truth. Pretty snazzy, huh? I was now free to tell the truth.

I also drew a visual pun in connection with my project (to reconcile good and evil).[4] [See fig. 8.1.]

Here I'm a little fish in a big pond. *Ankh* means the symbol of life; also I equated the symbol of the crucified serpent (notice the cross beneath the serpent) with life. Since I was evil, I had been crucified. But I was still alive, the symbol *Ankh* meaning "alive." But Jesus, too had been crucified; I could see myself then as an evil, crucified Jesus, the little fish on top of both of them. Disgrace also played into this. Jesus suffered disgrace; the serpent represents disgrace; and since each of these figures composed me, my identity, I too lived in disgrace. Everything about me came together in the images of disgrace. The pun (and I thought if people really looked at the figure, they would understand it)

4. The references here are as follows: the figure on top of the cross, Frank called the "little fish"; the serpent he saw as the Devil (evil), part of himself. *Ankh* meant alive; the cross symbolized Jesus and good, which was also part of himself. The little fish on top is the "whole" Frank: a "little fish in a big pond" is how he described it.

communicated this message. It all seemed clear. The story of my disgrace would be apparent in the drawing. Of course, now I realize it doesn't work that way; but then I believed that simply by showing the symbol, there would be immediate recognition. My whole story would become public knowledge.

The pun had several meanings: disgrace, suffering, evil, and reconciliation. Both Jesus and the serpent, each being a part of me, suffered; the cross suggests suffering. Since the serpent traffics in evil and since I'm evil, that must transform me into the serpent. Since the serpent is a beast, I must also be a beast. I convinced myself of my evilness. Satan is the Prince of Evil; the serpent is evil; I must therefore be very beastlike and very evil. If, though, I could reconcile Satan and Jesus, both parts of me, I might solve the contradiction between good and evil and there-fore please God. I would then be able to save myself from cer-tain annihilation at the hands of Satan. Yet if I'm part Satan, how could I possibly save myself from myself? See what puzzles I'm getting myself into?

The image of the serpent made me think about something else. It was the idea of twistedness; for some reason, I felt twisted, my body seemed to be wiggly like a snake. I "slid" over floors, through doors; my tongue seemed longer; occasionally I sensed myself as slimy, mucky and so on. I kept finding myself confront-ing images and scenes of evil, twistedness, beastliness. The visual pun would snap back at me like some judgment or attack. It sug-gested evil lurking in the room; it made everything I saw appear serpentine and snakelike. I thought of myself as a disgusting, wiggly "serpentina"; and then it occurred to me, maybe I was a serpentine. And to be serpentine, as a person, suggested wiggly, twisted, ugly images, a snake in the grass. And if I was all those things, I had to be warped.

Now in those days the word "warp" had the immediate asso-ciation to the T.V. show "Star Trek" and "warp speed." To be going very fast meant to be in "warp speed," and at times I felt myself being propelled at incredible speeds in this twisted con-figuration, the serpintina. It was a part of me; and I found myself propelled as if I were in warp speed in outer space. The serpent's twistedness, his evil, carried me quickly. I knew it was a desper-ate situation; I had to save myself from my own wickedness, my twistedness, my "self" as beast from the serpentina's evil. That's why the journey had increased to warp speed.

I also believed that since my project lay in telling the truth (remember cigarette smoking), people would be so shocked, so outraged, they would hate me. The hate would drive them to murder or mutilate my body, cut it up into pieces, torture me, and split me up the middle. I imagined every horrible depravity that could be done to my body. I had to save myself from all this accumulated hatred and anger. If people were to see me as the slimy, twisted serpent, I would be caught and then crucified for telling the truth. Every time I thought about this, I increased my warp speed. I had to outrun all the rage directed at me! What a price to pay for telling the truth! I felt compelled to move rapidly; it seemed unjust to be killed for my truth saying.

Why should people hate the truth?[5] Why should people want to kill me? For what? It was obvious. I should have seen it. I had the reasons ringing in my ears. It was jealousy! Jealously over the project of wanting to harmonize good and evil! If I had accomplished that project, I would be hated forever. Yet it was the only project I thought could save me. This time I had really painted myself into a corner; if I succeeded in pulling together good and evil, Jesus and Satan, I would be recognized as God, as all-powerful. Yet I was prevented from becoming what I knew I should be by the accumulated anger of people whose jealousy knew no bounds. To say the least, it put me in an impossible situation.

But there was another, even more serious problem. If the Prince of Devils caught me, then evil would have destroyed good. I had angered Satan for telling the truth, and if my warp speed failed me, not only would I be killed by the angry multitude, but Satan would probably be at the head of the pack. His victory would deprive me of my goal and put to rest, once and for all, the presence of good (which would of course mean a death of a part of me, which I was ferverishly trying to avoid). And the hope of reconciling good and evil would be over for eternity. That idea I found so frightening that my every waking moment was spent trying to fend off Satan and his crowds of bloodthirsty murderers. Hours would pass, days, months. I would sit quietly, without moving, in rapt concentration on the project. None of the staff knew what was happening. No one really seemed to care, since I was quiet and not disturbing any of the other patients. I imagined I looked catatonic. I went to meals, obeyed everyone; but the real action of my life lay in this race through nothingness trying to escape the clutches of Satan. If he caught me it would amount to eternal torment, the fires of hell; I would be damned forever.

I knew that I was outmatched; the struggle seemed futile, I simply could not outrun my own wickedness; it was bound to catch up with me in the end. But at that time the last thing I wanted was to recognize my badness or what I was calling evil. Yet I never experienced myself being caught. It was a matter of running, escaping the wickedness, the twisted serpent inside me. The faster I ran, the more exhausted I felt until I believed anni-

---

5. This reminded me somewhat of Plato's philosopher coming back from the sunlight with truth and knowledge; the people scorn and revile him for his message. This is possibly another element of identity in Frank's fascination with Plato.

hilation to be imminent. It was a pattern. My running increased; I lost my breath; I could see Satan coming up behind me. And the scenario would begin all over again. If Satan succeeded, if the action had allowed him to, it would have been all over. And Satan would have forced me to confess my wickedness to the universe, and held up to ridicule my project of fusing good and evil.

Nothing could save me; I felt I had been marked; the letters in trademark (t.m.) revealed the entire plan and what had been involved. And since the T.V. program "revealed" this knowledge to me through the letters t.m., I must then be the Beast of Revelation.

A lot of what I learned when I was psychotic was ephemeral. I thought I understood some important truths but most were silly and important only for my sense of identity, certainly not for anyone else. There appear in psychosis a number of astounding coincidences. They all pile up on each other and you receive the picture of the interconnectedness of all mankind. These connections make sense; they are real and immediate, then. The insights are always so present, so much in the here and now; and they seem, while they happen, so profound. It's amazing how much importance I attached to what were really inconsequential mind games.

"Welcome Back Kotter"

"Welcome Back Kotter" had special meaning for me; I recall at that time problems between the Russians and Chinese. The show designated me as mediator of the conflict, the chief negotiator between opposites. It's another example of word exchanges; here's how I got there.

Take the "sweathogs" [a group in the program]. Through "sweathogs" and its sounds, I came to the knowledge of my power and my central role as mediator. It went something like this: break down sweat into *swe*-at; substitute the v for the w because in my logic letters that have vertical lines can be substituted for each other. You then have *sve*-at. Now take sve-at and switch the e and the v, an acceptable sound change, due to roughly similar phonemes; s*ve* becomes s*ev*. With the substitution rule for vowels, first, s*ev* turns into s*ov*. You now have s*ov*-at; interchange i and e for a, and you end up with sov*iet*.

This is only one example; I processed all sorts of operations. No one saw them; they were secret, my own thoughts. I kept all knowledge of the rules to myself. All my identity, my knowledge of who I was, the Socratic "Know thyself," could be manipulated depending on my inventiveness in creating logics making words into what I wanted them to be. I literally leapt into the words. If I was the "sweathogs," my identity appeared hidden in that word depending on how I experienced the word's secret message. Identity, you see, always lay inside the linguistic structure of the word and the associations constructed on the manipulation of phonemes and letters. Sometimes the way phrases or letters were uttered would give them an identity, like sounds produced by the tongue up against the roof of the mouth: tu, du, nu, soo, doo and so on. There must have been forty or fifty logics governing the use of words and the substitution of letters and sounds. Everything I turned into during those years depended on how any word related to the action in my mind.

Well, to get back to Kotter. I knew I had been called by the Russians because of associations to "sweat." As for hogs and the Chinese, that's even more bizarre. Hogs I associated to the Chinese; how did I get there? Take again the word "sweat." Break it down phonetically into soo-wett; the sound *soo* resembles a Chinese word *zhu*, which, I believe, translates as "pork." Since *zhu* is Chinese, those who speak it would have to be "followers of Confucius." If hogs are understood as "followers of Confucius" and if "followers of Confucius" are Chinese, then hogs had to be Chinese. If hogs were Chinese and "sweat" also meant "soviet," the message in "sweathogs" delivers as "Frank mediate the conflict between the Russians and Chinese." It had to be that way because of the hyphenated character of the word sweathogs. Two distinct words put together; to me the position of the words meant mediation. If you take a line and put it between sweat and hogs, the separate but connected quality of the word is apparent. That line is actually me, the "line" or presence of mediation.

The program insisted I reconcile the Russians with the Chinese. After all the sweathogs didn't disappear. Whenever they were on the air, it would be a signal to me to resolve the conflict. I received the mediation message in yet another form. Take the image of Kotter playing chess. Now I play chess; and all Russians play chess; therefore the Russians were actually welcoming me back. Why else would Kotter play chess, if he were really not an extension of me playing at the game of chess? I absorbed Kotter; his presence on the screen simply disguised this extension of me. The message, then, in the title "Welcome Back Kotter" was, in my world, "Welcome Back Frank." The Russians secretly had been passing messages through this particular show welcoming me back as their emissary to deal with the Chinese.

The examples above give an idea of the complexity of Frank's inner life. It is not a universe that was undifferentiated or lacking in logic; rather, it is an example of an identity taken within an environment of language and a series of linguistic associations and transformations. Each delusion produced its own identity, but for Frank, within any given delusion, identity was certain and understood. He negotiated with the

Russians and Americans, won the 1980 election for Reagan, ran from the Devil, and mediated the dispute between the Russians and Chinese. Each of these activities coalesced as an identity dependent only on the ingenuity of his manipulation of words and his rules of grammar, syntax, and phonetics.

While Frank's mental operations appear intricate, their logic was not instrumental. It was not directed toward people, objects, or pursuits in the external world. It existed solely to construct the delusional defense. It was a universe of rules and words whose very utterance and invention served to keep Frank alive. The logics created his identity and significance as a person, even in the midst of psychosis. Without the word games, puns, and phonetic transitions, Frank would have possessed no reality. The games became his lived experience; they kept him attached to being. Although to the outsider Frank may have appeared out of touch, it is clear that he was anything but. He may have been removed from, as he put it, "secular concerns," but he was not without thought. His mental activity was intense and constantly functioning. Rather, his frame of reference was radically skewed to psychodynamic needs that created images of grandiosity and power. Frank's delusions came together as his identity in a process invisible to any outsider. Who Frank "was" remained hidden and inaccessible. Who, watching Frank riveted to the T.V., would have thought that he was carrying out complex negotiations, running from dreadful spirits, or playing at power games with world powers?

Other delusions preoccupied Frank during his psychotic phase. He believed that old people wanted to kill off "young people for having sexual impulses." He rewrote life in the Garden of Eden. In his view, the Elders ruled Adam's tribe. However, they discovered Adam's illicit sexual activity and decided to enforce a ban against fornication and licentiousness. The Elders found Adam's sin (his sexual desire) intolerable and punished him by banishing Adam from innocence and condemning him to a life of endless wandering. Frank also had his own version of the death of Jesus. According to Frank, Jesus suffered crucifixion because he took mankind's sexual sins onto himself. He allowed himself to be killed so others might enjoy their sexual impulses. Jesus' gift to mankind then lay in releasing sexual desire from the constraints of repression and morality. Frank identified with Jesus and felt certain that he, like Jesus, atoned for the world's violent sexual appetites, including his own. His suffering also became a stigmata, a sign of depravity and the sickness of his desire.

Isolation, banishment, the temptations of nature and sexuality, feelings of evil, omnipotence, and grandiosity: all defined Frank's inner world and the experience built upon it. His delusions included fantastic plans for destruction, political takeovers, messages hidden in body language, unspoken thoughts traveling through a telepathic medium, sacrifices for the sexual desires of mankind, and eternal battles between good and evil. Messengers, conspirators, and agents appeared to Frank wherever he went—in the hospital, on sidewalks, in buses, even for a period at Tenley House. He received communications through what he believed were prearranged signals and code words. If, say, he had been on a street corner and a stranger bumped into him, muttering a hasty "excuse me," for Frank, the utterance, no matter how informal, contained a message in code sent by a conspiracy ready to "destroy Chicago" or "attack the synagogues in Israel" or "free the hostages." Whoever said "excuse me" might in Frank's delusional world have been wearing a disguise. But Frank knew his identity; the language was intended for Frank and no one else.[6]

Table 8.3 describes the relative organization or lack of it in both consensual and psychotic identity. Each type of identity contains structure; the difference lies in the psychological environment that contains thought. An organized, consensual identity reflects historical, social, and interpersonal foundations; the psychotic identity, on the other hand, operates according to logics and connections peculiar to the existential field of the delusion itself, the "here and now" of delusional imagery and language.

The Movement Back: From Delusion to the Psychological Contract (Consensual Reality)

Frank's descent into psychosis was slow. It might be thought of as a movement through four tiers or levels, suggesting a deterioration in social and historical ego functions and a reorganization of awareness according to delusional logics and meanings (the development of hidden thoughts, structures, and operations; see table 8.4).

Tier 1 consists of activity in normal or consensual reality. It is characterized by the instrumental use of language; words do not contain intrinsic power nor can speaking them create identity. Language is tied to complex patterns of social and economic exchange. At this level Frank

---

6. Compare the following: for several days Frank walked around Hillwood with his arm outstretched and his thumb pulled inward against his palm. He felt he had to communicate, in this way, the teachings of the Fourth Commandment. He believed himself to be the spokesman for the commandment, God's emissary as vivid, walking gesture. Of course, the staff had no idea what Frank meant. Or in his mind, he would focus on a word such as "dollar"; while it had impure connotations for Frank, he also identified it with the Spanish word *dolor*, meaning pain, and then thinking, over and over, that money meant pain, then associating "penny" and "pain" and thinking, "So it's pain for the guy who gets the penny." This is just one example of thoughts merging into other thoughts. An idea is established and then innumerable associations arise from the idea's foundation. Thinking such as this absorbed Frank's awareness.

213

expects to make headway with his problems by "acting openly in the world. . . . agreements are made openly with people"; he hears no voices, his anxiety is manageable.

Tier 2 initiates transformations in reality perception; the changes are erratic; the T.V. appears to send out signals periodically; subliminal cues strike unexpectedly. Here Frank thinks less historically and more accord-

Table 8.3: Identity and Thought

Consensual identity	
Disorganized	Organized
a. causality confused	a. causal
b. historical references obscured	b. historical
c. sense of the past perceived as not important	c. social
	d. instrumental
d. disregard for feelings of others	e. interactional
e. high degree of narcissism	
f. "borderline" symptomatology	
g. inner and outer occasionally confused	
Similarity in lack of structure and logic	Similarity in possession of structure and logic

Psychotic identity	
Disorganized	Organized
a. lack of coherence	a. firm identity
b. fragmented thoughts	b. certainty as to system
c. looseness of associations	c. identifiable delusional subsets and actors
d. no patterning in language	
e. unconnected images	
f. confusion over meaning, time and place	d. secret languages committed to distinct purposes
	e. delusions as to theory of knowledge
	f. clear and decipherable language (if self chooses to speak)
	g. theory of omnipotence and grandiosity

Table 8.4: Movement from Normality
to Delusion

Tier 1: Normality	Tier 2: Skewed normality
• no voices	• changes come slowly
• no word games	• T.V. begins to talk intermittently
• expects to make headway with problems by "acting openly in the world"	• notices rising and falling inflections in voices of T.V. personalities
• "agreements made openly with people"	• high inflections tell Frank he is on "right track"
• normal linguistic communication	• low inflections reveal he is on "wrong track"
• no hidden meanings	• T.V. personalities become animated; hints of messages sent through airwaves

Tier 3: Part delusion/part normality	Tier 4: Delusion
• growing stockpile of odd ideas	• psychotic world becomes totally gratifying
• reality recedes; images assume increasing importance	• intense delusional preoccupations and obsessions
• message system develops more sophistication	a. "The 1980 Election"
• subliminal cues more and more intense	b. "The Beast of Revelation"
• great increase in non-specific anxiety and terror	c. "Welcome Back Kotter"
• withdrawal from people noticeable	• little real language exchange; speaks only in code
• begins to fear intentions of others	• word games
• isolates self	• word inversions, puns
• T.V. speaking to him on a regular basis	• telepathic communication
	• sexual fantasies and delusions

ing to existential perceptions. The rise and fall in voice inflection indicates hidden messages, particularly through such media as television and radio.

Tier 3 represents an intensification of the process: a steadily growing "stockpile of ideas" emerges and reality transforms itself into discrete and separate images that often seem confused and disjointed. Subliminal cues increase in intensity; interpersonal relationships and messages lose their importance and presence. Nonspecific anxieties and fears, induced by interaction with others, overwhelm the self; occasional fears of death or annihilation surface.

Finally, in tier 4, delusion or psychosis takes over completely and the self turns toward the inner world. Messages coming through the television, word games, puns, and private languages enclose psychical reality; the delusional universe is illuminated by secrets, hidden possibilities, and an unlimited potential for control. The omnipotent will assimilates the reality principle; all action defines itself through the delusional drama.

In relinquishing nature, in leaving his inner, delusional life, Frank cast his future in a world of embodied others, autonomous human beings whose reality, needs, and feelings had nothing to do with inner scripts or secret plans: "I'm working at tolerating the paradoxes of others." What depressed him, and formed a persistent theme in our conversations, was the loneliness of his condition, his inability to establish intimate relations. If the final transition from nature to the social contract lies in the creation of intimate bonds, Frank had still to take that step; he remained in an intermediate position, recognizing what he needed (or desired) but having yet to figure out how to realize an empathic or intimate relation.

Frank felt intensely isolated from others, although he continued to search. Nevertheless he repudiated psychotic reality and the identity that accompanied it and remained committed to the social world. He understood the terms of his new social contract and moved to embrace it on a fundamentally psychological level:

> I'm not quite sure how to live; I know I want to be close to others; that's my primary concern; nothing else really interests me; the relationships I have now make more sense than my psychotic fantasies. I know one thing: I will do anything I can to avoid becoming psychotic again. But I'm still somewhat afraid of others, of wanting to be in some kind of relationship.

Frank held back in terms of even experimenting with reciprocity, but even more in identifying with a community beyond himself. He longed for connectedness, but refused to move beyond the initial first stages of his psychological contract. In Rousseau's words, he was unable to give himself to the "whole community," nor was he ready to alienate his being "without reserve" (1950,14). Frank refused to give "himself to all" (ibid.). Both emotionally and politically, he fancied himself, I think, a "solitary walker," but he sought a closeness with a group greater than himself, with a will transcending the "will of all."

Frank often expressed a need to bind himself to a collective presence that would have the power to lift him from his intensely felt emotional isolation and give him new life. He searched quite consciously for an emotional or affective "General Will," but always returned to his fear of what is implied in giving the self completely over to a group identity: "I want to find a group, a community I can identify with; I try all sorts of things, but I'm always left with a sense of my own loneliness, my separateness." This feeling paralyzed his ability to move outward. The General Will remained elusive both conceptually and emotionally: "At times I feel the group never wants me; it excludes me and drives me away. I know that's irrational, but it's how it seems."

Frank referred to his exclusion primarily in emotional terms, but it affected his sense of self as a political being with reciprocal responsibilities to a given community. It would be difficult now to imagine him as a citizen or member of a group in the sense of the conditions Rousseau attributes to the community of the contract: "Each of us puts his person and all his power in common under the supreme direction of the General Will, and in our corporate capacity we receive each member as an indivisible part of the whole"(Rousseau 1950,15). Frank also did not see himself as being part of a "moral and collective body," not even in Tenley House. Whatever sharing or participation occurred there bore almost no relationship to a Rousseauian reciprocity between self and General Will. Frank was unable to construct what Rousseau sees as the "mutual undertaking between the public" (ibid., 16) and those individuals comprising the community. He did not commit himself to an obligation (or set of obligations) pertaining to, as Rousseau calls it, "a whole of which you form a part" (ibid.) other than by joining in the most rudimentary chores such as keeping his room clean, doing errands around the house, or eating at scheduled times.

It would be a mistake to see in Frank's life at Tenley House any evidence of what might even remotely be called a General Will. The residents, preoccupied with their own inner conflicts (but persistently demonstrating a real need for empathy) and the very real fear of making it in society, resisted a collective sense of being or body. The last thing the residents wanted was to be coerced into a participation that extended beyond what was necessary to survive. Rousseau's vision of being "forced to be free" would have been strongly resisted (in the same way, for example, that the psychotic self clings to its delusional identity as a defense against hidden needs). It was enough at this stage of their reemergence into society to cope with hostile surroundings and their own personal insecurities. Frank, however, could be quite critical of their attitudes:

> Tenley House provides me with a collection of people to talk to. But to feel connected, even capable of intimacy, I would probably have to leave and find another place to live. You see most residents are not concerned in having rules changed or in creating an environment that is their own, a product of spontaneous decision-making capacities. Most of them still act and feel like mental patients and show little interest in anything other than their own problems. They certainly take no emotional time to inquire about rules, why they are made, their purposes, who makes them, the reasons behind regulations.
>
> Yet at the same time rules are flouted and disobeyed; plenty of violations happen, but the breaking of rules demonstrates little or no political motive. Not that I'm interested in organizing, but I get angry when I see rule breaking done mainly to gratify selfish needs. Rules are seen around here only as impediments to gratification. No one is really interested in collectively rewriting rules, but only in getting away with what is wanted at the time. Sometimes I think I live in a menagerie of small, helpless children.
>
> It's hard living here, all of us have to deal with social ostracism, few jobs, and a continual reminder that our self-respect is on the line. Everyone feels desperate, abandoned, and isolated. Despair lies all around; it may not always be on the surface, but you can bet it's there. It would be ridiculous to think about political consciousness in this vale of tears. That idea simply does not occur to the residents. House meetings are pathetic affairs, a series of minor complaints about how the house is not being kept clean or somebody refuses to do the dishes or sweep the hallway or scrub the bathroom tub. Everyone sinks into collective pettiness, including the aides who sometimes are hardly emotionally better off than we are.

Frank clearly delineated the potentially rewarding and alienating aspects of community. He recognized social hostility, but remained committed to the belief that "out there" there was a community that would embrace him, gratify his desires, and fulfill his emotional need for closeness, a General Will without rules or constraints, a group of like-minded individuals searching for meaning in a world that rejected the indeterminate status of people like Frank. He attacked with great vigor the societal superego, his own moral upbringing, and the rigidity of social groups that bind through economic need and artificial inducements to security:

> I want something stronger than just belonging to an organization. That's not enough, or some simple social group who chats every Wednesday night. It's like being part of something larger than

yourself, being around individuals who reach underneath your
skin, who almost know intuitively who you are and what you
want. It's being common and uncommon at the same time, within
the folds of a community and apart from it. It's hard to explain,
but try to imagine yourself outside of yourself and being yourself
without losing your identity, your specialness.

Frank's critique of society, money, possessions, and materialism is
reminiscent of Rousseau's attack on egoism and "particular wills." For
example, his unhappiness with the residents of Tenley House derived
from what he saw as an environment of selfish claims and private needs
being put before common purposes. If Frank could have had his way, he
would have insisted that the retreat into privatism be replaced by a
recognition of their needs as individuals excluded from participation in
the mainstream of social and economic life. Yet Frank refused to act on
his critique of his fellow residents; he fantasized about "unity" but
showed little interest in carrying out the fantasy: "I don't see any point in
that; [the residents] just wouldn't listen; besides, no one is around here
that much. People come and go."

Issues such as these lay at the center of Frank's reflections on freedom
and power. While he admitted to being "freer" in delusion, he saw this as
an ephemeral freedom which in retrospect he found unacceptable. Frank
saw delusion as lacking an environment other than the contours of his
own mind; it was empty, unembodied, a life in images requiring no
exercise of will outside of the imagination. It was hermetic, sealed against
external others. He argued that it was otherwise in the social world. With
others, freedom involves a tremendous sense of responsibility, an activity
that presumes sharing and mutual respect. But to be free in a community
required difficult and sometimes demanding obligations:

> Most people have an urge to avoid freedom; freedom brings with
> it a certain responsibility and if things go wrong, then I'm the guy
> who caused it and I have to take the blame. This is actually more
> than most people want to hear. In delusion, though, my freedom
> had unlimited vistas; I could move wherever I wanted, do as I
> wished without ever having to think of responsibility. When I was
> psychotic, the whole idea of responsibility to others had no
> meaning; now I find myself surrounded by it.

Frank believed, then, that freedom in the consensual world implied
limits on action. It circumscribed Frank's sense of himself. To be free was
to be less grandiose but more connected, less isolated but more a part of
networks whose gratifications lie in cooperation and mutual undertakings:

> But I still find it difficult to work with others. I don't think about
> freedom too much, other than to be left alone, and to fulfill

whatever obligations I create. Outside of that, the idea has little utility for me. If someone asks me to do something or go some- where or just to sit and listen, I'll do it. I couldn't do that in de- lusion. So for me the responsibility of simply saying to someone else, "O.K., I'll go to the store with you" or take a bus ride or commiserate with your problems is being free. Now I can, at times, step out of myself; for fifteen years, I was consumed by myself; but now being around others gives me a great deal of pleasure. I suppose that's my conception of being free.

The concept of power fascinated Frank. In delusion, he could do whatever he wished; in his postpsychotic life, he found his power defined by others and the self's inner empathic capacities. For Frank, being powerful meant being able to sustain feelings of empathy and intimacy. Power necessitated encounters with others and the inevitable if some- times painful recognition that it was impossible for the self to control all aspects of being. But the power to be empathic had to do with psycholo- gical development, the expression of emotional needs without being threatened by them or being afraid to respond to similar needs in others:

> When I was powerful in delusion, I didn't have to think about
> my vulnerability, my dependency. I didn't have to worry about
> the feelings of others or how they would respond to mine. I
> didn't have any past or future to worry about . . . I needed only
> myself, my word. . . . You ask me what power is; power is to be
> able to grow as an individual in the way I should have grown as a
> kid . . . tiny little kids want to grow and they know what they
> want to do, but it gets stamped out, crushed.

Frank felt that his power to be himself had been annihilated by a past whose rigid moral injunctions and ever-present guilt acted like clamps. He experienced, himself, even in his postpsychotic life, as bound by guilt, inhibitions, and repressions that haunted him in memories of a childhood that was denied all forms of pleasurable activity. For Frank, then, the social concept of power and its reality as a bond between individuals could not be distinguished from its emotional conditions, the meaning of power as a projection of the self's capacity to be.

Frank rejected the argument that the defining elements of power are influence and manipulation. Although he accepted the existence of such operations in the social world, he simply was not concerned with power understood in these terms. Power for Frank was a process that binds the social order by lifting individuals out of their egoistic concerns. It was dependent on collaborative functions. If those functions were over- whelmed by self-seeking, then the entire basis of the social order was threatened. He saw his own withdrawal as an indication of the extreme consequences of a narcissistic selfishness. In this view of human interaction, power develops according to a reciprocity inherent in human needs and in the capacity of individuals to create intimate and empathic bonds. In this respect Frank shared vital Rousseauian assumptions.

Frank recognized that empathy brings contradictions; he struggled with the awareness of his need and his inability to resolve it: "I have no desire to be psychotic again, but I'm still trying to figure out what people want from me and what I want from them. How can I be intimate, belong, and still be myself?" It was not easy to realize practically an empathic power: "Being charitable in love makes me feel powerless . . . to feel love is to feel powerless, to be able to love and to feel power in that love creates incredible pressure because love is dependency. Yet I need to love someone, to have them love me." The tension between dependency and isolation frustrated Frank in his movement outwards.

While he was psychotic, Frank understood power to reside in the magical quality of words and their manipulation. Power and domination, synonymous concepts, had nothing to do with empathy, love, or the paradoxes of a self caught between dependency and autonomy. In his postpsychotic world, however, power or its lack appeared in day-to-day activities, in thinking about what to do, in the limitations of time, place, and history, in the failures of his present life compared to what he had been as a physicist and scientist. In delusion, his logics and symbolizations created power; his word inversions and phonetic laws allowed him to experience perfection. Yet all that was now lost; its memory became a relic of what was a dead and hopeless period in his life. Frank no longer conceived of power as omnipotence and domination; it was simply the ability of the self to reach, through empathy, the feelings and needs of another human being. From the perspective of Frank's past, these beliefs signified a radical shift in meaning.

For Frank, the importance of the social contract did not lie in its legal or juristic implications, which he tacitly accepted. Nor did he see the contract as particularly binding on him in terms of institutions, the requisites of voting, or participation in any public sphere. He disavowed the political dimension of community. His view of the contract lay solely in its capacity to realize and sustain empathic bonds within segments of his immediate community. In this sense, Frank's recognition of the contract was considerably more limited than Rousseau's. While I think he would have embraced enthusiastically the emotional content of Rousseau's theory, he would have been unsympathetic or even unconcerned about the more formal aspects of politics that Rousseau sees in the contract and the functions of the General Will. Frank shared with Rousseau a belief in trust, respect, and empathy, and would have agreed that "the social order is a sacred right which is the basis of all rights" (1950, 4). He would not have quarreled with the observation in the *Social Contract* that "this right does not come from nature, and must therefore be based

221

on conventions" (ibid.). He would, however, have expressed doubt concerning the meaning of the conventions, who interprets them, and what the intent is behind their enforcement. Indeed, Frank would have had serious problems with any convention unattached to the emotional conditions governing life in civil society.

Although Frank spoke of his desire to be part of a collective body, his contract with the General Will rested on a single overriding stipulation: that the General Will allow him to participate in an emotional life that would free his feelings from psychological inhibitions and guilt over which he had no control—a rather heavy burden to lay on the General Will, but one consistent with Frank's attitudes toward empathy and love. This demand reflected the intensely emotional quality of the conditions regulating Frank's entrance into some sense of community. This hope kept him going, along with the belief that the community of the group might release him from the emotional traps of his childhood[7] and provide him with the opportunity to learn new ways of coping with being human. Frank's hope had about it the quality of a fantasy, a wish that the group might rescue him from traps and contradictions. This fantasy became part of Frank's sense of self.

It may be that Frank imagined himself less vulnerable toward his own desires within boundaries established by the collective body or will. The safety of the group could also relieve him of responsibilities implicit in maintaining empathic relationships. Frank's dread of and desire for the possibility of intimacy not only accounted for his current impasse, but also provided him with the incentive to move outward, to try and solve the paradox, and by resolving it to tie himself further to the bonds of reciprocity and collaboration.

Conclusion

Table 8.5, which compares the psychotic and consensual world, is drawn from Frank's reflections. It suggests that the common theme of his narrative lay in the fundamental opposition between the omnipotence and isolation of the delusional world and the limited, troublesome, but outward aspects of consensual reality. The more the self experiences the environment of the social contract, the more receptive it is to the reality of others. The transition from nature to society, from the delusional universe to social life, thus releases a whole range of human and communal potential. It is that theme, in the final analysis a critique of the freedom of delusion and psychosis, that ran

---

7. "I take the traps with me wherever I go, trapped by isolation, by my fear of sex . . . my parents always told me sex ruined people's lives . . . sex would make you dead. To this day I fear that my sexual impulses will be punished . . . it makes me feel weak and helpless."

Table 8.5: Frank's Transitional Movements: From Psychosis to Consensual Reality

Experiential element	Psychotic	Present (post-psychotic)
Language	• private, hidden meanings • word games, inversions, puns • dropping of pronouns, adjectives, adverbs	• normal, consensual • words not invested with private meanings • follows conventional syntax • phonetic rules acknowledged
Body language	• no eye contact • hidden messages • body language never what it seemed to be	• eye contact • sensitivity to body language as used • no desire to find secret messages in movement
Attitudes toward caretaking staff	(Hospital) • hostility • refusal to obey; anger at restraint; flouting of rules	(Tenley House) • some hostility but not dominant • feels reactions sometimes are unfair, misunderstand his behavior • too strict regarding bathing • general acceptance; speaks and relates with others
Giving and receiving	• no sense of other • refuses to deal in money or gifts • preoccupation with self as center of universe; therefore no need to give	• awareness of need for reciprocity • enjoys giving small gifts (usually sees gifts as his "time") • sees empathy and giving as inter-related

223

Table 8.5 (*Continued*)

Experiential element	Psychotic	Present (post-psychotic)
Giving and receiving (cont.)		• finds the giving and receiving of emotion difficult
Sharing	• none with real others • none in delusions • refused to share content of delusions to avoid loneliness • refused to share words or meanings	• an activity integral to life • shares time and space • sharing as function of information giving (such as conversation) • frightened of sharing as emotional vulnerability
Cleanliness	• dirt and sexuality related • "odor makes me more carefree" • to be dirty means to have power, particularly sexual power • "If I could perceive my body as completely dirty, I'd be that much healthier and happier" • no sense of shame about his dirtiness	• keeps body clean • still finds it difficult to accept social obsession with cleanliness • required to bathe and change his clothes every day; resents this • upholds his end of the cleanliness bargain • not particularly concerned about being shamed by dirtiness
Eating	• food polluted body • Italian foods corrupt • often believed that if stopped eating would win his delusional struggles	• food necessary; eats when hungry • no enjoyment in food; viewed as substance to sustain life • no favorite foods

Table 8.5 (*Continued*)

Experiential element	Psychotic	Present (post-psychotic)
Eating (cont.)	• refused to eat anything with sugar • would often be force-fed with a tube	• eating purely functional; no social meanings attached
Sex	• autoerotic gratification • fantasies (about female patients, staff, sex during group therapy) • more attuned to sexual messages • all sexual feelings held within • never spoke about sex to anyone • world more sexually animated in his mind	• major preoccupation • no sexual activity in halfway house • feels he will never find a sexual partner • connects sexuality with feeling powerful • feels powerless at times because he finds himself frustrated in finding a partner • sex and intimacy seen as part of same emotional process • occasionally will fantasize about sex orgies, always in groups (his defense against intimacy)
Freedom	• rule breaking • lack of limits in delusion • felt unconstrained by anything hospital ordered him to do • risk and excitement heightened	• more docile • more obedient • feels less interesting, therefore more unfree • freedom amid others more limited, but other satisfactions

Table 8.5 (*Continued*)

Experiential element	Psychotic	Present (post-psychotic)
Freedom (cont.)	• freer in taking risks (but all risks product of delusional imagination • "At Hillwood I didn't break the rules against having sex, so I wasn't entirely free even then."	• having "sex with a woman" would be a sign of his freedom • struggles with freedom involve climbing over emotional roadblocks
Work	• refused all work • disavowed all economic and financial connections to society • transferred to Grovehaven State Hospital because of refusal to pay bill at Hillwood (to sign the necessary insurance reimbursement papers)	• accepts its utility, but refuses work • lives on a small annuity • would not work unless he enjoyed what he was doing • volunteers several hours a week to a local nursing home
Relationships	• relating a great deal but only in delusion • seem full, but only illusory; never speaks to anyone • everyone seems interesting and humorous; makes people laugh by use of strange language, but never really engages the other	• actual, real, varied • invariably feels them to be less interesting because has to cope with real human beings • often seem flat and lackluster • people appear dull • finds it difficult to take an interest in mundane affairs or in the interests of other human beings

Table 8.5 (*Continued*)

Experiential element	Psychotic	Present (post-psychotic)
Relationships (cont.)	• sense of self grandiose and omnipotent; relationships therefore always with imaginary projections of powerful figures	• recognizes this as contradiction since if he is ever to be in an intimate relationship will have to deal in the "mundane"
Community	• nonexistent; only in mind • telepathic groups • extensions of self all over the place • never lonely; too many "Franks," too much activity, busy in negotiations • artificial communities built around specific words	• Tenley House; a few social groups in the community • volunteer work • experience of community as imperfect and dull • impatient with details of cooperation and collaboration, yet constantly speaks about their need • not as much going on as there is in delusional projections • existing communities less interesting than delusion
Power	• internal, not shared • activities centered on resolving dichotomies, oppositions • sense of self as having unlimited power	• realizes he is "just a man"; therefore power limited by others • believes himself to be ineffectual most of the time (has to do with self-esteem and his focus on his worth or lack of it in the real world)

Table 8.5 (*Continued*)

Experiential element	Psychotic	Present (post-psychotic)
Power (cont.)	• power as capacity to dominate a political relationship	• despair over ever finding "true" power (the power to love, to be empathic)
	• would experience self as son of God, or powerful historical figures like Jesus, Caesar, or Henry VIII	• "It's a struggle to just get out of the pit; it takes all my energy."
		• forced to look at personal power in terms of social purposes and values; leads to periodic feelings of estrangement

through Frank's understanding of his experience and his attempts at resolution.

This view implicitly accepts vital oppositions central to Rousseau's political thought: isolation versus association; private languages versus public utterance; narcissistic withdrawal versus shared understanding; lack of ambiguity in nature versus contradiction, perplexity, frustration, and imperfection in community; seeming indifference to external environment versus engagement with contingent, consensual reality; emotional isolation from others versus reliance on an intersubjective empathic reason.

Finally, I kept asking myself through the ten months of our meeting together if there was anything left for a person like Frank, who at one time had enjoyed a reputation as scholar, teacher, and scientist. He seemed genuinely to regret his loss, but it was without bitterness, just a kind of sad resignation that things turned out as they did. Yet there was something about Frank that lent him a certain charisma. I could imagine him as a brilliant lecturer or convincing a colleague of his point of view, or devising ingenious experiments and proofs. That aspect of Frank, what remained inside him, had not disappeared. With all that happened, with the shambles of his life, this fifty-year-old man still displayed an enthusiasm and a frankness about himself and his desires that I took to be a sign of an essential tenacity and strength.

It has been six years since Frank last experienced a psychotic regression, and I feel he came to recognize what Rousseau saw as so essential to human and political life: the capacity to develop relations whose foundations lie in empathic understanding and communication. It was Frank's intuitive grasp of this truth, and its importance in his attempt to move outwards, that gave him the endurance (as he put it, quoting from *I Never Promised You a Rose Garden*) to "hang with the world . . . full weight."

nine

The Rousseauian Integration:
Empathy and Being

Frank's need for empathic understanding was
not unusual. His orientation was one I found articulated in different ways
by many ex-schizophrenics. The observations of Ellen, a resident at
Tenley House, are typical. She spoke of her experience at the hospital as
one of sharing, cooperation, and friendship: "I've had a life of death and
losses . . . I felt dead inside . . . I had a desperate need and love was
created." Before she entered Hillwood, she felt "deeply hurt; it was like a
hole; when someone touched me it made me angry. My anger had me
completely out of control . . . the feeling I had was of loss; and I
responded through rage and helplessness." Ellen's initial tendency was to
withdraw, to spend time watching T.V., engaging in silent dialogues with
characters in the programs. She created her own community, particularly
through family shows: "They were real to me; I loved them and they
loved me back. I thought all these shows were about me, and the families
were welcoming me into their arms."

Therapeutic intervention at Hillwood encouraged her to communicate, to become involved with others. Eventually, the delusions receded
and the friendships established on the ward replaced a delusional world
dominated by T.V. figures. She described this process in Rousseauian
terms, as if she were being forced to be free. It was not something she
wanted:

> At first, I refused to leave the T.V. I saw [other patients and
> staff] as intrusive. I hated them for turning off the programs and
> getting me involved in hall activities. I was under pressure to be
> social, to talk and relate. I would force myself to talk to other
> patients. But after a while, I discovered my responses were uni-
> quely my own. And people liked me for who I was. At that point
> I began to acknowledge their problems.

Ellen seemed to thrive on close, face-to-face encounters, as is apparent in
her psychiatric records: "Mrs. _____ adjusted very well to the patient
community on the ward. She became something of a leader, serving as an
articulate spokeswoman on important ward issues. It is noted however,
that Mrs._____ had adapted well in previous inpatient settings."

Ellen discovered her empathic community within the environment of
the mental hospital. It was the only place she could experience herself as a

human being. When she first arrived at Hillwood, she said, "all I wanted was to go to bed; to be away from people. Hillwood forced me to stay awake. I could have stayed there forever." But the transition from Hillwood to a local halfway house brought up all sorts of feelings of abandonment and separation. She feared she would lose the empathic community; finding a "friend in the outside world" seemed to be a persistent preoccupation: "Where will I find others responsive to me? Where will I be that I might be responsive to others?" Ellen appeared to be genuinely frightened. No one would be there to acknowledge her reality. She yearned for "a friend to share myself with without being self conscious . . . love balances you out. When you lose that source, feelings get muddled . . . it makes you feel together. . . . If you lose that [love] the ship goes down. Before I came to Hillwood I felt like the angel of death."

Both Ellen and Frank articulated a fundamental Rousseauian position: empathy as the foundation for understanding. Both were at one time inside "nature" (delusional reality), and both became extremely distrustful of a social and economic world that operates according to hypocritical, deceitful, and unethical rules. Before she entered the hospital, Ellen felt that her body "was moving" and her "spirit had been killed . . . I became a machine. I cranked myself up in the morning. Did you ever wake up and find you couldn't get out of bed? I didn't want to do anything for myself. I felt like going out and getting hit by a car. I had lost my soul, my will to live. Part of me was dead inside." Ellen and Frank each felt victimized by the regulations and assumptions of a surrounding civil society, and each resisted those regulations. As Frank observed, "there is an internal, moral critical judgment inside my soul that I'd like to rip out." And each felt powerless in relation to what society constructs as models of efficacy and success.

It was the pressure of the inner world that in some respects gave them this awareness of the need to isolate the self from prevailing social currents. Ellen and Frank lived outside the mainstream of social interaction because of their sensibility, what they saw in others and in themselves. And what they saw may indeed be a modern translation of a Rousseauian virtue: both refused to make compromises with an uncaring social order or to engage in relationships requiring complex social operations such as deceit, manipulation, conniving and so on. Both avoided dependent relationships and interpersonal "games." Both were hesitant to tamper with this virtue, and neither was capable of an ounce of guile; they became modern-day Emiles without the Tutor. While they recognized the existence of the Hobbesian world, their concern was to maintain their innocence and incorruptibility. This made for some helplessness, but Ellen and Frank were adept at protecting themselves from the intrusiveness of others. Frank carefully arranged his life around the halfway house and his volunteer work. Ellen, rather than trying to find a job that would take advantage of her administrative skills, hid from the world as a cashier in a small book store. Both Ellen and Frank withdrew from what they experienced as an oppressive society. Each in the past embraced the stark internality of nature, and each later attempted a new social contract that placed them on the fringes of the existing social order. Neither has found the perfect community; they still search for the ideal social contract.

Many ex-mental patients describe their experience as a series of Rousseauian recognitions: disenchantment with hypocrisy; a refusal to dissemble or disguise; a distaste for and distrust of instrumental relationships; a feeling of great distance between themselves and the social order; and the primacy of empathy and compassion among emotional responses. It is the latter that creates so many difficulties, since empathy, at least in today's narcissistic, Hobbesian society, is not highly rewarded.

In this chapter, therefore, I would like to focus on aspects of Rousseau's political thought that touch on the experience of ex-patients like Ellen and Frank: the theory of integration into community, the empathic foundations of that integration, and the role of philosophical knowledge in creating the terms and conditions of the new compact. What Ellen and Frank endured is illustrative of the extent to which consciousness can "leave" society and of the trials involved in "coming back." Further, if the experience of other patients spoken about in this book is any indication, the natural condition, an awareness of self in a precivil or nonsocial environment, is a very real one.

For Hobbes, nature teaches paranoid defensiveness; it is a condition of pure fear; nothing else. But if one looks at delusion from a Rousseauian perspective, the psychotic world reveals a sense of self that sets the foundation for all postpsychotic relationships. Ellen and Frank rejected their prepsychotic universe and had no wish to go back. Yet no matter how painful and horrible their psychotic life may have been, the experience profoundly transformed their view of self and other through a series of recognitions that at its core is Rousseauian.

When Frank launched into a diatribe against "civilization" or the "superego," it was a Rousseauian attack—not an ideological one or one coupled with a demand for class consciousness, nor was it a militant call for organization or for a political program for the rights of ex-mental patients. Rather, it was a straightforward moral plea for acknowledgment of the humanity of the self, a demand for empathic understanding. His unwillingness to translate this plea into action limited his effectiveness; his was a Rousseauian claim without the political or visionary dimension.

Frank's observations began from the acceptance of his distance from all types of organization, while at the same time he expressed a yearning for contact or relatedness that might lift him out of his self-absorption. His critique, like Ellen's, was theoretical and abstract. It was as if both existed outside of prevailing social concepts and pursuits and saw themselves as witnesses describing the decline and decay of a corrupt culture but incapable of concrete action or organizational commitment. Each survived in the world as a lonely wanderer.

The Appearances of Civil Society: Rejection and Need

Ellen rejected everything that civil society represents:

> I have a fantasy of living off the land, being alone, without the
> telephone or any social communication. I might be able to do
> meditation, draw, paint. At least I would be away from the rat
> race. . . . Whatever we paint and draw, it's the soul . . . my need
> to give is strong, I respond, but I pace it. . . . When I was at
> Hillwood I felt I was the only person in the world. I had no trust
> in anything ever being permanent; everybody and everything was
> out of control. . . . Freedom? You ask me what I think freedom
> is all about? I suppose freedom to be within love, freedom to be
> at peace with sadness instead of judging myself so harshly, free-
> dom from worrying what people feel about me, freedom from the
> fear of rejection, self-blame . . . freedom from pain, anguish,
> helplessness, from criticism.

Ellen disliked the imperfections of others, the demands of social necessity, the neediness of dependency:

> I'm happier if no one's around; people are like vultures out
> there. Give them an inch and they'll take a mile. But it's not
> their fault; by the time society's finished with them, it has made
> them into monsters. I want nothing of that monster world. It's
> such a shame because people give in all too easily; if they would
> simply defend their interests as human beings, instead of being
> all the time caught up in the race, they would be much better off.

Paradoxically, though, while Ellen spurned dependency in terms of human relationships whenever she found herself in deep emotional trouble, she turned for support to her belief in God:

> He confronts me like a perfect mother and perfect father. Some-
> times He's the soft, nourishing, caring, gentle mother. Other
> times, he's the ideal father, full of strength, anger. . . . He
> teaches me things, skills, like sewing or putting things together. If
> I'm having trouble, He'll tell me what to do. His hands come
> down onto mine and guide them. He takes my loneliness away.
> It's not my will, not possession exactly, to surrender to somebody
> else's plan for me. I really need Him, He keeps me, here, my
> constant yearning is away from things of daily life. He pulls me

233

> back. It's like having my mother again where I was safe [Ellen's
> mother died when she was eight]. When He's inside me guiding
> my actions, I often feel like I'm a three- or four-year-old being
> put on its own. I remember painting faces. I couldn't get it right
> and He showed me how to do it. I had never done eyes, or a
> mouth before and He taught me. I sensed I was receiving a gift. I
> chose to think of it as a gift. At that moment I felt I was being
> guided from without.

Ellen struggled with human relationships. She rejected the connotative
world with its economic and manipulative assumptions. Like Rousseau,
she attacked possessiveness, ownership, and dependency, both economic
and personal, although this was a thorny issue she resolved through the
projection of an omnipotent and nurturing God. Ellen had little need to
define the world in terms of mine and thine, although she did want
everyone to recognize that her sense of privacy and isolation was real and
necessary. She rejected the values and commitments accompanying
property, the requirements of accumulation, obligation, debt, and dealing with the other as a thing or client. She refused to find any gratification
in power-oriented social operations. With Rousseau, she believed that as
social life becomes more complex, the self's chance for inner renewal
declines and the further alienated it becomes from an inner meaning or
virtue: "I find myself hating to go out and buy things or listen to people
trying to sell me something or get me to do something because they see in
me something they can profit from whether it's my money, my body, or
my feelings." Ellen saw all the structures of civil society (specialization of
function; social and political organization; rational, sophisticated thinking) as traps. Politics, she believed, only makes you more "confused";
political life responds only

> to the needs of the politicians; it's a game they play with no
> ending. There's nothing in that for me; it just makes you feel
> bad. I don't want to think or act in the way "they" want me to, I
> just want to be left alone to find a few people I can share some-
> thing with.

For Ellen, even the mental operations connected with civil society
brought pain, estrangement, and unhappiness:

> I used to think I was really smart; I was a straight "A" student,
> good at numbers. I would work out all sorts of deals for my
> bosses. Boy, they needed me! I was the highest-paid administra-
> tive assistant in _____. Everyone was after me. But I look
> back on that now and I hate myself for doing it, for using what-
> ever intelligence I had to accomplish such shallow objectives. I'd
> rather live with pennies; their world is no longer worth it to me.

Ellen's sentiments here are Rousseauian in all respects. She withdrew not only from egoism but also from the instrumental thinking inevitable in an egoistic community. She repudiated the manipulative dimension of social acts. It is not that Ellen refused to think; rather, she shifted her field. She left the psychological environment where connotative thought is the beneficiary of all kinds of rewards. She still thought quite clearly, but had no desire to put thinking to use, to earn from it, to use other people to gain, materially or emotionally, from her intelligence. Her feelings suggested an almost total rejection of socially established exchange relations. But she managed to survive; it was as if she unconsciously internalized the Rousseauian rejection of civil society. Like Emile, she experienced herself in an alien world.

If Ellen had had her way, she would have transformed her world into an extension of the intense empathy she felt at Hillwood. This was obviously unrealistic and in many respects indulgent. But her sentiments expressed the extent of her alienation from surrounding social forms, her Emile-like being in the world. She refused to participate on any terms but her own, and she made her own "contract" with a God who fulfilled whatever need she had for belonging and identity. There was little room for anyone or anything else. God functioned for Ellen much as the Tutor functioned for Emile.

What should be emphasized here is not the resolution of Ellen's dependency on a God figure but the nature of her critique of society and its Rousseauian foundations. It is not that Ellen refused even to entertain the idea of community; rather, she was so discouraged and felt so hopeless that she found it impossible to imagine that an empathic community could even exist "out there," that there were enough trusting individuals around who might, through whatever agency, find themselves drawn together. Her empathic needs were met through her relationship with God, which cut her off from people.

Ellen's approach to civil society was critical and often cantankerous, but she did not feel she had to withdraw completely from the world. She had no desire to return to delusion. What Rousseau found in nature, and Ellen found in her discovery of internal, empathic resonances through her relationship with God is a principle that repudiates the kinds of power dynamics that accompany social exchange and instrumental behavior. Without empathy and its regulation of value and intersubjectivity, thought, language, and logic become corrupted through the human project of accumulation, domination, and appropriation. What Ellen and Frank did then was reject a "politics"—a way of seeing self and other as well as a historical approach (classical liberalism) to the organization of the material world.

Philosophy and Human Nature: The Conditions of Transformation

In the Rousseauian critique, it is society—which comprises a set of relationships having its origins in the division of labor, necessity, and property—that destroys human potential. Nothing short of a fundamental transformation in human nature, Rousseau argues in the *Social Contract*, can remedy the terrible deprivations society imposes on consciousness, action, and self. What that transformation in human nature means from a contemporary perspective may perhaps be understood by looking at Rousseau's concept of transformation as a psychological phenomenon, an integration of self in a world free of what civil society regards as valuable and social. Such a task—the construction of a psychic and political environment that transcends existing socialization—may be considered a therapy, since for Rousseau no change makes sense unless it is accompanied by a radical alteration in the nature of feeling, response, and most particularly in the use and purposes of language and the instruments of social exchange. Philosophy for Rousseau acts as the inspirational source for that therapeutic intervention, and the philosopher functions as a kind of master therapist, capable of mediating the relationship between knowledge and self. Implicit in Rousseau's argument, then, is a therapeutic vision; it has to be drawn out, but it is there. For Rousseau, the therapeutic vision involves (as it does for ex-mental patients like Ellen and Frank) questioning the root of culture itself.

Rousseau's social contract is a statement about human possibility, the consequence of radically altering the motivations and substance of human nature. The community of the contract depends on face-to-face relations, on an organization untainted by egoism or "particular wills." The Rousseauian community assumes the existence of a different kind of self from the one we meet in corrupt civil society, the *bete noire* of Emile's Tutor. The new citizen acts not to defend himself from others, but as a responsive human being, with and for others, in a state of mutual exchange and respect. Most importantly, the Rousseauian community contains a vision of institutions that assure greater equality, within which the internal or psychological being of individuals ceases to exist in an estranged relationship with others. To be aware, to be an integral participant in a political event, means that each individual regards the other not as a threat or competitor, but as a person whose humanity appears through the "virtue" and courage of common action. What occurs in the *Contract* suggests a radical alteration in values and meanings, the appearance of a field of being complete with novel signs, references, and consciousness.

Throughout the first book of the *Social Contract*, and especially in the early chapters, Rousseau points to the nature of the startling transformation accomplished in "human nature"—the new self as perfected citizen. But each hint appears in the guise of a metaphor or fiction; individuals leave the state of nature; they contract with others. Each person invests the General Will with a determining influence over behavior, and each transformatory process in the movement of a new nature (and politics) assumes descriptive form as metaphor. We see nothing of what might actually happen within the psyche of the person who assumes the political identity implicit in the community of the contract. The fact of that identity is never questioned; it is a given, a proposition about human nature that omits any discussion of the internal processes accompanying a change in the structure of the self.

While Rousseau weaves a complex metaphoric argument, the terms appropriate to an understanding of what he means for a contemporary audience sound vague in the abstract, contractarian language of the eighteenth century. It may be useful, therefore, to look more closely at some of Rousseau's theories—not so much in their own terms as literal representations, but as signs suggestive of psychological processes which, for a modern understanding, might be described in terms that acknowledge the existence of unconscious structures.

The abstract figures of contract theory are insufficient to explain such a complex and traumatic event as the remaking of human nature. It makes little interpretive sense simply to state that human nature "changes," nor is it easy to intervene in the structure of the self. If the patients at Sheppard/Pratt and the residents of Tenley House are those who have undergone the retreat from society (a process that seems to be a precondition for changing human nature), the psychological event of rejection must stem from tortuous expressions of human need, a painful shedding of the social ego. For Rousseau, theory responds to the reality of human suffering, and to think about his theory without raising issues about the status of the self and the relationship between consciousness and the constraints of culture would be to deny critical realities important for our own age.

Constructing a new human nature means altering not only conscious perception and the ego's priorities, but also shifting the context and energy of "affect," feelings generated at the level of the unconscious, the site of what I have been calling delusional knowledge. For the political philosopher, concepts not only exercise power over conscious choice, but also have the capacity to alter the kind of affect generated by the unconscious. The philosophic task becomes one of restoration, to heal the psyche wounded by entropy and the forces of cultural transformation. Rousseau seeks health, balance, a refuge from the frenzy inherent in history; thus to think about political form implies an equally important commitment to the welfare of the self and to a therapeutic objective. A group that internalized the Rousseauian message would of necessity find itself with a novel set of perceptual orientations. Any concept or thought that intervenes therapeutically in both conscious and unconscious structures reaches into the self; it penetrates the being of the person and transforms existing values. Sense, intuitions, even formal thinking undergo transformation. Frenzy, selfishness, hypocrisy, weakness, laziness—traits Rousseau associates with a decadent culture—disappear (or ought to) as a consequence of this kind of philosophical therapy. The philosopher as therapist alters the relationship between need and affect by replacing a corrupt set of signs with those that regenerate experience; he severs the reality of the self from acts that induce an entropic, alienated existence.

In the *Social Contract* Rousseau describes a human being whose psychological roots no longer adhere to the antecedent social order. Something traumatic occurs during what seems to be the innocent move from nature to community. Those who forge the contract do not suddenly discover reason. What seems more likely is that the self emerges from a deep, narcissistic preoccupation. It experiences a restoration of intersubjective consciousness, but with a strongly attached empathic sensibility that bears little or no resemblance to the selfish energy produced by decadent cultural forms. The kind of psychological universe that Rousseau labels as decadent and sick (in other words the prevailing civil society) disintegrates, and the hold of that universe on consciousness disappears; its bonds or gestalt relationships are broken or split off from the self. That movement suggests the appearance of an ego that rejects the values of necessity and property. The making of the contract means the founding of a community based on transformed assumptions about politics and self.

Rousseau never directly argues that the movement from civil society to nature suggests ego disintegration. He provides no picture of the socialized ego breaking up. He relies on an intellectual environment that addresses itself to specific historical and theoretical concerns. Yet if we look at his theory of nature and empathy or compassion from a psychoanalytic perspective that assumes the psychological reality of narcissistic absorption and its function in delusional experience, it appears that the movement from nature to community demonstrates processes of ego disintegration and reintegration, the construction of an alternative form of intersubjectivity.

Natural man, for example, appears in several psychic poses throughout the *Discourse on the Origins of Inequality*. His development moves gradually from autistic withdrawal to a highly differentiated consciousness. He recognizes autonomous others separate from self; he feels compassion at the sight of the dead or dying, "a natural repugnance at seeing any other sensible being, and particularly any of our own species suffer pain or death" (Rousseau 1950,193). Nature, not the artifice of social convention, teaches the self its first or core emotional response. Empathy is not learned; it arises from within, spontaneously. As Rousseau describes it, the sensation of compassion derives from the presence of a nonsocial event. It is a psychic moment existentially bound up with an immediately felt reality, specifically the sight of the dead or dying, and it takes natural man out of his self-absorption. Compassion or empathy, understood as an oceanic sense of what is, infuses the self without any assistance from artificially constructed motivations or needs. It is this feeling that distinguishes what is artficial in human nature from what is original. Empathy in the state on nature acts as the foundation of the core self, it is the emotion that lies at the center of human responsiveness; most importantly, it is the emotion that pushes the self toward recognition of the other.

Compassion is not an intended or calculated sentiment. It is not instruction in social knowledge. It comes to consciousness directly. It is a purely natural or innate experience whose origin cannot be traced to any social process. It provides the emotional environment for a language generated by nature and not by the needs of the social ego. As natural man moves from the isolation of nature toward more complex psychic states, he develops increasingly sophisticated perceptual mechanisms. In his most regressed moments in nature, his "imagination paints no pictures; his heart makes no demands on him. . . he can have neither foresight nor curiosity. The face of nature becomes indifferent to him as it grows familiar." He lives within a bounded present: "His soul, which nothing disturbs, is wholly wrapped up in the feeling of its present existence, without any idea of the future, however near at hand"(ibid., 211).

Empathy lifts him from this withdrawn, almost mute state; the emotion engages the world and others and creates the first understanding of nature's "universal language." Before he becomes corrupted by social possessiveness, property, and the division of labor, natural man has the potential to experience a sense of relation that has nothing to do with what Hobbes sees as instrumentality or value. It is this empathic relation that becomes submerged in the necessity of social exchange. The recognition of empathic presence and vitality, for example, in Ellen and Frank's situation begins a process of reintegrating ego and establishing some connection with a life-sustaining intersubjectivity.

For Rousseau, philosophy has the power to intervene in fragmented human situations, in the alienation produced by a corrupt sociality. Concept or theory contains a restorative potential, a therapeutic dimension; and philosophy seeks its justification by addressing itself to the human project, by intervening in the human self and bringing consciousness from its isolation and solitude in nature. When Ellen described her helplessness and sadness, the theme of solitude ran throughout her discourse. She felt completely cut off from everyone. Therapy for her duplicates what Rousseau sees as essential to the theoretical function: the creation of a relation in language with others that can offer the self another set of emotional and existential possibilities. Rousseau, refusing to be an apologist for withdrawal, never intends to leave natural man in nature:

> What progress could be made by mankind, while dispersed in the woods among other animals? And how far could men improve or mutually enlighten one another, when, having no fixed habitation, and no need of one another's assistance, the same persons hardly met twice in their lives, and perhaps then, without knowing one another or speaking together? [Rousseau 1950,213]

It is not Rousseau's intention to encourage withdrawal by leaving his audience perpetually condemned to an autistic state of nature. Similarly, neither Frank nor Ellen expressed a desire to remain in or return to delusion, to be out of touch with other human beings, or to relinquish any kind of intersubjective discourse. Rousseau's theory rests on the eventual integration of the self into community, but a community shaped by the therapeutic interventions of philosophic knowledge.

The Legislator's Therapeutic Function and the Reintegration of Ego

For Rousseau, the critical task of theory lies in devising a set of prescriptions or concepts that, while appealing to consciousness can reach into the unconscious and fundamentally alter the structure of the self. Such theoretical activity implies not only the reordering of conscious political priorities and the correction of imbalances in political structure (the recommendations in the *Social Contract*, especially the later books), but also the much less categorical (and more elusive) task of reconstructing a human intelligence unattached to what Rousseau sees as decadence, hypocrisy, and property.

Philosophy here addresses itself to the transformation of human nature in its entirety. It is an immense task: to offer a theory that can lift the self from nature and create an emotional and political environment institutionalizing an empathic politics requires a superintelligence or, better, a supertherapist.

Rousseau invents the legislator for this purpose, but from a modern perspective it is a thoroughly unrealistic suggestion. If therapy with schizophrenics is any indication, then moving an entire society from its corruption to a renewed political environment would be an improbable project. The ideal community, political or otherwise, as Frank so clearly recognized, remains a fantasy, an unattainable dream. It is difficult enough for individuals to get along together on a personal level. If shedding the old beliefs and values of civil society is a precondition for entering into the community of the General Will, then this goal, given the complex psychodynamics involved, would appear to be unattainable. It can, however, serve as a model of human nature. The *Social Contract* provides a criticism of an existing pattern of arrangements, and its usefulness lies in its critical perspective. It offers a theory of self that derives from natural or innate impulses, not from social sources. In his isolated condition, natural man represents a basic structure of existence, the critical beginnings in the development of intelligence and thought. It is not a unidimensional state; he moves from complete isolation and regression to complex forms of thought, to "languages" that provide security, intersubjectivity, meaning, attachments, and purposes (see, for example, Rousseau's argument in part 2 of the *Second Discourse*). The different psychological stages in the hidden, inner life of the delusional self form an analogous situation (see table 9.1).

Delusion is not a single phenomenon; rather, it moves through different stages. It may appear as thoroughly autistic, (stage D, or Rousseau's natural man at his most primitive). Or it may appear as fragments and

Table 9.1: Modalities of Delusional
Experience: Psychological Moments
in Nature

Consensual reality	Delusional reality (stages in a psychological state of nature)
Instrumental and scientific logics, social manipulation	A. Complex delusional systems and logics (most sophisticated)
	B. Unsystemic but recognizable utterances, logics, and observations
	C. Fragments, discrete images lacking any coherence
	D. Muteness, refusal to speak, physical rigidity, no awareness of surroundings, absolutely no self control (least sophisticated)

Examples of A: Mary, Ann, Ted, and Frank; examples of B: Chuck, Jenny, and Tom; examples of C: Louise; example of D: only one patient resembled in any respect the withdrawn, mute "hebephrenic." He was a young man of around twenty who for several months had been kept in one of Sheppard's seclusion rooms. Almost all evidence of civilized reality and habit had disappeared from his gesture, behavior, and language; he had absolutely no control over his impulses. He lived in what could be described as a psychological state of nature.

discrete images, (stage C, natural man emerging from his linguistic and interpersonal cocoon). Or delusion may come together in language as unsystematic but recognizable utterances and logics, (stage B, natural man forming bands, uttering the rough and rudimentary sounds of nature). Or delusional thought may emerge as well-formulated parables or narratives possessing a rich and highly structured mythic quality (stage A, natural man banded together as tribal group with complex language and imagery).

Perhaps the ego-destructive properties of schizophrenic withdrawal illustrate what it means totally to deny the prevailing social order. Because of the anguish and pain that accompany the fragmentation of the social ego (and the "indwelling" in delusional nature), it may very well be that schizophrenics who return to the consensual world possess a knowledge about empathy and its structures that is inaccessible to nonschizophrenics (the "indwellers" of civil society). Frank's and Ellen's most moving and intense reflections centered on how to live and survive in a world that, at least to them, discouraged empathic communication. To survive delusional reality and to forge a compact with consensual reality is no small victory.

In some respects, both Frank and Ellen would make fine citizens in a Rousseauian community. But at the stage of their lives when I interviewed them, their awareness and needs still centered on deeply personal issues. They became (and I believe will remain) hostile to any political sense of being. Prior to their psychoses, both had been involved in the activity and demands of civil society. Each had been integrated into the activities, goals, and assumptions of the economy; each considered himself or herself a participant in prevailing social efforts. Their postpsychotic universe was different. Ellen would not even look for work that resembled her prepsychotic occupation. Frank disdained teaching or research in mathematics or physics. Both were content, with minimal finances, to remain on the fringe of the social order, to refuse work appropriate to their talents and energies. It was, however, their choice not to engage in any job that violated very strong feelings about the organization and structure of the social world as they experienced it. They craved privacy, invisibility, a lack of entanglements, and yet they fantasized about being part of communities that might lift them out of their loneliness. Perhaps they are like Rousseau's "solitary walker," alone with their thoughts, distant from the prevailing political winds of change. Each was a living example of what Rousseau idealized as the simple virtuous life. Yet their lives were far from easy; their complex task was to sort out internal issues, to come to terms with their pasts and failures.

For Ellen and Frank, the social contract is a hedged bet. It is tentative; it could come unraveled at any moment. As long as they are left alone, they will do what is necessary to survive physically. They have no desire for wealth, fame, power, glory, or entanglements of any kind. But to be within Rousseau's social contract assumes not only disenchantment with social organization, but a corresponding willingness to build a political or public reality according to different terms. It is this choice or movement that Ellen and Frank have refused. They want nothing of the public; they may accept the General Will as the empathic dimension of a readily identifiable group consciousness, but not as the foundation for a set of new political arrangements.

It is, of course, different for Rousseau, who envisions a complex *political* community. The agent for this transformation is the legislator, that "great personage" who takes upon himself the making of institutions. What is psychically important is the claim that the legislator should "feel himself capable, so to speak, of changing human nature, of transforming each individual, who is by himself a complete and solitary whole, into part of a greater whole from which he in a manner receives his life and being" (1950,38). (Ellen resolved the issue by identifying the greater whole or community with God; Frank constructed a fantasy of a group consciousness and participation that would diminish his sense of alienation and emptiness.) The legislator alters "man's constitution for the purpose of strengthening it" (ibid.). He substitutes an interdependent and "moral existence for the physical and independent existence nature has conferred on us all" (ibid.). Such power is therapeutic, in the sense that the philosopher (through his legislator imago) directly intervenes in the structure of the self. Further, in making it impossible for the influences of civil society to intrude in the philosophic project (by removing from the psychic field all evidence of a degenerate socialization), the philosopher constructs a set of conceptual relationships whose effect on consciousness will be ideally to bring health and transcendence, what might be understood in a mythic sense as attaining a sacred space, a sense of untouched place (Ellen's idea of God, for example).

That hope remained elusive for Frank. For him, there were no more sacred spaces. Grovehaven State Hospital cured him of that fantasy. As he put it, "I now understand how things are; no one will save me; I am as I am; it's unfortunate, but we live in a world of greedy animals." The Rousseauian call to arms is the vision of a new political order, a commitment to an entirely novel set of institutional arrangements. Frank and Ellen were resigned. Life would remain as it is; dreams belonged to the past. This stoicism departs considerably from the moral fervor of Rousseau's political theory. For these ex-mental patients, the world had shrunk; the Rousseauian legislator had been reduced to therapeutic interventions on a small scale.

But Rousseau's vision remains grandiose: theory has an objective in the world and in the social order, not just in the individual psyche. If we take Rousseau's legislator at his word, he sounds like a god (maybe even Ellen's God). Rousseau even leads us to believe that the figure possesses a godlike power. But given the experience of delusional reality, it is not generally a god figure that attains therapeutic success but the active caring of a therapeutic agent in situations of confusion, pain, and suffering. To make the figure of the legislator (who is Rousseau's agent of transformation) sensible or believable, it might be helpful to look at his actions not as those of a god, but as the philosophical equivalent of a shamanic therapy. A shaman is sucessful to the extent that he banishes evil from his diseased patient (Glass 1974). It is precisely this function that the legislator accomplishes. Like the shaman, he drives away pain from a corrupted body, (for Rousseau, corruption lies in the historical and social roots of the body politic). A shaman works through psychological penetration; his song enters the diseased patient, and he participates with his audience until evil disappears from the organism.

It seems more reasonable to see in the legislator's task a process closely aligned with the therapeutic objectives of a shamanic therapy, than simply to conceive his function as the traditional giving of law in the manner of a Moses, Lycurgus, or Solon. Even though these parallels seem historically obvious (and undoubtedly they meant a great deal to Rousseau), nonetheless, in psychological terms the historical analogies do little to explain the phenomenon involved in "transforming human nature." The success of the legislator's message depends on his capacity to induce a cure, to build an ego without any of the pain associated with the frenzy of a decadent historical process. If an audience or patient willingly internalizes such understanding in its consciousness, and if that same understanding appears in the unconscious as affect (a sense or implicit understanding of empathy), it may indeed be possible to speak about a fundamental change in human nature. The power of a therapy that can accomplish such a cure comes not from any abstract source removed from concrete suffering nor from any omniscient lawgiver, but from the incantatory effect of a knowing (or healing) reaching into the deepest levels of the self. The true shaman, an individual who stands in a special relationship to the collective or tribal group and who claims extraordinary powers (and Rousseau certainly claims the power to "see"), performs cures. He devises therapies; he responds to the felt need of an audience caught up in forces beyond its own powers of rational or historical explanation.

For the political philosopher, that "cure" manifests itself as a conceptual project, and Rousseau's legislator, by lifting consciousness from its subjectivity and isolation in nature, opens up the self to an objectivity (or consensual foundation) bounded by empathic communication. The complete and solitary individuals of nature become interdependent through a knowledge that integrates self-knowing with choices made in the presence of other. For Rousseau, founding a political community means, in addition to creating new institutions, transforming the nature and quality of psychological relationships. As a process that affects the psyche, founding occupies a position for Rousseau similar to the sense of renewal the shaman induces in his patient. Shamanic intervention regenerates. This sense of beginning, what Mircea Eliade (1967) calls "an *incipit vita nova*" gives the philosopher's audience a feeling for its potential, its capacity to internalize the psychological 'cure' (the knowledge of the philosopher-therapist) and to recover an ethics that rejects the destructiveness of the corrupt civil society.

In this context, where the past has been transcended psychically, therapy means nurturing consciousness out of its isolation, leading the sick or wounded self away from the influences that cause pain. In Rousseau's argument, the movement of the self from the primitive condition of nature to a full and complete existence within the community suggests a therapy that derives from the capacity of philosophic knowledge to transcend the corrosive effects of a historical past. Therapy in the social contract brings both communal *and* political awareness; it institutionalizes empathy in voting, participation, action, and legislation. It founds not only a new self, but a new citizen. It operates in an universe untouched by history and socialization.

In Rousseau's conception, however, therapy is ideal in the sense that the philosopher relies only on his awareness or wisdom to formulate a cure. And the act of therapy for a philosopher like Rousseau entails thinking of the therapeutic task as a political event, along with the assumption that the sickness of the psyche is intimately involved with the general degeneration in the culture itself. The following observations by the Finnish psychiatrist Marti Siirala have much in common with the Rousseauian position: "The prophecies [of the delusional self] are the insights into our collective sickness, into the unnoticed murders among us. These lie deeply buried, away from our 'healthy' minds; we have then protected ourselves against them, perhaps for many generations already." Delusion emerges from a "common soil of sickness" and "appears as a message about possibilities which have not yet entered a process of realization through reciprocity between the individual and his fellow men" [Siirala 1963,43,45]

But for Frank and Ellen, the Rousseauian vision failed precisely because of its dissociation from convention and what exists, what Frank saw as "the world where we live, the grittiness of the streets." Both seemed much more comfortable with the existential Rousseau, the wanderer, the social critic, the defender of compassion and empathy. For Frank and Ellen, thinking about the General Will or community as a political form suggested an unrealistic and dangerous sense of human possibility. It was hard enough for them even to speak to another human being, let alone participate in a world of common and shared interests built around political concerns. "How can I possibly think about politics," Ellen asked,

> when all I see around me is distortion and despair? Look at the people living here [Tenley House]; for them the political world, whether it is in the form of family, schools, relationships with peers, is part of the problem. If we have anything to hope for, it has to be some recognition that all human beings want to be desired, respected, and loved. That speaks more strongly to me than any political program.

Thus it is the human subject that stands at the heart of Frank and Ellen's "Rousseauianism." It was simply premature in their conception of things even to consider the process or structures of renewal as a political event.

ten

Conclusion: Where Should Political Theory Be Now?

Political Theory and the Self

I am not sure there can be an answer to the question posed by the title of this chapter. Of course, political theory should be timely; it should look at the classical issues of authority, participation, the meaning of action, community, and the like. (Modern themes of community, for example, might include identity, boundary, generation and disintegration.) Political theory should be what it always has been: an activity of theoretical construction that tries to say something meaningful about how individuals organize their lives. It is an activity, a process, a conversation that situates the observing or theoretical self within a phenomenological world that involves speculation and some separation from the ongoing processes of political life. Current academic or professional theorists are influenced by paradigms of study that presume a measure of separation from the political process, from the "first-order" experiences that generate theory. These theorists are primarily observers of political life who place considerable importance on history, philosophy, and historical patterns of knowing, and take upon themselves the historical task of reminding their audiences that the concept of the political includes more than corrupt or jingoistic politicians.

In my view, political theory should be an activity that focuses on the relationship between the self (particularly its unconscious structures) and political life. I am not saying that this should be the only or even the primary aim of political theorists. The issue is, however, a critical one, and one that lies at the heart of much in the historical tradition of political thought. The self is a reality; it exists. It is not a fiction, any more than the psychological operations by which individuals orient action and perception in the world are fictions. To argue that there is no such thing as human nature or the unconscious would be to dispense with the meaning of dreams, slips of the tongue, erratic or unusual behavior, sexuality, the flows of appetite and desire, and, as I have argued in this book, the languages of delusion. Not only does the notion of an unconscious situate the individual in a social and economic matrix, but unconscious dynamics infuse the knowledge and perception that form the core of ethical and philosophical systems. Political theory has often been a response to the theorist's perception of the self's energy, its direction, and the ways to

247

contain or embody it in political form. In the *Republic*, for example, Plato writes: "Recall the general likeness between the city and the man" (1975,80). It is this relationship that for Plato pushes the ideal polity toward a catastrophe provoked by unbalanced psyches ravaged by desire: "The tyrant is. . . filled with multitudinous and manifold terrors and appetites. . . convulsions and pains" (ibid.,806).

Plato, Machiavelli, Rousseau, and Marx all reflect an almost obsessive concern with the ways in which the human self relates to surrounding forms of political and social life. Each calls for a reformulation of the structure of human character and the pattern of need and desire that defines the community's relation to history. Each confronts a history that erodes human value, twists human purposes, and rewards viciousness and brutality. Each formulates a concept of beginnings that recovers identity in human nature and the historical community. What compels the theoretical imagination lies in this sense of urgency, the recognition that the political universe has been consumed by madness.

When in the *Republic* Plato describes the decline of the ideal state, he focuses attention on the way in which the lust for power and private wealth corrupts the human character. This etiology (or pathology) sees the disintegration of the self as intimately related to the emotions and needs of the community. Plato links forms of psychological life with forms of political life: they weave in and out of the images of political justice and virtue. The consequence of a disintegrating reason is the descent into madness or delusion, with the political community dominated by a wolflike tyrant and the self at the mercy of incessant violence. Plato's conception of a community-in-psychosis is violent; the political universe faces annihilation and the tyrant's insatiable unconscious gives rise to grim images of destruction.

Should not political theory be concerned with what is within the self, with the psychological dynamics that propel people into participatory relationships, into effective citizenship? If individuals lack internality or if talk of "inside" and "outside" distorts human action, then whether political theorists take seriously the idea of the unconscious, of hidden or inaccessible parts of the self, makes little difference. If the self is fully manifest in external appearances, then there is no value in studying such concepts as the unconscious, the intrapsychic, the splitting of the ego, the delusional introject.

I accept the proposition that feelings derive from complex interactions between intrapsychic events and external objects; that the human self is a bundle of defenses that may inhibit or interfere with the creation of relationships or the sense of connectedness. What Otto Kernberg calls the "psychoanalytic exploration of character pathology" means locating one arena of political struggle in "the intrapsychic relationship that arises between the patient's ego and superego." (1976,79) From this perspective, the nature of character or the self depends on events that happen "inside" and on the ways in which "a past pathogenic internalized object relation (representing a particular conflict) has become 'frozen' into a character pattern" (ibid.). Further, the outcomes of these interactions are often "forgotten," repressed, and inaccessible to consciousness. To bring to consciousness what has been forgotten, particularly in the patterns and structures of delusional utterance, is to uncover (or recover) what is unconscious in the self. It is this activity that contributes to self-governance.

This implies, following theorists like Freud and Ricoeur, that the self possesses a "history" written in each stage of development by events that are acted out on an internal field. This process may be summarized in Kernberg's words as three dynamics: the "internalization of interpersonal relations" beginning at birth; the contribution of such relations to "normal and pathological ego and superego developments"; and the reciprocal effect or "mutual influences of intrapsychic and interpersonal object relations" (ibid., 56) The ego is subjected to great stress and trauma throughout its growth. Certain feelings that threaten its stability, its ability to survive and hold itself together, may be split off and repressed. In the form of affect, these become "recognitions" that may later come back to haunt the self through unusual behavior, thoughts, or sensations.

Psychodynamic Interpretations and Dialogue in Political Theory

Why are current political theorists reluctant to look at methodologies, terminologies, and perspectives directed toward understanding and analyzing internal psychological states? Why are theorists and political scientists now so skeptical of and often hostile toward the theoretical implications of psychoanalytic methodology? For me, these are crucial questions about the current condition of political theory and its objects of inquiry.

This reluctance derives primarily from two sources. First, political theory has become the study of political thought, so that (even in its philosophical projects) it is now dominated paradigmatically by historical methods of analysis. Second, political theorists assume that it is somehow unphilosophical to assimilate a clinical language to theoretical discourse (Glass 1979). Historians of political theory object to psychoanalytic methodology primarily because its clinical language is thought to distort the "meaning" of history and the language environment in which theorists should work. How, they ask, can we reach toward intentions in political theory if we must continually translate from one language game (the texts and contexts studied) to another (psychoanalytic methods of study)? They worry that differences in assumptions, values, traditions, and intellectual habits make it highly unlikely that the gestalt of any current methodology (with psychoanalysis as but one example) can respond well to perceptions that generate meaning, value, and choice in earlier environments. Clinical languages not only distort the theorist's intention, so the argument goes, but also obscure the historical foundation and matrix of any act of theory construction. For historians of political theory, what matters is accuracy of description and attribution of meaning, and they doubt that any depth-psychological theory can be an adequate tool for discovering meaning.

The clinical literature, however, (not to mention this book), suggests that psychoanalytic methodology is indeed sensitive to history. Psychoanalysis studies the generation of meaning structures in a particular past; as Ricoeur argues, "the patient is both the actor and the critic of a history which he is at first unable to recount" (1977,862) I do not argue that historians of political theory are intolerant of nonhistorical languages of analysis. The issue is whether clinical languages can penetrate intentionality and recover historical meaning. The debate centers on how to approach and represent intentions, how to make sense out of the relation between an idea and its historical field. For the psychoanalyst, history is meaningful in two forms: in its capacity to produce symbolic manifestations of meaning (symptoms) and in its constitution as a relationship between the content of symptoms and the order of unconscious reasons that motivate incapacitating mental states.

The usefulness of psychoanalytic method in studying delusion lies in its ability to recover the sources of intention. In this respect, it becomes an investigative or hermeneutic activity committed to uncovering a historical relation: the knowledge of those processes and structures that give rise to specific psychological events. In looking at a political theory, psychoanalytic method is far from insensitive to intentions. What motivates the psychoanalytic technique is an extraordinary sensitivity to the structures that provoke the self's historically indentifiable behaviors. For the psychoanalyst, the true meaning of intentionality is hidden; intention is a product of both unconscious and conscious factors. Moreover, intentions reveal truth not so much through the symptoms themselves (which may be defenses against recognizing the truth), but through the pathways that symptoms provide to the largely inaccessible areas of the psyche. For the psychoanalyst, history is the reason for the therapeutic dialectic. But history disguises and hides. Psychoanalytic investigation thus views history as two-sided: as both the conscious formulation of meaning (symptom) and as the dissembler of truth.

In the latter respect, the conscious and recognizable history of the self can be seen as a mask for the unconscious "reasons" that contain the self's historical truth. And on this basis, the psychoanalyst argues that the true objectivity of the self is to be found in what is hidden: the unconscious. Cannot the same argument be made about political theory?

If theory is approached as symbolization, then the search for intention in the history of political theory is much like the search for meaning in the psychoanalytic investigation of delusion. What is true about intentionality is not what is immediately visible. There may be unconscious states in political theory much as there are in individuals, and reaching an understanding of this unconscious means assuming that the theoretical statement or formulation represents or symbolizes what Ricoeur calls "psychical reality." It also means adopting a methodology compatible with this assumption. Theoretical concepts such as the Hobbesian natural condition, then, become ways of speaking about unconscious contents in the theory itself. Thus theoretical constructions may studied as symbolizations of psychological states.

Such states are accessible through a language that translates classical statements into modern interpretive frameworks. This is done in an attempt to discover the common tie between theory as symbolic representation of mind (for example, the Hobbesian natural condition of mankind as delusional pathology) and the implications of such a reading of those theoretical symbols for a contemporary audience. This is an analysis of meaning, but it treats theoretical symbolizations much as the analyst would treat symptoms in the patient. It is what Ricoeur calls an "interrogation of the text." But here the text is not some historical fact or historians' debate but a psychological production that moves on an unconscious level.

In Hobbes, for example, what is important about the concept of narcissistic withdrawal is not only its clinical background, but its usefulness in drawing out the implications of an important statement in the political tradition. Narcissistic states relate to demands for political order, control, and dominance; the concept of narcissism translates Hobbesian theory into a modern context. It forges a connection between internal states and politically significant behavior. This is not to deny the importance of understanding or pursuing political theory as a historical investigation of meaning and cause. Rather, it is to add another dimension to that inquiry. Hobbes demonstrates that narcissistic isolation motivates conceptions of political rule, choice, and power. He provides theoretical evidence of the importance of intrapsychic states in recommending structures for political rule. Is it not appropriate, therefore, to look at Hobbes (who places tremendous importance on the self conceived as an isolated monad locked into its own needs and "secret thoughts") through the perspective established by psychoanalysis in dealing with similar psychological structures?

At this point I would like to address the objection that clinical languages are unphilosophical. Psychoanalytic theory consists of more than

techniques for dealing with specific character disorders: it provides philosophical justification for conceptions of mind that posit unconscious or
hidden layers. It is metapsychological in providing frameworks or points
of view that move beyond strictly clinical issues. One obvious example is
Freud's analysis of the relationship between human happiness and the
interests of civilization on the one side and struggles between sexuality,
instinct, and demands for order on the other. *The Future of an Illusion*
(1969), *Civilization and Its Discontents* (1961), and *Moses and Monotheism* (1939) all attend to philosophical, cultural, and political questions
that move beyond a strictly clinical focus. And it is not unusual in recent
times to see considerable philosophical interest directed toward the unconscious. Examples abound in works by Paul Ricoeur (1970), Jacques
Lacan (1968), Geza Roheim (1943), Harold Lasswell (1930), Herbert
Marcuse (1955), Max Horkheimer and Theodor Adorno (1944), Jurgen
Habermas (1971), and Alexander Mitscherlich (1963). Philosophical and
clinical projects move along many common lines, such as the interpretation of perceptual structures, the analysis of influences on the self, and
the evaluation of connections between emotion and action.

To argue that psychoanalytic theory is unphilosophical not only distorts its origins (in nineteenth-century dialogues over the meaning of
mind), but also neglects its metapsychological importance (especially
with respect to the reevaluation of traditional political concepts). To look
at mind only as an outgrowth of purely rational processes and historical
modes of generating understanding is to form a judgment of what mind is.
It makes just as much sense to study mind as only a function of symbolic,
metaphoric, repressed, and irrational psychological states. What mind is
remains an open question; the analysis of unconscious dynamics and
delusional states can at least contribute to alternative conceptions of its
structure.

If the unconscious does not exist, then mind indeed becomes an extension of strictly rational processes. If distinctions between rational and
irrational are discredited, then the very concept of human nature, particularly of a precivil human nature, is banished or reduced to mere processes, reactions, and unlimited energies. This would be nihilism. Any
human act that reflects passionate feeling would have to be conceived as
coming from random impulses. Identity, no matter what its bases, would
arise not from the complex interaction of the intrapsychic and interpersonal, but from past psychosocial events such as the effect of socialization
on consciousness and immediate reactions in the form of defenses to
external stimuli. We could only say that identity is because it is present,
that what we are consists of whatever specific situational influences
happen to affect us. The self in this view would be like a sieve: experience
runs right through it; what remains is an empty vessel. Nothing is stored
up—no layers, no sediments of the self, no human archeology. Identity

appears as stark energy embodied only through what it encounters in chance meetings.[1] A human nature such as this could be comprehended only through a nihilistic theory of indeterminacy.

In this conception, the self is monad; not a Hobbesian monad, because Hobbes at least granted an autonomy to the "secret thoughts that run over all things without praise or blame," but an alienated monad without dimension. It is human energy without meaning, purpose, choice, or commitment, the individual as raw material to be shaped by whatever situation confronts it, psychic energy without structure, or identity, a chaotic "indwelling." To do away with any sense of an unconscious is to eradicate the very concept of human nature, if only because the unconscious self is that aspect of the human being neither fully outside nor fully inside, neither fully determining nor fully determined: it is the abiding structure of human nature, bridging effective humanity and affective being. To speak of an unconscious even in the form of delusion is to posit that human experience encompasses a generativity or intentionality not subject to the molding influence of social reality, environment, or habit.

It seems to me difficult to construct a theory of liberty without a conception of human nature and the purposes of human desire. What is Freud speaking about if not the liberty of the self, the inner capacity for self-governance, the right to be free of crippling anxiety? Are not individuals as incapacitated by emotional disorders as they are by external threats? Are not "introjects," tormenting superego formations, the tyrannies of delusional reality, as painful in restricting freedom as unjust laws? Should not political theorists be sensitive to the ways in which the self is enchained by *internal* sources of domination?

The Autonomy of the Inner: Psychical Reality as Truth

If there is no human nature, then we exist as monads in the existential universe, mirrors for the datum of consciousness. In this view we have no interior, no objects for whatever powers govern social exchange. To dispense with the notion of an interior self means to accept that we are either completely determined beings, thoroughly conditioned by behavioral forces (systems distinguished by inputs and outputs) or transcendent energies unbound by anything other than the facticity of the will to power (a kind of fantasy Übermensch).

I find these three alternatives unacceptable. The first two reduce the individual to a cipher of external influences; the third glorifies narcissistic

---

1. Chauncey Gardiner (Chance) in Jerzy Kosinski's *Being There* (1976) is a caricature of this kind of identity.

grandiosity. To release the self from a psychological past, an inner history, is to do away with the need for any limitation. The struggle between the unconscious and the conscious creates limits; it suggests the need and potential for ethics as a restraint on impulse. Without the unconscious, there is no superego, no sense of conscience, and it is difficult to ignore the possible complicity of the unconscious with an overly restrictive superego, which may come back to haunt and torment the self in the form of delusion. Furthermore, to do away with the superego altogether would be exceedingly dangerous, for it would preclude any sense of limitation and cast the self into a nihilistic emptiness. To deny the unconscious would be to deny not only the ego, leaving the self no reflection in the world, but also conscience, which encircles the self in meaning.

As Otto Rank suggests, truth and reality depend on internal modes of knowing. The psychological interior is a place: it creates and projects life. Delusion, for example, possesses its own identity; it is a hermetically sealed environment of meaning, logic, and structure, a radical example of the projection of inner onto outer. The world of affect and desire lies "inside," the product of an inner history written in the nuances of unconscious languages. There is a great deal in Rank's assertion that affect defines what is true for the self. Truth is recovered through an inward movement—an exploration of the complex pathways of desire—and not through intellectual abstraction or romantic projection.

Similarly, will is not just "there." Rather, as Rank puts it, "our own act of will" derives from the self's interior. It is the consequence of the "inner pressure after truth" (1936, 25). In Rank's view, there is little sense in knowing psychological facticity without mediating that material through the inner sources of will; will *is* psychical energy. In turn, this conception depends on the generative sources of an unconscious, on the "truth" of the self. For Rank, then, knowledge of will is knowledge of the unconscious.

From this perspective, it is inevitable that individuals will impose on their worlds a conception of reality that comes from unconscious sources. At one extreme, this is exemplified by the delusional symbology of schizophrenics. Indeed, it is unclear to what extent a consensual universe is affected by unconscious sources of knowing. The case of Ann, for example, indicates how truth involves the psychological operations of projection: she believed that all machines wanted to have sex with her. She was terribly frightened of these machines when they were operating or emitting noise (the medium for communicating messages about sexuality). These feelings, along with the attribution of sexual desire and will to machines, were not random utterances, nor was Ann responding randomly to her confusion. Her language contained meaning, structure, and purpose. Her thoughts were intended and, in their own context, logical.

Ann's belief in machine sexuality was part of a complex inner epistemology that regulated self-consciousness and action. In fact, machine sexuality formed only a part of her complex inner system. Ann's assertion created her reality, and what she spoke mirrored a "will" that assimilated the external world through powerfully expressed fears of penetration by machines. Such messages did not originate in a socially constructed or consensually defined universe. Her utterance was couched in "ordinary" language but her frame of reference differed radically from the traditional, conventional, and social, and what she meant and inferred in her delusional language was the product not of convention or history, but of a *willed* truth buried deeply within herself. Ann's symbology included communicating with alien spaceships, turning into a cat, and experiencing her lover as an airplane descending. Such symbols convey information about the self's interiority, its conception of desire, and the relationship of desire to thought. They reveal the structure of unconscious thought.

This kind of discourse, with its many variations, is relevant to the study of political life. Inner dialogues, the languages of delusion, and internal epistemologies can all be seen to raise philosophical questions about the origins of ethics, conceptions of good and evil, structures of power and perception, judgments of fact, and (most importantly) relationships between the meaning of "truth" and unconscious sources of knowledge. Thus a knowledge of internal states may illuminate value assumptions and psychological forces with origins in the historical patterns of the self. Although delusion breaks contact with socially generated, historical meanings, it remains an index of certain historical contradictions and struggles within the self's ontogenetic history.

Schizophrenia and Political Theory:
Thematic Parallels

The desires generated by unknown forms of psychic energy, the possibilities that such desires might break through boundaries (as they do in delusion), and the dynamism and violence of a self lacking political identity all constitute themes central to the theoretical tradition and interests of political philosophy. For example, how might Plato's cave be understood as a metaphor for unconscious states of being? We might ask whether the fear of extremes is a reaction against what Otto Rank has described as "self tormenting introspection," a state of mind that turns the self away from the polity (with its administrative apparatus, activity, and values) as the preeminent touchstone for personal identity. Does knowledge of truth as a function of psychological interiority (consider the "cave" Plato refuses to show us as the abode of unconscious knowledge) diminish the importance and role of "politics"

or "the political" as a set of standards to guide consciousness and behavior?

From this perspective, the study of political theory, or at least one
dimension of the study, involves connecting historical and current expressions of human nature. How, for example, is a political theorist to
enter human nature, to listen to what Rousseau called the "languages of
the heart?" Or to put it another way, what are the properties of language
and utterance that might allow the political theorist an empirical experience of what is designated by the concept of human nature? What would
constitute first-order evidence of the existence of a human nature that
precedes civil and social forms of knowing, interaction, and identity?
Where should political theorists look for confirmation and specification
of the concept of human nature? Might a psychoanalytically informed
language, using notions of conscious and unconscious, ego and superego,
provide a more coherent and better definition for a term so important in
the history of political thought? Where is the theorist to find evidence of a
human nature?

In a psychoanalytic sense (as Lacan has forcefully argued), language
embodies the unconscious. Utterance makes unconscious conflict and
struggle visible and places feeling in a public or consensual context. It
therefore makes sense to look for the facticity of human nature in
language, indeed, in a peculiar kind of language, with frames of reference
that sharpen the distinction between conscious and unconscious forms of
knowledge. This distinction is characteristic of delusional symbology. It
represents long-buried unconscious conflicts and desires in an imagery
that, to be sure, possesses a logic, but one organized according to the
terms of unconscious knowledge.

Such language generally is not seen to possess any ontological significance; political theorists and philosophers ignore it. In everyday life, we
have pejorative words for such utterance: crazy, lunatic, mad. But there
are also technical terms: asyndetic speech, concrete thinking, paleological thought, and so on. Delusional language is not pretty or soothing; its
emotions are neither uplifting nor regenerative. It is the language of
despair, hopelessness, and, at times, death. Most importantly, it is language that represents a period of human development prior to the acquisition of formal linguistic structures.

In Platonic terms, schizophrenics live in the cave, in darkness. It is not
a happy state; it is no pathway to redemption. But it is a condition that
testifies amply to the existence of a human nature that precedes social and
civil forms. In particular, the language of delusion provides empirical
evidence for both Rousseau's concept of the languages of the heart (the
deeply felt drive for empathic communication) and the Hobbesian experience of chaos, violence, and imminent annihilation. Perhaps the
delusional self's journey from Hobbesian terror to the Rousseauian

recognition of empathy and pity mirrors psychological developments in the maturation of the human self: the violence and indeterminancy of a Hobbesian nature precedes the emergence of the complex affective states of empathy and relatedness. Certainly Frank and Ellen's movement from nature to community suggests that it is empathy that restores the self's social and relational being.

In schizophrenic utterances, knowledge is the product of interiority. Significantly, this interior form of knowledge is obsessed with political concepts: boundary, identity, power, good and evil, domination, violence, justice. As language expressing the self's earliest emotional and psychological experience, as symbols prior to the acquisition of formal linguistic structures, delusional language represents precivil thought and reality. Thus schizophrenics may be said to recover an ontogenetic past through their production of language.

If the utterances of schizophrenia are any indication, the natural inclination of human nature is toward narcissistic gratification. This first-order, intimately charged knowledge appears in a narcissistic framework that remains (although repressed) in the human self. In the stories of schizophrenics, it is not at all clear that impulses toward sociality are stronger than more regressive, narcissistic trends. Narcissistic structures remain within the self throughout development, and it may be that all forms of maturation and individuation depend on a persistent struggle between the interests of sociality and the more underlying or unconscious narcissistic energies that periodically achieve prominence in the internal life of the self or psyche. (It should be noted that especially destructive aspects of narcissism are also visible in individuals who would not normally be classified as psychotic or schizophrenic [see Kernberg 1976; Masterson 1976]).

Many of the concerns of schizophrenic epistemologies mirror themes in the history of political thought. Boundary, identity, power, and reason and its uses are all thematic structures of political thought. I do not say that theoretical statements in the tradition are schizophrenic or that they reflect or represent schizoid dynamics, although it may be interesting to look at certain statements in political theory from such points of view. I do argue, however, that the stories, fables, and "theories" implicit in schizophrenic delusions reflect ideas that historically have been of concern to political theory. For example, is not the *Republic* a treatise on identity, on the meaning of passion and desire, on the nature and organization of power? Although it does not make the same sort of statement about identity as does the schizophrenic's "possession" of reality, the *Republic* is still similar in being a fable: it unfolds as an imaginative construction. The point is not that delusional symbology should be compared to theoretical imagination, but that political theorizing may be occasioned by many of the same issues and motivated by many of the same forces that unconsciously preoccupy schizophrenics. Of course, the two remain distinguished by their separate kinds of intellectual production. The political philosopher is obviously better able to express the contents and structures of identity (both personal and political), boundary (what constitutes human nature, what separates individuals, what feelings or needs hold communities together, how "reason" provides or takes away from a sense of boundary), and power (images of grandiosity and omnipotence, agents charged with transforming political and historical life, actors of great presence of mind and will).

The philosophic *mythos* reflects images of omnipotence, whether that quality is expressed in the symbology of a philosopher king, a prince, Leviathan, the legislator, or the proletariat. What is unmistakable in these imaginative projections are both alternative theories of knowledge and meaning as well as, in their historical contexts, radically different images of power and regeneration. It may even be possible to refer to certain conceptualizations in the tradition as symbols of transformation that have effects and consequences as significant for the constitution of psychical reality as for the structures of political reality.

Therapy as a Form of "Political Life"

Let us look briefly at another issue that spans the worlds of schizophrenics and political theory: therapy and the role of the therapist. Those who work with (rather than manage) schizophrenic patients, who believe in the potential of verbal communication, accomplish on an intimate level what political theorists discuss in collective or historical terms. Psychodynamic psychotherapy addresses itself to issues of boundary, identity, and self, and therapists emphasize the interaction of the intrapsychic and the interpersonal.

Both the philosopher and psychotherapist are troubled by a history that produces pain, that projects falsity and alienated representations of the self (whether in a personal or political sense). Each searches for reasons in a repressed history, a time lost to consciousness. Each is committed to restoring fragmented identities to a state of unity and health. Each attempts to locate in values, patterns, traditions, styles, and habits some recognizable potential, an identity that might provide a link between the historically repressed past and the construction of a viable future, a way to break through the impediments of history. Each moves to mediate between the inner and outer, to bring to an end the historical alienation between what appears to be and a core or cohesive identity.

It is this concept of a culture that exists in a schizoid relation to itself (in other words, that inhibits a dynamic relation between political identity and the motivations of human nature) that distinguishes major paradigmatic statements in the tradition. The distinction might be drawn in

258

terms of how a theorist identifies psychotic tendencies in the political objects under examination. For example, in clinical terms a hysterical character disorder differs from the schizophrenic's false self system. In the schizophrenic the fragmented and distorted masks, the radical separation of inner and outer, and the prominence of delusion require a therapy that can reconstruct the ego by reaching to the core of the self. However, the type of alienation that defines a hysterical relation to experience poses less of a threat to the prevailing social order. A hysterical personality moves within existing frames of reference; the order of time is not necessarily confused (although it certainly may be); the distinction between outer and inner is firm, and the self suffers from more specific (and less global) conflicts. For the schizophrenic, the major problem is identity, an overwhelming confusion about the meaning of the self. Hysteria, and the whole range of the behaviors classified as neurotic, require a form of therapy aimed at a particular problem in adaptation, sexuality, or behavior control. This kind of psychological condition does not reflect the shattering confusion and dislocation of the schizophrenic's anguish. Neurotic conflict or character disorders that evolve around oedipal issues rarely distort the self's basic or core identity.

Following on this argument, is it possible then to distinguish political theories in terms of their sensitivity to uncovering schizophrenic aspects of a culture or social order? I am not saying this is the only way to evaluate or understand political theory and philosophy; it may, however, be a useful way, and add a psychodynamic dimension to interpretation. For example, are theorists who focus on the organization of human nature asking what from a modern perspective would be clinical questions that bear directly on the structure of identity? It is one thing to speak of a culture as plagued by the corruption of history and by fragmentation in meaning, patterns of value, and the motivations of human nature; it is, however, an entirely different theoretical task to treat issues that touch on adjustments in the society's visible political arrangements. In the latter case the interest is not so much in transforming the conditions of being, the very roots of human character, as it was for Rousseau, as in ministering to identifiable evils that interfere with political and economic exchange. Such theorists (and this is particularly true of post-Hobbesian liberalism) tend to ignore unconscious or schizophrenic aspects of human experience.

It is possible then that the paradigmatic quality of political philosophy may derive from the ways in which theory conceptualizes delusional invasions of the "body politic," uncovers conflicts in the personal and collective unconscious, and translates those conflicts into a conceptual symbology. It may be this activity that separates paradigm-creating theory from the more historically limited "normal" theorizing (in the sense that Kuhn [1962] refers to "normal science"). For the paradigm-innovative theorist (such as Plato, Machiavelli, Hobbes, Rousseau, or Marx), the issue is more than the alteration of existing political arrangements, the administration of laws, or concern over responsibilities and obligations. The arguments of this kind of theorist suggest more than a plea for an effective citizenship, although the task of conceptualizing an alternative form of citizenship is certainly central to the theoretical objective. What the philosopher demands, however, is a thorough reconstruction of self, political form, and being; the human and existential task is monumental and is directed primarily at a history that threatens human and social survival.

Similarly, the schizophrenic personality cries out for more than limited psychotherapy. What is necessary for the schizophrenic (and the schizoid political community) is a therapy aimed at *a massive reordering of internal psychological structures*. This is definitely not the task of theorists in the tradition of modern liberalism, but it is the therapy intended by a philosopher who confronts a culture that is seen as psychotic or delusional. It would be inappropriate for the psychotherapist to treat a schizophrenic patient like a hysteric. Psychotherapy for schizophrenics requires a commitment to the therapeutic reconstruction of identity. The techniques of necessity have to be adapted to a human being whose emotional reality has been subject to incredible pressure, violence, and distortion. The situation is similar for the paradigm philosopher: it is simply not possible to conceive of a political theory in terms of readjusting laws or institutions; change becomes meaningless unless it reaches to the structure of motivation and desire, to unconscious and psychical reality. The theorist's purpose is to create a political ego; the psychotherapist's is to integrate an ego so fractured that the self has no normally recognizable identity. Theorist and therapist alike work to found self-sustaining and responsible identities; both seek to break down identities built on nonconsensual reality; both seek to establish relationship within some form of community or civility. For the theorist, the aim is political civility; for the psychotherapist, the goal is civility premised on a dyadic relationship and sense of trust. Eventually, both depart from their respective environments.

What is the therapeutic function if not ridding the body politic of a diseased self tormented and persecuted by its own introjects? Therapy (for example, the type represented by Rousseau's legislator) is an intervention that encourages movement toward the foundation of new ego structures. Ideally, the transformed, integrated ego, now capable of sophisticated differentiation, decides or acts through "political" recognitions, beliefs that situate the self in a renewed ethical context whose assumptions have little to do with the historically corrupt civil society. Consciousness develops a sensitivity to justice and trust, a commitment to the ties among human beings, an awareness of the limitation and possibility of authority, and an appreciation of the forms in which authority exercises its rights.

Like Rousseau's precivil self, schizophrenics possess little sense of consensual validation in their psychological state of nature. Aware of the depths and costs of their alienation and withdrawal, they experience intense isolation and exclusion. The idea and meaning of connection with a larger, participatory community of human beings holds little comfort or promise for them. Reentering community, rediscovering sociality, renewing trust, and learning how to become part of a greater whole, however, require a certain political sensibility. This involves several issues that arise out of interaction with the psychotherapist: the therapist's autonomy, the nature of power in delusional imagery, the therapist's own power, the self's emerging sense of cooperation and justice, and the discovery of boundaries. Let me add that the creation of identity is vital in therapy with schizophrenics as it is in "therapy" with wounded polities. In some ways, it is the central issue of therapy, since the schizophrenic is terribly confused about what the self contains and means in relation to others. Even sexual identity (which in a psychodynamic sense is considered fundamental) is often in doubt.

It is not uncommon to find schizophrenic patients who feel possessed by alien spirits, who believe that something outside is tearing the self apart, who know their bodies to be inhabited by forces beyond their control, and who see the therapist as an other to rescue them from torment. Such tormenting introjects echo Plato's drones, Machiavelli's *condottiere*, Rousseau's particular wills, and Marx's capitalists, all of whom drive the community (and the self) toward death and disintegration. This also suggests that the political theorist and the psychotherapist fight historical forms of identity and impositions of given histories on the "body," whether it is the body politic or the body psychological. In the case of the political state, it is history understood as collective identity; in the case of the schizophrenic, it is history understood as the psychophysiological past of the self. For both the political theorist and the psychotherapist, the goal is to restore health to "bodies" ravaged by the effects of historical time.

In what direction, then, should political theory be going? It is naïve in these times even to imagine a grand theory emerging. Still, it is necessary to pursue theory that asks questions of our institutions and that looks at the past to see what messages make sense for our own age. Yet it is also important for political theorists to remember that their activities derive inspiration from realities and expectations situated in feelings, needs, and desires. Political theory studies individuals: living, sentient presences who breathe, eat, engage in sexual relations, and experience friendship, disappointment, pain, and sorrow. We should not lose sight of the *human* basis of political theory. We should not forget that to think about politics as a life world is to imagine people acting and interacting in all their rationality and irrationality, with thoughts that take shape along the pathways of desire.

References

Adler, A. 1954. *Understanding human nature*. Greenwich: Fawcett.
American Psychiatric Association. 1980. *DSM III: Diagnostic and statistical manual of mental disorder*, third ed.
Arendt, H. 1958. *The human condition*. New York: Doubleday.
Arieti, S. 1964. Acting out and unusual behavior in schizophrenia. *Am. J. Psychotherapy* 18:329–41.
———. 1967. *The intrapsychic self*. New York: Basic Books.
———. 1974. *Interpretation of schizophrenia*. New York: Basic Books.
Benedetti, G. 1979. The structure of psychotherapeutic relationship in the individual treatment of schizophrenia. In C. Muller, ed., *Psychotherapy of schizophrenia*. Oxford: Excerpta Medica.
Burnham, D.L., Gladstone, A.I., and Gibson, R.W. 1969. *Schizophrenia and the need-fear dilemma*. New York: International Universities Press.
Cameron, N. 1938. Reasoning, regression, and communication in schizophrenics. *Psychological Monographs* 50:1.
———. 1939. Deterioration and regression in schizophrenic thinking. *Journal of Abnormal and Social Psychology* 34:265.
Cohen, P.S. 1969. Theories of myth. *Man* 4:337–53.
Edelson, M. 1971. *The idea of a mental illness*. New Haven: Yale University Press.
Eliade, M. 1967. *Myths, dreams, and mysteries*. New York: Harper.
Fairbairn, W.R.D. 1952. *Object relations theory of the personality*. New York: Basic Books.
Ferenczi, S. 1916. *Sex in psychoanalysis*. Boston: Badger.
———. 1938 *Thalassa: A theory of genitality*. New York: Psychoanalytic Quarterly.
Firth, R. 1960. Twins, birds and vegetables: Problems of identification in primitive religious thought. *Man* 4:1–17.
Forrest, D.V. 1965. Poiesis and the language of schizophrenia. *Psychiatry* 28:1–18.
———. 1969. New world and neologisms, with a thesaurus of coinages by a schizophrenic savant. *Psychiatry* 36:44–73.
———. 1973. On one's own onymy. *Psychiatry* 36:266–90.
Forbush, B. 1972. *The Sheppard and Enoch Pratt Hospital: 1853–1970*. Philadelphia: Lippincott.
Foucault, M. 1961. *Madness and civilization*. New York: Random House.
Freud, S. 1920. *Beyond the pleasure principle*. Standard Edition 18.

References

———. 1927. *The Future of an illusion*. Standard Edition 21.

———. 1930. *Civilization and its discontents*. Standard Edition 21.

———. 1939. *Moses and monotheism*. Standard Edition 23.

Glass, J.M. 1974. The philosopher and the shaman. *Political Theory* 2:181–96.

———. 1976. Machiavelli's prince and alchemical transformation: Action and the archetype of regeneration. *Polity* 8:504–28.

———. 1979. The language of analysis: Theory as defense against the internal. *Polity* 12:127–42.

Green, H. 1965. *I never promised you a rose garden*. New York: New American Library.

Habermas, J. 1971. *Knowledge and human interests*. Boston: Beacon Press.

Hill, L. 1955. *Psychotherapeutic intervention in schizophrenia*. Chicago: University of Chicago Press.

Hobbes, T. 1968. *Leviathon*. Ed. C.B. MacPherson. New York: Penguin.

Horkheimer, M., and Adorno, T. 1944. *Dialectics of enlightenment*. New York: Herder and Herder.

Jacobson, E. 1964. *The self and the object world*. New York: International Universities Press.

James, W. 1971. *Essays in radical empiricism and a pluralistic universe*. New York: E.P. Dutton.

Kasanin, J.S. 1964. *Language and thought in schizophrenia*. New York: Norton.

Kernberg, O. 1975. *Borderline conditions and pathological narcissism*. New York: Jason Aronson.

———. 1976. *Object-relations theory and clinical psychoanalysis*. New York: Jason Aronson.

Klein, M. 1950. *Contributions to psychoanalysis, 1921–1945*. London: Hogarth Press.

Kosinski, J. 1974. *The devil tree*. New York: Bantam.

———. 1976. *Being there*. New York: Bantam.

Kuhn, T.S. 1962. *The structure of scientific revolutions*. Chicago: University of Chicago Press.

Lacan, J. 1968. *The language of the self*. Baltimore: Johns Hopkins University Press.

Laing, R.D. 1978. *The divided self*. New York: Penguin.

———. 1980. *Sanity, madness and the family*. New York: Penguin.

Lasswell, H. 1930. *Psychopathology and politics*. Chicago: University of Chicago Press.

Levi-Strauss, C. 1967. *The scope of anthropology*. London: Jonathan Cape.

———. 1969a. *The raw and the cooked*. New York: Harper.

———. 1969b. *The savage mind*. Chicago: University of Chicago Press.

———. 1973. *From honey to ashes*. New York: Harper.

Lévy-Bruhl, L. 1928. *The soul of the primitive*. New York: Macmillan.

Lidz, T. 1965. *Schizophrenia and the family*. New York: International Universities Press.

Loevinger, J. 1977. *Ego development*. San Francisco: Jossey Bass.

Mahler, M. 1968. *On human symbiosis and the vicissitudes of individuation: Infantile psychosis*. New York: International Universities Press.

References

Mahler, M., Pine, F., and Bergman, A. 1975. *The psychological birth of the infant: Symbiosis and individuation.* New York: Basic Books.

Marcuse, H. 1955. *Eros and civilization.* New York: Random House.

Marx, K. 1964. Alienated labor. In T.B. Bottomore, ed., *Marx's early writings.* New York: McGraw Hill.

Masterson, J.F. 1976. *Psychotherapy of the borderline adult.* New York:Brunner/ Mazel.

Mendel, W.W. 1974. A phenomenological theory of schizophrenia. In A. Burton, *Schizophrenia as a life style.* New York: Springer.

Mitchell, S.A. 1981. The origin and nature of the "object" in the theories of Klein and Fairbairn. *Contemporary Psychoanalysis* 17:374–98.

Mitscherlich, A. 1963. *Society without the father.* New York: Schocken Books.

O'Brien, B. 1975. *Operators and things: The inner life of a schizophrenic.* New York: Barnes.

Pao, P.N. 1979. *Schizophrenic disorders.* New York: International Universities Press.

Piro, S. 1967. *Il linguaggio schizofrenico.* Milan: Feltrinelli.

Plato. 1961. *Republic.* Trans. P. Shorey. In E. Hamilton and H. Cairns, eds., *Collected dialogues.* New York: Bollingen.

Rank, O. 1936. *Truth and reality.* New York: Knopf.

Rank, O., and Ferenczi, S. 1925. *The development of psychoanalysis.* New York: Nervous and Mental Disease Publishing Co.

Rank, O., and Sachs, H. 1968. *Psychoanalysis in art and in science.* Detroit: Wayne State University Press.

Reich, A. 1960. Pathologic forms of self-esteem regulation. *The Psychoanalytic Study of the Child* 15:215–32

———. 1973. Pathologic forms of self-esteem regulation. In *Psychoanalytic contributions.* New York: International Universities Press.

Reich, W. 1972. *Character analysis.* New York: Simon and Schuster.

Ricoeur, P. 1970. *Freud and philosophy.* New Haven: Yale University Press.

———. 1977. The question of proof in Freud's psychoanalytic writings. *J. Am. Psychoanal. Assn.* 25:835–73.

Roheim, G. 1943. *The origin and function of culture.* New York: Doubleday.

Rousseau, J.J. 1950. *The social contract and discourses.* New York: Dutton.

———. 1966. *On the origins of language.* New York: Unger.

Schulz, C.G. 1980a. The all or nothing phenomenon. In J.S. Strauss, ed., *The psychotherapy of schizophrenia.* New York: Plenum.

Schulz, C.G. 1980b. The contribution of the concept of self-representation object-representation differentiation to the understanding of the schizophrenias. In S.I. Greenspan and G.H. Pollock, eds., *The course of life: psychoanalytic contributions towards understanding personality development, vol. I: Infancy and early childhood.* Washington, D.C.: NIMH Publication.

Schulz, C.G., and Kilgalen, R.K. 1967. *Case studies in schizophrenia.* New York: Basic Books.

Searles, H. 1960. *The nonhuman environment.* New York: International Universities Press.

———. 1965. *Collected papers on schizophrenia and related subjects.* New York: International Universities Press.

————. 1979. *Countertransference and related subjects*. New York: International Universities Press.

Sechehaye, M. 1951. *Symbolic realization*. New York: International Universities Press.

————. 1956. *A new psychotherapy in schizophrenia*. New York: Grune and Stratton.

Siirala, A. 1965. *The voice of illness*. Philadelphia: Fortress Press.

Siirala, M. 1963. Schizophrenia: A human situation. *Am. J. Psychoanal.* 23:29.

————. 1969. *Medicine in metamorphosis: Speech, presence, and integration*. London: Tavistock.

————. 1972. Psychotherapy of schizophrenia as a basic human experience, as a ferment for a metamorphosis in the conception of knowledge and the image of man. In A. Rubenstein, ed., *Psychotherapy of schizophrenia*. Amsterdam: Excerpta Medica.

————. 1976. Delusional possession of reality—the normal madness. Milan: International Congress of Psychoanalysis on Madness.

Spitz, R. 1965. *The first year of life*. New York: International Universities Press.

Sponitz, H. 1969. *Modern psychoanalysis of the schizophrenic patient*. New York: Grune and Stratton.

————. 1976. *Psychotherapy of preoedipal conditions*. New York: Jason Aronson.

Storch, A. 1924. *The primitive archaic forms of inner experience and thought in schizophrenia*. New York: Nervous and Mental Disease Publication Co.

Sullivan, H.S. 1952. *Schizophrenia as a human process*. New York: W.W. Norton.

————. 1953a. *Conceptions of modern psychiatry*. New York: W.W. Norton.

————. 1953b. *Interpersonal theory of psychiatry*. New York: W.W. Norton.

————. 1954. *The psychiatric interview*. New York: W.W. Norton.

Tausk, V. 1948. On the origin of the "influencing machine" in schizophrenia. In R. Fliess, ed., *The psycho-analytic reader*. New York: International Universities Press.

Vygotsky, L.S. 1962. *Thought and language*. Cambridge: MIT Press.

Werner, H. 1957. *Comparative psychology of mental development*. New York: International Universities Press.

Willis, R.G. 1967. The head and the loins. *Man* 2:514–34.

Winnicott, D.W. 1965. *The maturational process and the facilitating environment*. New York: International Universities Press.

————. 1975. Transitional objects and transitional phenomena. In *Through pediatrics to psychoanalysis*. New York: Basic Books.

Wittgenstein, L. 1969. *On certainty*. Oxford: Basil Blackwell.

Index

Adler, A., 79
Adorno, Theodor, 252
Alienation, Marxist, 115–20, 128–30
American Psychiatric Association, *Diagnostic and Statistical Manual of Mental Disorders*, 40
Arendt, Hannah, xviii n. 107
Arieti, S., 1, 19, 27, 35, 39
Aristotle, 11; *Politics*, 132
Authoritarianism, xiii, 38. *See also* Power relations

Benedetti, G., 176
Burnham, D. L., 54

Cameron, N., 25, 27n
Catatonia, 24–25
Clinician. *See* Therapist
Cohen, P. S., 33n
Countertransference, 89

Delusion, xiii, xiv–xv, 2–4, 80, 115–17, 130–31; absolute character of, xiii, 54–55, 59–61, 69; and alienation, 115–20; and consensual reality, 14–15, 75, 81–82, 222–28; cure of, 91–94, 106–7, 108–9, 144–46; and fanatic, xiv; and freedom, 99–101, 219–20; function of, 16–17, 87–88, 119, 125, 141, 146, 212; and infantile states, 54–55, 58–59; and knowledge, 14–18, 48–50, 61–66, 72–77, 133–35, 138–46, 254–55; and sexuality, 73–77, 79; and state of nature, 125–27; and time, 52, 62, 112–15
Demystification, 86, 90
Desymbolization, 25

Edelson, M., 2, 3
Eliade, Mircea, 245
Empathy, 152–54, 182–83, 230–32; and power relations, 220–21, 234–35; and state of nature, 238–40, 256–57
Empiricism, 138–46

Entrapment, 98–100
Ethics, 38; and state of nature, 127
Evaluation, psychiatric, 162–68

Fairbairn, W. R. D., 60n
Fanatic, xiv–xv
Ferenczi, S., 84n
Firth, R., 33n
Forbush, B., 5
Forrest, David, 26
Freud, Sigmund, xvi, xix, 3, 253; *Civilization and Its Discontents*, 252; *The Future of an Illusion*, 252; *Moses and Monotheism*, 252

Glass, J. M., 244, 249
Green, H., *I Never Promised You a Rose Garden*, 229

Habermas, Jürgen, 252
Hill, Lewis, 39, 56
Hobbes, Thomas, 24, 30, 182, 251, 253, 256–57; *Leviathan*, 11, 124–28, 132, 134; and phantasms, 132–39, 146; and state of nature, 99–100, 125–27, 131, 148–53, 178–80, 232
Horkheimer, Max, 252

Identity, delusional, xiv–xv, 83–84, 120, 176; and delusional speech, 141, 142–46, 201–13; and ritual, 95–98; and symbolization, 88; and therapy, 261
Imagery, delusional, xiii–xiv, xviii–xix, 117; and power relations, xiii–xiv, 52–53, 64–66, 77–80. *See also* Speech, delusional
Infantile states, 53–61; and delusion, 150–51, 152; and mothering, 55–57; and splitting, 54, 57
Introjection, 56, 57, 60n

Jacobson, E., 53
James, William, 136, 138–39, 143, 146

Index

and delusion, 81–82, 91, 98–99, 119–20, 121–22, 222–28; and delusional speech, 86–88, 107–12, 155, 160–62, 167–68, 174–75; and language, 108, 213–14; and schizophrenic, 15–17, 36, 68

Regardie, 123

Regression, 19, 20–21, 22, 27, 55, 119

Reich, A., 54, 55, 57

Reich, Wilhelm, 23

Relations, in delusional speech, 139, 141, 142

Resymbolization, 122n

Ricoeur, Paul, 112, 121, 122, 250, 251, 252

Ritual, 95–98, 102–4

Roheim, Geza, 252

Rousseau, Jean-Jacques, xvi, 153, 180, 182–83, 228–29, 230–35, 248, 256–57, 261; and General Will, 216–19; and state of nature, 11, 68, 238–40; and transformation, 236–46.

Rousseau, Jean-Jacques, works: *Discourse on the Origins of Inequality*, 238–39; *Emile*, 132; *The Origin of Languages*, 194; *Second Discourse*, 193–94; *Social Contract*, 132, 221–22, 236–37, 238, 240, 241

Schizophrenia, xiii-xiv, xvii–xviii, 19–24, 27–28, 259; definitions of, 39–41; etiology of, xvi–xviii, 14, 19, 39–40, 55–57; and family, 154–55, 175–76; and infantile states, 55–57, 60–61; and political theory, 257–58; symptoms of, xvii n, 40–42, 58, 64

Schizophrenic, xiii-xiv, xix–xx, 4, 260; and anger, 58–60; and Marxist alienation, 115–20; and social contract, xix–xx, 68–69; and socialization, xxi, 21; and society, 14–16, 217–22, 231–35, 242, 261. *See also* Speech, delusional

Schulz, C. G., 54, 58

Searles, Harold, 25–26, 60n, 71, 89, 120n, 147, 154, 161

Sechehaye, Margaret, 14, 61

Self, and society, 248–49

Sexuality, 73–77, 79

Sheppard, Moses, 5

Sheppard and Enoch Pratt Hospital (Sheppard/Pratt), 5–10; patient population at, 7; procedures at, 158n, 168–69; treatment at, 5–6, 7–9, 148, 149n, 150n, 153–54, 175

Siirala, A., 2

Siirala, M., 105–6, 245

Social contract, 11, 216–17, 236–38; and empathy, 221–22, 232, 242–43; and schizophrenic, xix–xx, 68–69

Society: and delusional speech, 17, 23–24, 68, 111–12, 128; and language, 17, 21–22; and schizophrenic, 14–16, 217–22, 231–35, 242, 261

Speech, delusional, xiii, xvi, xx–xxi, 1–3, 66–67, 82–83; associational content of, 84–88; and consensual reality, 86–88, 107–12, 120–21, 140–43, 194–95; and empiricism, 138–46; function of, 48–49, 50, 77, 101–4, 111–12; and infantile states, 56–57; and introjection, 60–61; and language, 71, 109, 124–25, 136, 137–38, 192–93; logic of, 10–11, 13–14, 17–18, 27, 34, 48, 62–63, 74–77, 84–90, 200; and Marxist alienation, 128–30; meaning of, 15–17, 25–28, 31–32, 71, 135, 139; and myth, 22, 29–31, 32–35, 36; and narrative, 112–15; and phantasms, 134–37; and political theory, xv–xvi, 11, 256–57; and politics, 12–15, 38–39; and power relations, 38–39, 59, 62, 63–66, 69–70, 71–72, 75–77; and regression, 27; and ritual, 95–98, 102–4; and society, 17, 23–24, 68, 111–12, 128; and symbolization, 71–72, 108; and therapist, 105–7. *See also* Imagery, delusional

Spitz, R., 53, 61

Splitting, 57, 69, 151; infantile, 54, 56, 57

Spotnitz, H., 41

State of nature, 4; Hobbesian, 99–100, 131, 125–27, 148–53, 178–80, 232; Rousseauian, 11, 68, 238–40

Storch, Alfred, 20

Suicide, 100

Sullivan, Harry Stack, 5, 71, 108, 109, 112, 121n; and schizophrenia, 26, 40, 122n

Synaesthesia, 21

Szasz, Thomas, xv–xvi

Taboo, 33, 34

Tausk, V., 74

Therapist, xviii n, 244; and delusion, 81–82, 88–90, 90–91, 95, 96, 98–99; and delusional speech, xv–xvi, 105–7; and political philosophy, 132, 133, 236

Therapy: and language, 9, 134–35, 138; and political philosophy and theory, 237–38, 239–42, 243–46, 258–61; and society, 245; stages in, 81–94, 105–9, 121–22, 153

Index

"Theriology," 133–34
Time, 52, 62, 112–15

Unconscious, xiii, xvi, 11–12; and identity, 252–55
Utterance. *See* Speech, delusional

Victimization, xiii–xiv, xix, 3, 59
Vygotsky, L. S., 22, 25, 27n

Werner, Heinz, *Comparative Psychology of Mental Development*, 20–22
Willis, R. G., 28
Winnicott, D. W., 53
Wittgenstein, Ludwig, *On Certainty*, 15–16